ISBN: 9781314517323

Published by:
HardPress Publishing
8345 NW 66TH ST #2561
MIAMI FL 33166-2626

Email: info@hardpress.net
Web: http://www.hardpress.net

THE MASTERPIECES OF

Catholic Literature, Oratory and Art

CONTAINING

Choice Selections by the Most Celebrated Writers, Orators and Painters, both Ancient and Modern

INCLUDING

Selections and Contributions from His Holiness, Pope Leo XIII; Cardinals Gibbons, Logue and Vaughan; Archbishops Ryan, Keane, Ireland, Messmer and other distinguished authorities.

———

EDITED BY

HYACINTHE RINGROSE, LL.B., A. M.

———

ALSO THE

Sublime Passion Play of Ober-Ammergau, as performed in Bavaria at its last presentation, splendidly illustrated.

———

VOLUME I, II, III

———

1910
PUBLISHED BY
E. J. SWEENEY & COMPANY
NEW YORK. CHICAGO. SAN FRANCISCO

SPECIAL NOTICE

The Publishers will not offer this book for sale in Book Stores. It is published exclusively for subscribers, and can only be obtained by ordering it of our Authorized representatives for this great work.

Mess. E. S. Sweeney & Co

Gentlemen. Your enterprise in publishing three volumes of Catholic Literature is worthy of generous patronage. I am glad that you included in the table of contents some of the best productions of several of the Fathers' - Doctors of the Church.

Faithfully yours in Xt.

J. Card. Gibbons.

INTRODUCTION.

The purpose of this work is, as its title suggests, to present in three convenient volumes to the Reverend Clergy and Faithful Laity of our Holy Church selected masterpieces of Catholic Literature, Oratory and Art.

The Church of Christ has stood the searchlight of criticism and opposition for nearly nineteen centuries, proving to the race that, as an institution, it is founded on a Rock, and that the Gates of Hell cannot prevail against it.

James Anthony Froude, an Anti-Catholic and Anti-Irish historian, writing of the Catholic Church, laid aside his deep-rooted prejudices long enough to say "The Roman Church has once more shot up into visible and practical consequence. While she loses ground in Spain and Italy, which had been so long exclusively her own, she is gaining in the modern, energetic races, which have been the stronghold of Protestantism."

This book is primarily intended for true believers, those who can say with the earthly martyrs, "Christianus Sum!" "I am a Christian!"

To our separated brethren we trust a perusal of the sublime pictures, eloquent orations and masterly essays which are gathered together here will act as guide posts and beacon lights, pointing to the Church Holy and Beautiful.

We may possess all the riches of the Orient and yet be entirely destitute of the unsearchable riches of Christ.

We may know by name every star and constellation in the firmament, and yet know nothing of the Bright and Morning Star. We may be acquainted with every flower in the domain of botany, and yet be ignorant of the Rose of Sharon, and the Lily of the Valley.

The Catholic Church has ever been the Alma Mater of all that is beautiful in music, poetry and art. The world's greatest painters, sculptors, orators and poets have been among the most devoted sons of the Church. When we examine the art treasures of the earth we find the most sublime illustrations of genius are dedicated to the service of God. He who would paint a perfect man, can find no loftier or more illuminating ideal than the Man, Christ Jesus; he who would fashion out of marble a perfect woman, can find no ideal more glorious and true than Mary, the Mother of our Lord. In the realm of music we find the most ravishing and inspiring melody is used as a medium for praising God in His Holy Church. What a foretaste of the Angelic Choir is offered us in the sweet strains of Gounod's Mass of St. Cecilia, and the introductory march from "La Reine de Saba."

In the Republic of Letters Catholics have more than done their share; and the world's greatest orators have laid their golden gifts of eloquence at the foot of the cross.

We have, editorially, looked over the magnificent field of spiritual and intellectual Catholic wheat, and selected for harvesting the best and most pleasing grain. After gathering the sheaves, we have taken the grain to the mill of literary criticism, where, by a careful process, the kernels were separated from the chaff and the beautiful and strengthening flour of spirituality and thought was prepared for the Catholic mind and heart. In garnering our precious grain, many beautiful sheaves have been left in the harvest field, but this has been occasioned simply by the economy of space.

A book containing all the noble masterpieces of Catholic expression would be larger in size than one of the Himalaya Mountains. Besides, there is a wide contrariety of judgment and opinion concerning many of the splendid specimens of art and literature in the Catholic Church. Only those masterpieces which are unanimously acknowledged by experts to be gems of the first water are here reproduced.

In our endeavor to give newness and attractiveness to the work, we have purposely omitted many ideal treatises, orations and pictures, well deserving of being classed as masterpieces, but which have already become so familiar to the Catholic reader as to render unnecessary their reproduction here.

Every ten years the gentle peasants of the Bavarian village of Ober-Ammergau produce that wonderful theatrical presentation of the Passion of Christ, known as "The Passion Play." Thousands of Catholics and Protestants crossed the Atlantic in the Summer of 1910 to witness the production of this sublime tragedy. In view of the world-wide interest in this truly Catholic drama, we have deemed it fitting to include in this book a "Passion Play" chapter from the pen of a distinguished Catholic traveller and writer.

All through this work the desire of the publishers and editor to please our readers is plainly manifest; but our paramount object is that which illuminates and makes masterly all our contributions, namely, to further the Cause of Christ and His Holy Church.

HYACINTHE RINGROSE.

VOLUME I.

LIST OF ILLUSTRATIONS.

CONTENTS.

CONTENTS—Continued.

HIS EMINENCE CARDINAL GIBBONS

TRUTH AND SINCERITY OF CHARACTER.

Contribution by

His Eminence Cardinal Gibbons.

There are certain natural virtues which our young men are habitually called upon to exercise in their relations with one another as students during their academic career, and afterwards as citizens and priests in their intercourse with their fellow-beings in the world. Among these virtues, I shall single out three, because being leading and fundamental, they have a dominant influence on the others. These virtues are, Truth, Self-respect, and Fraternal Charity. They will be treated in the four following chapters.

The highest compliment that can be bestowed on a man is, to say of him that he is a man of his word; and the greatest reproach that can be cast on an individual is, to assert that he has no regard for the virtue of veracity. Truth is the golden coin with God's image stamped upon it, that circulates among men of all nations and tribes and peoples and tongues; its standard value never changes nor depreciates.

> "Truth has such a face and such a mien,
> As to be loved, needs only to be seen."

Like all valuable commodities, truth is often counterfeited. If it is a crime to counterfeit money, it is a .greater crime to adulterate virtue. The more precious the genuine coin, the more criminal and dangerous is the spurious imitation; and as truth is more valuable than specie, its base resemblance is more iniquitous and detestable: "Corruptio optimi pessima."

As truth is the medium of social and commercial intercourse, so high is the value which civilized society sets upon it that, for its own protection, it metes out the severest punishment to any one who violates it in commercial transactions. Some time ago, a citizen, who had boasted of owning more property than any other person in the neighborhood of a large city, was afterward sent to the penitentiary for telling a lie on a scrap of paper, or for forging another man's name on a note.

If it is a sin to prevaricate in business transactions, how much more grievous is the offense to lie in religious matters! Ananias and Saphira were suddenly struck dead at the Apostle's feet, because they had made a false return of the price of their farm. Their transgression did not consist in giving the Apostle only a part of the price of the land they sold, for he declared that, as it was a free gift, they were at liberty to do what they pleased with it. But they sinned by telling a deliberate lie about it.

The virtue of veracity is so indispensable an element in the composition of a Christian gentleman, that neither splendid talents, nor engaging manners, nor benevolence of disposition, nor self-denial, nor all these qualities combined, nor even the practice of religious exercises, can atone for its absence. They all become vitiated, they lose their savor, if the salt of truth and sincerity is wanting.

The vice of lying and hypocrisy is so odious and repulsive that it is obliged to hide its deformity, and clothe itself in the garment of truth.

While we feel at our ease and are disposed to be open and communicative in the presence of an upright and candid man, we are instinctively reserved and guarded before a deceitful person. He diffuses around him an atmosphere of distrust, and we shun him as we would a poisonous reptile. "There is no vice," says Bacon, "that so covereth a man with shame as to be false and perfidious."

So damaging and infamous in public estimation is the imputation of falsehood that, when we charge a man with unveracity, we rarely go so far as to call him a liar to his face; but we tell him in less offensive language that he has a vivid imagination, that his memory is defective, or that he has been betrayed into an error of judgment.

All men, Pagans and Jews, as well as Christians, pay homage to truth. They all profess to worship at her shrine. Pagan Rome supplies us with noble examples of fidelity to truth even at the sacrifice of life. When Regulus was sent from Carthage to Rome with ambassadors to sue for peace, it was under the condition that he should return to his Carthaginian prison if peace was not proclaimed. When he arrived in Rome, he implored the Senate to continue the war, and not to agree to the exchange of prisoners. That implied his own return to captivity at Carthage. The Senators and the chief priest held that, as his oath had been extorted by force, he was not bound by it. "I am not ignorant," replied Regulus, "that tortures and death await me; but what are these to the shame of an infamous action or the wounds of a guilty mind? Slave as I am to Carthage, I have still the spirit of a Roman. I have sworn to return. It is my duty to go." Regulus returned to Carthage and, it is said, was tortured to death.

When Eleazar was threatened with death if he did not violate the law of God, he was urged by his friends to save his life by an act of dissimulation. But he replied: "It doth not become our age to dissemble; whereby many young persons might think that Eleazar, at the age of four-score and ten years, was gone over to the life of the heath-ens. For though, for the present time, I should be deliv-ered from the punishments of men, yet should I not escape the hand of the Almighty neither alive nor dead. Where-fore, by departing manfully out of this life, I shall shew myself worthy of my old age. And I shall leave an example of fortitude to young men if, with a ready mind and con-stancy, I suffer an honorable death for the most venerable and most holy laws. And having spoken thus, he was forth-with carried to execution."

If there is one virtue reflected more clearly than another on the pages of the New Testament; if there is one virtue for which Christ and His disciples were eminently conspic-uous in their public and private life, it is the virtue of truth, candor, ingenuousness, and simplicity of character; and if there is any vice more particularly detested by them, it is hypocrisy, cunning, and duplicity of conduct.

So great is our Saviour's reverence for truth, so great His aversion for falsehood, that He calls Himself "the way, the truth, and the life." His Holy Spirit, He names "the Spirit of truth," while designating the devil "a liar, the father of lies and of liars."

Even His enemies could not withhold their admiration for His truthfulness and sincerity: "Master," they said, "we know that Thou art true, and teachest the way of God in truth; neither carest Thou for any one; for Thou dost not regard the person of men."

"Let your speech," says our Lord, "be yea, yea, nay, nay," as if He would say: Let your conversation be always frank and direct, free from the tinsel of embellishment and exaggeration, divested of studied ambiguity with intent to deceive.

I can recall but two instances in which Christ pronounces the eulogy of any man outside of the apostolic circle. He extols John the Baptist for his constancy and austerity, and He praises Nathanael for his guilelessness and sincerity of character: "Behold an Israelite, indeed, in whom there is no guile." When He was instructing His disciples for their future mission, He told them to be "wise as serpents and simple as doves." While they were to be wary and reserved among a hostile and captious people. He never allowed them to prevaricate or deflect one iota or tittle from the truth even to save their lives. As the serpent is said to expose his whole body to protect his head, so the Apostles were admonished to surrender not only their goods and their body, but even to sacrifice their life, rather than betray the truth.

Christ is the martyr of truth as well as of charity. Caiaphas said to Him: "I adjure Thee by the living God that Thou tell us whether Thou be the Christ, the Son of God." How easily could Jesus have saved His life on this occasion by His silence or by an evasive answer! But by openly avowing that He was the Christ, He signed His own death-warrant.

It was not without a purpose that Christ gives us a little child as our model in our relations with our neighbor. "Unless ye become as little children, ye shall not enter into the kingdom of heaven." Now, a child, until perverted by its vicious elders, is artless, open, and truthful. It speaks from the heart. It deals not in equivocations or mental reservations.

There was one class of persons toward whom our Lord was unsparing in His reprobation, and these were the scribes and Pharisees. He calls them a generation if vipers. "Wo to you, scribes and Pharisees, hypocrites," He says, "because ye make clean the outside of the cup and of the dish; but within you are full of rapine and uncleanness. * * * Ye are like to whited sepulchres, which outwardly appear to men beautiful, but within are full of dead men's bones and of all filthiness. So you also outwardly indeed appear to men just, but inwardly you are full of hypocrisy and iniquity." His language toward them is a scathing denunciation of their insincerity, selfishness, and perversion of the truth. We may judge how odious is deceit in His eyes when He says to the Pharisees: "Amen I say to you that the publicans and the harlots shall go into the kingdom of God before you."

St. Paul says: "Putting away lying, speak ye the truth every man with his neighbor, for we are members one of another." There is so absolute a trust and confidence between the members of the human body, that when the heart, or hand, or foot suffers pain, the head never suspects the afflicted member of practicing deception. The same trustworthiness that subsists among our physical members should, extend also, to the domestic, collegiate, and social body. Without this mutual confidence, there could be no official nor friendly relations among men, and the wheels of social intercourse and commercial communication would suddenly stop. Nearly all the information that we acquire is obtained from the testimony of others. Although we may at times be imposed upon, we have an instinctive faith in the veracity of our fellow-being.

So great is the esteem in which truth is held at West Point Academy that, if a cadet deliberately makes a misstatement to any of his superior officers, he is punished by expulsion. What a reproach would be the life of a Christian student who does not live up to the West Point standard! In Cornell, Harvard, Yale, and other universities, the same punishment is inflicted on students found guilty of presenting as their own essays, the compositions of another. If the virtue of truth is inviolably upheld in commercial life, in secular colleges, and military circles, it should, undoubtedly, be not less cherished by those that aspire to be the official heralds of the Gospel of truth, and the most honorable members of that mystical body of which Christ is the Head. If it is a shame, as St. Bernard declares, to be effeminate members under a Head crowned with thorns, surely it is not less revolting to be a lying mouthpiece under a Head that is the Oracle of truth.

St. Peter says: "Laying aside all malice and all guile and dissimulations and envies and all detractions, as new-born babes, desire the rational milk without guile that thereby you may grow unto salvation." We are the spiritual children of a mother that never deceives us. So undoubting is our trust in her that we receive from her hands the bread of truth with as unquestioning a faith as the infant receives the milk at its mother's breast. The children should resemble the mother especially in her characteristic features of truth and sincerity.

St. Thomas a Becket was conspicuous from his youth for inflexible veracity. Even in his childhood he always chose to suffer any blame, disgrace, or punishment rather than to tell an untruth, and in his whole life he was never found guilty of a lie in the smallest matter.

St. Alphonsus, pleading a case before a court of justice, was accidentally betrayed into an error by interpreting the meaning of a document against the adverse party. When convinced of his mistake, so delicate was his sense of truth, so great his aversion for even the semblance of a lie, that he abruptly abandoned the legal profession and embraced the religious state.

There is no time nor place in which the soldier of Christ is permitted to lay aside the armor of truth. The breast of God's minister, like that of the priest of the Old Law, should be the depository of doctrine and truth.

The disciple of Christ should be the organ of truth not only when robed in the sacred vestments, but also in the secular garb; not only in the sanctuary and pulpit, but in the public and private walks of life as well; in gay and festive, as well as in serious moods:

"Ridentem dicere verum quid vetat?"

Purchasers view with suspicion even genuine cloth offered for sale by those who are known to deal in shoddy merchandise.

Seneca says that the untruthful man must have a good memory, because the falsehoods that he has once uttered, must be kept in mind so as to be propped up with additional misstatements.

One may be guilty of falsehood in many ways. He may lie by telling a half-truth, omitting a circumstance essential to the fidelity of the narrative. He may lie by a shrug of the shoulders, by a gesture, by a deceitful silence, or by palming off in class as his own production the fruit of another's brain; for the essence of a falsehood consists in the intention to deceive. His life may be a colossal lie by being false to his profession or calling, appearing to be rich in grace and good works in the sight of men, but being poor and blind and miserable in the sight of God. There are others who have a habit of exaggerating from a morbid desire of imparting a relish to the conversation, and of attracting the attention of their hearers. The incidents they describe are usually of a startling and phenomenal nature, and their adventurous experiences have the flavor of a Gulliver or a Baron Munchausen.

The pernicious habit of retailing jocose lies and sensational stories, or making inaccurate statements, and of talking at random without weighing his words, will impair the offender's reputation for veraciousness in grave matters, and expose him to the penalty of not being believed even when he tells the truth. He will be an illustration of the boy in the fable, who had repeatedly given false alarms about the approach of the wolf; but when the wolf had actually invaded the fold his outcry remained unheeded.

The two chief causes that lead men to prevaricate, are prejudice against their neighbor, and inordinate self-love. Prejudice warps our judgment, and jaundices our mind, so that we view in an unfavorable light our neighbor's words and actions. Self-love and vanity prompt us to exaggerate our good deeds, and to underrate or palliate our own shortcomings.

Charity and humility are the guardians of truth. They are the two angels that defend the temple of the soul against the approach of the demon of falsehood. Charity counsels us not to judge our neighbor unjustly or to magnify his defects; and humility inspires us not to extenuate our own.

If we cannot be martyrs, let us be confessors of the truth. If we have not the courage, like our Master, to endure death for its sake, we should at least be prepared to suffer for it some passing humiliation or confusion.

Let it be the aim of your life to be always frank and open, candid, sincere and ingenuous in your relations with your fellow-man. Set your face against all deceit and duplicity, all guile, hypocrisy and dissimulation. You will thus be living up to the maxims of the Gospel, you will prove yourself a genuine disciple of the God of truth, you will commend yourself to all honest men. You will triumph over those that lie in wait to deceive, for the intriguer is usually caught in his own toils.

THE CATHOLIC CHURCH AND THE MARRIAGE TIE.

By His Eminence Cardinal Gibbons.

MARRIAGE—THE MOST SACRED OF ALL CONTRACTS.

Marriage, in the view of the church, is the most inviolable and irrevocable of all contracts that were ever formed. Every human compact may be lawfully dissolved but this. Nations may be justified in abrogating treaties with each other; merchants may dissolve partnerships, brothers will eventually leave the parental roof, and, like Jacob and Esau, separate from one another; friends, like Abraham and Lot, may be obliged to part company: but by the law of God the bond uniting husband and wife can be dissolved only by death. No earthly sword can sever the nuptial knot which the Lord has tied, for "what God hath joined together let no man put asunder."

Three of the evangelists, as well as the apostles of the gentiles, proclaim the indissolubility of marriage and forbid a wedded person to engage in second wedlock during the life of his spouse. There is, indeed, scarcely a moral precept more strongly enforced in the gospel than the indissoluble character of marriage validly contracted.

The pharisees came to Jesus, tempting him and saying, "Is it lawful for a man to put away his wife for every cause?" who, answering, said to them: "Have ye not read that he who made man from the beginning made them male and female? And for this cause shall a man leave father and mother and shall cleave to wife and they two shall be one flesh. Therefore now they are not two but one flesh.

What, therefore, God has joined together let no man put asunder." They say to him: "Why then did Moses command to give a bill of divorce and to put away?" He said to them: "Because Moses, by reason of the hardness of your heart, permitted you to put away your wives; but from the beginning it was not so. And I say to you that whosoever shall put away his wife, except it be for fornication, and shall marry another, committeth adultery, and he that shall marry her that is put away committeth adultery."

NO LEGISLATION DEVISED BY MAN CAN VALIDLY DISSOLVE IT.

Our Saviour here emphatically declares that the nuptial bond is ratified by God himself and hence that no man, nor any legislation framed by man, can validly dissolve the contract.

To the Pharisees interposing this objection, if marriage is not to be dissolved, why then did Moses command to give a divorce, our Lord replies that Moses did not command, but simply permitted the separation, and that in tolerating this indulgence the great lawgiver had regard to the violent passion of the Jewish people, who would fall into a greater excess if their desire to be divorced and to form a new alliance were refused. But our Saviour reminded them that in the primitive times no such license was granted. He then plainly affirms that such a privilege would not be conceded in the new dispensation, for he adds:

"I say to you: Whosoever shall put away his wife and shall marry another committeth adultery."

Protestant commentators erroneously assert that the text justifies an injured husband in separating from his adulterous wife and marrying again. But the Catholic Church explains the gospel in the sense that while the offended consort may obtain divorce from bed and board from his unfaithful wife he is not allowed a divorce a vinculo matrimoni, so as to have the privilege of marrying another.

TESTIMONY OF SCRIPTURE.

This interpretation is confirmed by the concurrent testimony of the Evangelists Mark and Luke and by St. Paul, all of whom prohibit a divorce a vinculo without any qualification whatever.   In St. Mark we read:

"Whosoever shall put away his wife and marry another committeth adultery against her, and if the wife shall put away her husband and be married to another she committeth adultery."

The same unqualified declaration is made by St. Luke:

"Every one that putteth away his wife, and marrieth another committeth adultery: and he that marrieth her that is put away from her husband committeth adultery."

Both of these Evangelists forbid either husband or wife to enter into second wedlock, how aggravating soever may be the cause of their separation.   And surely if the case of adultery authorized the aggrieved husband to marry another wife, those inspired penman would not have failed to mention that qualifying circumstance.

Passing from the gospels to the Epistle of St. Paul to the Corinthians we find there also an unqualified prohibition of divorce.   The apostle is writing to a city newly converted to the Christian religion.   Among other topics he indicates the doctrine of the church respecting matrimony.   We must suppose that, as an inspired writer and a faithful minister of the word, he discharges his duty conscientiously, without suppressing or extenuating one iota of the law. He addresses the Corinthians as follows:

"To them that are married, not I, but the Lord commandeth that the wife depart not from her husband.   And if she depart that she remain unmarried, or be reconciled to her husband. And let not the husband put away his wife."

Here we find the apostle, in his Master's name, commanding the separated couple to remain unmarried, without any reference to adultery. If so important an exception existed, St. Paul would not have omitted to mention it; otherwise he would have rendered the gospel yoke more grievous than its founder intended.

We therefore must admit that, according to the religion of Jesus Christ, conjugal infidelity does not warrant either party to marry again, or we are forced to the conclusion that the vast number of Christians whose knowledge of Christianity was derived solely from the teachings of Saint Mark, Luke and Paul were imperfectly instructed in their faith.

The Catholic Church, following the light of the gospel, forbids a divorced man to enter into second espousals during the life of his former partner. This is the inflexible law she first proclaimed in the face of pagan emperors and people and which she has ever upheld, in spite of the passions and voluptuousness of her own rebellious children.

HISTORIC DIVORCES AND THE CHURCH.

Henry VIII, of England, once an obedient son and defender of the church, conceived in an evil hour a criminal attachment for Anne Boleyn, a lady of the Queen's household, whom he desired to marry after being divorced from his lawful consort, Catherine of Aragon. But Pope Clement VII, whose separation he solicited, sternly refused to ratify the separation, though the Pontiff could have easily foreseen that his determined action would involve the church in persecution and a whole nation in the unhappy schism of its ruler.

Had the Pope acquiesced in the repudiation of Catherine, and in the marriage of Anne Boleyn, England would, indeed, have been spared to the church, but the church herself would have surrendered her peerless title of Mistress of Truth.

When Napoleon I repudiated his devoted wife, Josephine, and married Marie Louise of Austria, so well assured was he of the fruitlessness of his attempt to obtain from the Holy See the sanction of his divorce and subsequent marriage that he did not even consult the Holy Father on the subject. A few years previously Napoleon applied to Pius VII to annul the marriage which his brother Jerome had contracted with Miss Patterson of Baltimore. The Pope sent the following reply to the Emperor:

"Your Majesty will understand that upon the information thus far received by us it is not in our power to pronounce a sentence of nullity. We cannot utter a judgment in opposition to the rules of the church, and we could not, without laying aside those rules, decree the invalidity of a union which, according to the word of God, no human power can sunder."

SOCIAL REFLEX OF FAMILY LIFE.

The family is the source of society; the wife is the source of the family. If the fountain is not pure, the stream is sure to be foul and muddy. Social life is the reflex of family life.

And if we would clearly understand whither, as a nation, we are drifting when we forsake the Christian standard of morals and the Christian precepts concerning the indissoluble nature of the marriage tie, the history of woman in pagan countries should enlighten us. Woman in pagan countries, with rare exceptions, suffered bondage, oppression, and moral degradation. She had no rights that the husband felt bound to respect.

WOMAN AND MARRIAGE IN PAGAN LIFE.

The domestic life of Greece, it is true, was founded on monogamy. But whilst the law restricted the husband to one wife as his helpmate and domestic guardian, it tolerated, and even sanctioned the hetairai who bore to him the relation of inferior wives and who enjoyed his society more frequently and received more homage from him than his lawful spouse.

And whilst the education of the wife was of a most elementary character, the greatest care was lavished in cultivating the minds of the hetairai, that they might entertain their paramour by their wit while they fascinated him by their charms. The wife was the beast of burden; the mistress was the petted and pampered animal. These hetairai derived additional importance from being legally chosen to offer sacrifice on certain public occasions.

This demoralizing system, so far from being deplored was actually defended and patronized by statesmen, philosophers, and leaders of public opinion, such as Demosthenes, Pericles, Lysias, Aristotle and Epicurus.

A MERE CHATTEL, MARKETABLE AT WILL.

Solon erects in Athens a temple to Venus, the goddess of impure love. Greece is full of such temples, whilst there is not one erected to chaste, conjugal love. No virtuous woman has ever left a durable record in the history of Greece. The husband could put away his wife according to his capricious humor, and take a fairer, younger, and richer bride. He could dissolve the marriage bond without other formality than an attestation in writing before an Archon; and the wife had practically no power to refuse, as she was completely under the dominion of her husband. She was a mere chattel, marketable at will; nor had she any power to dissolve the marriage without her husband's consent.

In a word, the most distinguished Greek writers treat woman with undisguised contempt; they describe her as the source of every evil of man.   One of their poets said that marriage brings but two happy days to the husband— the day of his espousal and the day on which he lays his wife in the tomb.

Hesiod calls woman "an accursed brood and the chief scourge of the human race."   The daily prayer of Socrates was a thanksgiving to the gods that he was born neither a slave nor a woman.   And we have only to glance at the domestic life of Turkey today to be convinced that woman fares no better under the modern Mohammedanism than she did in ancient Greece.

THE MOHAMMEDAN BOND.

The Mohammedan husband has merely to say to his wife: "Thou art divorced," and the bond is dissolved.   To his followers Mohammed allowed four wives; to himself an unlimited number was permitted by a special favor of heaven.

The moral standard of the Lacedæmonian wives was far lower than that of the Athenians.   They were taught when maidens, to engage in exercises that strengthen their bodies and impart grace to their movements, but at the sacrifice of female modesty.   The ideal of conjugal fidelity was not seriously entertained.   Adultery was so common that it was scarcely regarded as a crime.   Aristotle says that the Spartan wives lived in unbridled licentiousness.

Passing from Greece to Italy, we find that monogamy was, at least nominally, upheld in Rome, especially during the earlier days of the republic. But while the wife was summarily punished for the violation of the marriage vows, the husband's marital transgressions were committed with impunity.

Toward the end of the republic, and during the empire, the disorders of nuptial life increased to an alarming extent. There was a fearful rebound on the part of Roman wives, particularly among the upper classes, from the restraints of former days to the most unlimited license. They rivaled the wantonness of the sterner sex.

DISSOLVED AT WILL.

So notorious were their morals in the time of Augustus that men preferred the unfettered life of celibacy to an alliance with partners bereft of every trace of female virtue. The strict form of marriage became almost obsolete, and a laxer one, destitute of religious or civic ceremony, and resting solely on mutual agreement, became general. Each party could dissolve the marriage bond at will and under the most trifling pretext, and both were free to enter at once into second wedlock.

Marriage was accordingly treated with extreme levity. Cicero repudiated his wife, Terntia, that he might obtain a coveted dowry with another ; and he discarded the latter because she did not lament the death of his daughter by the former.

Cato was divorced from his wife Attilia after she had borne him two children, and he transferred his second wife to his friend Hortensius, after whose death he married her again.

Augustus compelled the husband of Livia to abandon her, that she might become his own wife. Sempronius Sophus was divorced from his wife because she went once to the public games without his knowledge. Paulius Aemilius dismissed his wife, the mother of Scipio, without any reason whatever. Pompey was divorced and remarried a number of times. Sylla repudiated his wife during her illness, when he had her conveyed to another house.

If moral censors, philosophers, and statesmen such as Cato, Cicero and Augustus discarded their wives with so much levity, how lax must have been the marriage bond among the humble members of society, with examples so pernicious constantly before their eyes?

Wives emulated husbands in the career of divorces. Martial speaks of a woman who had married her tenth husband. Juvenal refers to one who had had eight husbands in five years. St. Jerome declares that there dwells in Rome a wife who had married her twenty-third husband, she being his twenty-first wife.

"There is not a woman left," says Seneca, "who is ashamed of being divorced, now that the most distinguished ladies count their years not by consuls, but by their husbands."

THE MISSION OF CHRISTIANITY.

It was a part of the mission of Christianity to change all this. By vindicating the unity, the sanctity, and the indissolubility of marriage the church has conferred the greatest boon on the female sex. The holiness of the marriage bond is the palladium of woman's dignity, while polygamy and divorce involve her in bondage and degradation.

The church has ever maintained, in accordance with the teachings of our Saviour, that no man can lawfully have more than one wife and no woman more than one husband. The rights and obligations of both consorts are correlative. To give to the husband the license of two or more wives would be an injustice to his spouse and destructive of domestic peace. The church has also invariably taught that the marriage compact, once validly formed, can be dissolved only by death, for what God hath joined together man cannot put asunder.

LEGITIMATE CAUSE FOR SEPARATION ; NONE FOR ABSOLUTE DIVORCE.

While admitting that there may be legitimate cause for separation, she never allows any pretext for the absolute dissolution of the marriage bond.

For so strong and violent are the passion of love and its opposite passion of hate, so insidious is the human heart, that once a solitary pretext is admitted for absolute divorce, others are quickly invented, as experience has shown. Thus a fearful crevice is made in the moral embankment and the rush of waters is sure to override every barrier that separates a man from the object of his desires.

A FEARFUL CREVICE.

It has again and again been alleged that this law is too severe; that it is harsh and cruel; and that it condemns to a life of misery two souls who might find happiness if permitted to have their marriage annulled and to be united with more congenial partners. Every law has its occasional inconveniences, and I admit that the law absolutely prohibiting divorce A VINCULO may sometimes appear rigorous and cruel.

But its harshness is mercy itself when compared with the frightful miseries resulting from the toleration of divorce. Its inconvenience is infinitesimal when contrasted with the colossal evils from which it saves society and the solid blessings it secures to countless homes. Those exceptional ill-assorted marriages would become more rare if the public were convinced once for all that death alone can dissolve the marriage bond. They would then use more circumspection in the selection of a conjugal partner. Hence it happens that in Catholic countries where faith is strong, as in Ireland and Tyrol, divorces are almost unheard of.

SUCCESSIVE POLYGAMY.

The reckless facility with which divorce is procured in this country is an evil scarcely less deplorable than Morman- ism—indeed, it is in some respects more dangerous than the latter, for divorce has the sanction of the civil law, which Mormonism has not. Is not the law of divorce a virtual toleration of Mormonism in a modified form? Mormonism consists in simultaneous polygamy, while the law of divorce practically leads to successive polygamy.

Each State has on its statute books a list of causes—or, rather, pretexts—which are recognized as sufficient ground for divorce A VINCULO. There are in all twenty-two or more causes, most of them of a trifling character, and in some States, as in Illinois and Maine, the power of granting a divorce is left to the discretion of the Judge.

STARTLING STATISTICS.

In his special report on the statistics of marriage and divorce made to Congress by Carroll D. Wright in February, 1889, the following startling facts appeared:

YEAR.	DIVORCES.
1867	9,937
1868	10,150
1869	10,939
1870	10,962

YEAR.	DIVORCES.
1871	11,586
1872	12,390
1873	13,156
1874	13,989
1875	14,212
1876	14,800
1877	15,687
1878	16,089
1879	17,083
1880	19,663
1881	20,762
1882	22,112
1883	23,198
1884	22,994
1885	23,472
1886	25,535
Total	328,716

From this table it will be seen that there was a total of 328,716 divorces in the United States in the twenty years, 1867-1886. Of these there were 122,121 in the first half of the period and 206,595 in the last half.

That is to say, the divorces in the latter half were 69 per cent. more than those in the first half. The population between 1870 and 1880 increased only 30 per cent. The divorces in 1870 were 10,962 and in 1880 they were 19,663, and, as the table shows, they were in 1886 more than two and one-half times what they were in 1867. I have not at hand the figures for the last decade, but there is no reason to believe that they show any decrease in the awful industry of the divorce courts.

THE CANCER SPREADING—HEROIC AND SPEEDY REMEDY NEEDED.

From the figures I have quoted it is painfully manifest that the cancer of divorce is rapidly spreading over the community and poisoning the fountains of the nation. Unless the evil is checked by some speedy and heroic remedy, the existence of family life is imperiled. How can we call ourselves Christian people if we violate a fundamental law of Christianity? And if the sanctity and indissolubility of marriage does not constitute a cardinal principle of the Christian religion, I am at a loss to know what does.

AN HONEST APPICATION OF THE TEACHINGS OF THE GOSPEL CURE.

Let the imagination picture to yourself the fearful wrecks daily caused by this rock of scandal, and the number of families that are cast adrift on the ocean of life. Great stress is justly laid by moralists on the observance of the Sunday. But what a mockery is the external repose of the Christian Sabbath to homes from which domestic peace is banished, where the mother's heart is broken, the father's spirit crushed, and where the children cannot cling to one of their parents without exciting the jealousy or hatred of the other.

And these melancholy scenes are followed by the final act of the drama when the family ties are dissolved and hearts that had vowed eternal love and union are separated to meet no more.

This social plague calls for a radical cure, and the remedy can be found only in the abolition of our mischievous legislation regarding divorce and in an honest application of the teachings of the gospel. If persons contemplating marriage were persuaded that once united they were legally debarred from entering into second wedlock they would be more circumspect before marriage in the choice of a life partner and would be more patient afterward in bearing the yoke and in tolerating each other's infirmities.

JAMES, CARDINAL GIBBONS.

THE VILLAGE OF OBER-AMMERGAU.

THE PASSION PLAY OF OBER-AMMERGAU.

I. THE VILLAGE.

Ober-Ammergaus is a quaint Bavarian village nestling in the Tyrolese Alps, and situated about fifty-three miles southwest of Munich. Its inhabitants are engaged mainly in the manufacture of toys and the carving of wooden crucifixes, images of saints and rosaries. Many of the houses are adorned with beautiful frescoes of Biblical subjects. The chief interest of Ober-Ammergau to the outer world is derived from the magnificent presentations of the Passion Play which take place in the great amphitheatre of the village every ten years, and are attended by thousands of European and American visitors. The play is performed by the villagers themselves, and is one of the chief wonders of the world. The last presentation of this sacred drama took place in the summer of 1910 and attracted the. greatest throngs ever known in the history of Ober-Ammergau. Produced anywhere else but in this romantic Alpine village, performed by any others than these gentle Christian peasants, and the Passion Play would be a blasphemous and sacrilegious exhibition; but here in this gentle vale, far removed from the commercialism of our great cities, with God's eternal hills as a background, and played by a gentle pastoral folk whose highest ambition is to love and worship their Redeemer, the Passion Play becomes a spectacular and impressive religious service. The actors by the River

Ammer have been repeatedly approached by enterprising theatrical managers and promoters with offers to produce the drama in England and America, only to receive the same refusal to play anywhere else but in their beloved hamlet. "We could not perform the Passion Play in England," said one of their burgomasters, "without taking Ober-Ammergau with us." The actors are easily recognized on the streets of the village after the performances, for it is one of the strictest rules of the presentation that no false wigs or beards shall be used on the stage of the Passion Play, and none of the performers are permitted to use grease paints, rouge or other facial make-up. It has been remarked that the performance, for three hundred years, of this play, by succeeding generations, seems to have exercised a psychical influence on the looks, manners and modes of thought and speech of the Ammergauites. Their occupation for an equal length of time, as carvers of crucifixes and holy images, and the omnipresence of such images in the town wherever one turns, have no doubt exercised an equal influence on the physical and spiritual nature of these people. The mountain scenery of the locality is almost Palestinian in its character, and the village has the appearance of a bit of Judea transplanted into the heart of the Bavarian Alps. The people seem to belong more to the past than to the present. There is a seriousness in their faces that is striking. They who impersonate noble parts, do not only act their roles on the stage, they live them, and live them in their daily lives. Anton Lang, the village potter, and Anna Flunger, the postman's daughter, seem as much the Jesus and Mary off the stage as on it. They play neither for entertainment or profit. It is not a matter of gold with them, but of religion. They have their ambitions like other people, but no ambitions of a worldly nature.

A PASSION PLAY ACTOR, AT HOME.

Their fondest hope is to be found worthy to play a leading part in the Passion Play; their highest ambition is some day to play the part of Christus or of the Virgin Mary. For these parts the children seem to be trained from their very cradles. Life has no higher object; heaven itself but fewer honors. If we could read the hearts of the Ober-Ammergau mothers, I have no doubt but that we would find graven there most fervent prayers that they might live to see their children as actors on the stage of the Passion Play. Just as the pious mother of Israel of old was in the habit of praying that the expected Messiah might be born of her, so the peasant woman of this lovely village hopes to see her son perform the glorious role of the Christ in the famous drama. I verily believe that if the Parliament of Bavaria were to come to some of these villagers and give them the choice between becoming King of Bavaria or playing the part of Christ in the Passion Play they would answer without a moment's hesitation: "Rather one day the role of Jesus than a lifetime a real king."

II. THE PILGRIMAGE.

We had a grand railway ride from Munich to Oberau. We passed by the beautiful Lake of Starnberg just as the sun was setting and gilding with gold the little villages and pleasant villas that lie around its shores. It was in the Lake of Starnberg, near the lordly pleasure house that he had built for himself in that fair vale, that poor, mad Ludwig, the late King of Bavaria, drowned himself. Poor King! Fate gave him everything calculated to make a man happy excepting one thing, and that was the power of being happy. Fate has a mania for striking balances. I knew a little shoeblack once who used to follow his profession at the corner of Westminster Bridge. Fate gave him

an average of sixpence a day to live upon and provide himself with luxuries; but she also gave him a power of enjoying things which kept him happy all day long. He could
buy as much enjoyment for a penny as the average man
could for a ten-pound note—more, I think. He did not
know he was badly off any more than King Ludwig knew
he was well off; and all day he laughed and played and
worked a little—not more than he could help—and ate and
drank. The last time I saw him was in St. Thomas' Hospital, into which he had got himself owing to his fatal passion for walking along outside the stone coping of Westminster Bridge. He thought it was "prime" being in the
hospital, and told me that he was living like a "duke," and
that he did not mean to go out sooner than he could help.
I asked him if he was not in pain, and he said, "Yes," when
he "thought about it."

Poor little chap, he only managed to live like a "duke"
for three days more. Then he died, cheerful up to the last,
so they told me, like the plucky little Irishman he was.
He could not have been more than twelve years old when
he passed away. It had been for him a short life and a
merry one. Now, if only this poor little fellow and poor old
Ludwig could have gone into partnership, and so have
shared between them the shoeblack's power of enjoying and
the King's stock of enjoyments, what a good thing it would
have been for both of them, especially for King Ludwig.
He would never have thought of drowning himself then—
life would have been too delightful. Soon after losing sight
of Starnberg's placid waters we plunged into the gloom of
the mountains and began a long, winding climb among
their hidden recesses. At times shrieking as if in terror, we
passed some ghostly hamlet, standing out white and silent
in the moonlight against the shadowy hill, and now and then

THE TRIUMPHAL ENTRY.

THE CHRISTUS AND JOHN—PASSION PLAY.

a dark still lake, or mountain torrent, whose foaming waters fell in a long white streak across the blackness of the night. We passed by Murnau, in the Valley of the Dragon, a little town which possessed a Passion Play of its own in the olden times, and which, until a few years ago, when the railway line was pushed forward to Partenkirchen, was the nearest station to Ober-Ammergau. It was a tolerably steep climb up the road from Murnau over Mount Ettal to Ammergau—so steep, indeed, that one stout pilgrim, not many years ago, died from the exercise while walking up. Sturdy-legged mountaineer and pulpy citizen both had to clamber up, side by side, for no horses could do more than drag behind them the empty vehicle. The railway now carries him round Mount Ettal to Oberau, from which little village a tolerably easy road, as mountain roadways go, of about four or five English miles, takes him up to the Valley of the Ammer. It was midnight when our train landed us at Oberau station, but the place was far more busy and stirring than on ordinary occasions it is at mid-day. Crowds of tourists and pilgrims thronged the little hotel, wondering, as did the landlord, where they were all going to sleep, and wondering still more, though this latter consideration did not trouble their host, how they were going to get up to Ober-Ammergau in the morning in time for the play, which always begins at eight A. M. Some were engaging carriages at fabulous prices to call them at five, and others who could not secure carriages, and who had determined to walk, were instructing worried waiters to wake them at half-past two, and ordering breakfast for a quarter past three sharp. I had no idea there were such times in the morning. We were fortunate enough to find our landlord, a worthy farmer, waiting for us with a tumble-down conveyance, in appearance something between a

circus chariot and a bath chair, drawn by a couple of pow-
erful-looking horses; and in this, after a spirited skirmish
between our driver and a mob of twenty or so tourists, who
pretended to mistake the affair for an omnibus, and would
have clambered into it and swamped it, we drove away.
Higher and higher we climbed, and grander and grander
towered the frowning moon-bathed mountains round us,
and chillier and chillier grew the air. For most of the way
we crawled along, the horses tugging us from side to side
of the steep road; but whenever our coachman could vary
the monotony of the pace by a stretch-gallop, as, for instance, down the precipitous descents that occasionally followed upon some extra long and toilsome ascent, he thought-
fully did so. At such times the drive became really exciting,
and all our weariness was forgotten. The steeper the
descent, the faster, of course, we could go. The rougher
the road, the more anxious the horses seemed to be to get
over it quickly. About half-way up we passed Ettal at the
entrance to the Valley of the Ammer. The great white
temple standing, surrounded by its little village, high up
amid the mountain solitudes, is a famous place of pilgrimage among devout Catholics. Many hundreds of years ago
one of the early Bavarian kings built here a monastery as
a shrine for a miraculous image of the Virgin that had
been sent down to him from Heaven to help him when in
a foreign land he had stood sore in need, encompassed by
his enemies. The old church and monastery, which latter
was a sort of ancient Chelsea Hospital for aged knights,
was destroyed one terrible night some hundred and fifty
years ago by a flash of lightning; but the miraculous image
of the Blessed Virgin was rescued unhurt, and may still
be seen and venerated by tourists. From Ettal the road is
comparatively level, and, jolting swiftly over it, we soon
reached Ober-Ammergau.

THE BETRAYAL.—PASSION PLAY.

THE VOW.

During the Thirty Years' War a terrible plague, as if half a dozen armies were marching up and down the country, swept over Bavaria, devastating each town and hamlet. Of all the highland villages Ober-Ammergau, by means of a strictly-enforced quarantine alone, kept for a while the black foe at bay. No soul was allowed to leave the village; no living thing to enter it.

But one dark night Caspar Schuchler, an inhabitant of Ober-Ammergau, who had been away working in the plague-stricken neighboring village of Eschenlohe, creeping low, passed the drowsy sentinels and gained his home, and saw what for many a day he had been hungering for—a sight of his wife and bairns. It was a selfish act to do, and he and his fellow villages paid dearly for it. Three days after he had entered his house he and all his family lay dead, and the plague was raging through the valley, and nothing seemed able to stay its course. Then it was that the good Catholic peasants who dwelt by the side of the Ammer vowed that if the plague left them they would, every ten years, perform, in a theatrical manner, the Passion of our Blessed Lord. After their vow and earnest prayers the most skeptical admit that the plague disappeared as if by magic. So every ten years, in fulfillment of their solemn vow, and as an act of thanksgiving to Almighty God for their deliverance from the plague, the Ober-Ammergauites present for the edification and wonder of the world the famous Passion Play. Before each performance all the characters gather together on the stage around their pastor, the village priest, and kneeling, pray for a blessing upon the work then about to commence. The profits that are made, after paying the performers a wage that just compensates them for their loss of time—wood-carver **Lang,** who played the Christ in 1900, only received about two hundred and fifty dollars for the whole of the thirty or so performances given during the season, to say nothing of winter rehearsals—is put aside, part for the temporal benefit of the community and the rest for the benefit of the Church. From burgomaster down to shepherd lad, from the Mary and the Christus down to the humblest supernumerary, all work for the love of their religion, not for money. Each one feels that he or she is helping forward the cause of Christianity.

In writing of the Passion Play, one must not forget grand old Father Daisenberger, the gentle, simple old priest, "the father of the valley," who now lies in silence among his children he loved so well. It was this saintly priest who shaped the rude burlesque of a coarser age into the impressive, reverential drama that we saw yesterday. He taught the wood carvers of Ober-Ammergau that the Passion Play was intended not as an entertainment, but as a religious service.

THE PLAY.

The crowded audience in which we sat yesterday looking at the Passion Play of Ober-Ammergau saw Christ of Nazareth nearer than any book, however inspired, could bring Him to them; clearer than any words, however eloquent, could show Him. They saw the sorrow of His patient face. They heard His deep, rich tones calling to them. They saw Him in the hour of His so-called triumph wending His way through the narrow streets of Jerusalem, the multitude that thronged round Him waving their branches of green palms and shouting loud hosannas. What a poor scene of triumph! A poorly-clad, pale-faced man, mounted upon the back of a shuffling, unwilling little

THE SCOURGING. PASSION PLAY.

gray donkey, passing slowly through the by-ways of a city busy upon other things. Beside him a little band of worn, anxious men, clad in threadbare garments, fishermen, petty clerks and the like; and following a noisy rabble, shouting as crowds in all lands and in all times shout, and as dogs bark, they know not why—because others are shouting or barking. And that scene marks the highest triumph won while He lived on earth by the Divine carpenter of Galilee, about whom the world has been fighting and thinking and talking so hard for the last nineteen hundred years. They saw Him angry and indignant, driving out the desecrators from the temple. They saw the rabble, who a few brief moments before had followed Him shouting "Hosanna " slinking away from Him to shout for His foes.

They saw the high priests in their robes of white, with the rabbis and the doctors, all the great and learned in the land, sitting late into the night, beneath the vaulted roof of the Sanhedrim's council hall, plotting His death.

They saw Him supping with His disciples in the house of Simon. They saw poor, loving Mary Magdalene wash His feet with costly ointment that might have been sold and the money given to the poor.

They were present at the parting of Mary and Jesus by Bethany, and it will be many a day before the memory of the scene ceases to vibrate in their hearts. It is the scene that brings the humanness of the great tragedy most closely home to us. Jesus is going to face sorrow and death at Jerusalem. Mary's instinct tells her that this is so, and she pleads to Him to stay.

Poor Mary To others He is the Christ, the Saviour of mankind, setting forth upon His mighty mission to redeem the world. To loving Mary He is her son; the baby she has suckled at her breast, the little one she has crooned to sleep upon her lap, whose little cheek has lain against her heart, whose little feet have made sweet music through the poor home at Bethany: He is her boy, her child; she would wrap her mother's arms around Him, and hold Him safe against all the world. Never in any human drama can be witnessed a more moving scene than this. Never has the voice of any actress (and I have seen some of the greatest, if any great are living) stirred my heart as did the voice of Anna Flunger, the postman's daughter, who played the role of the Blessed Virgin. It was not the voice of one woman, it was the voice of Motherdom gathered together from all the world over.

Oliver Wendell Holmes, in "The Autocrat of the Breakfast Table," I think, confesses to have been bewitched at different times by two women's voices, and adds that both these voices belonged to German women. I am not surprised at either statement of the good Doctor's. I am sure if a man did fall in love with a voice, he would find, on tracing its source, that it was the voice of some homely-looking German woman. I have never heard such exquisite soul-drawing music in my life as I have more than once heard float from the lips of some sweet-faced German fraulein when she opened her mouth to speak. The voice has been so pure, so clear, so deep, so full of soft, caressing tenderness, so strong to comfort, so gentle to soothe, it has seemed like one of those harmonies musicians tell us they dream of but can never chain to earth.

As I sat in the theatre listening to the wondrous tones of this mountain peasant woman, rising and falling like the murmur of a sea, filling the vast sky-colored building with their yearning notes, stirring like a great wind stirs aeolian strings, it seemed to me that I was indeed listening to the voice of the Mother of God.

We saw Him, as we have so often seen Him in pictures, sitting for the last time with His disciples at supper. But yesterday we saw Him not a mute, moveless figure, posed in conventional attitude, but a living, loving man, sitting in fellowship with the dear friends that against all the world had believed in Him, and had followed His poor fortunes, talking with them for the last sweet time, comforting them.

We saw Him bless the bread and wine and heard Him say: "This is My body; this is My blood."

We saw His agony in the Garden of Gethsemane, the human shrinking from the cup of pain, the Divine, ready to do His Father's will. We saw the false friend and disciple, Judas Iscariot, betray Him with a kiss.

We saw Him, pale and silent, dragged now before the priests of His own countrymen, and now before the Roman Governor, while the voice of the people—the people who had cried "Hosanna" to Him—shouted: "Crucify Him! Crucify Him!" We saw him bleeding from the crown of thorns. We saw Him, still followed by the barking mob, sink beneath the burden of His cross. We saw the woman, St. Veronica, wipe the bloody sweat from off His face. Then the last long, silent look between the mother and the Son as, journeying upward to His death, He passed her in the narrow way through which He once had ridden in brief-lived triumph. They heard her low sob as she turned away, leaning on the Mary Magdalene. We saw Him nailed upon the cross between the two thieves. We saw the blood start from His side. We heard His last cry to His God. We saw Him rise victorious over death.

Few believing Christians among the vast audience but must have passed out from that strange playhouse with their belief and love strengthened. The God of the Christians, for his sake, became a man and lived and suffered and died as a man; and as a man living, suffering, dying among other men, he had that day seen Him. The man of powerful imagination needs no aid from mimicry, however reverent, to unroll before him in its simple grandeur the great tragedy on which the curtain fell at Calvary some nineteen centuries ago. A cultivated mind needs no story of human suffering to win or hold it to a faith. But the imaginative and the cultured are few and far between, and the peasants of Ober-Ammergau can plead, as their Master Himself once pleaded, that they seek not to help the learned but the lowly. The unbeliever also passes out into the village street full of food for thought. The rude sermon preached in this hillside temple has shown to him, clearer than he could have seen before, the secret wherein lies the strength of Christianity; the reason why, of all the faiths, this faith, born by the Sea of Galilee, has spread the farthest over the world and struck its note the deepest into human life. And that reason is the Divine personality of Jesus.

Experienced professional stage managers, with all the tricks and methods of the theatre at their fingers' ends, find it impossible out of a body of men and women born and bred in the atmosphere of the playhouse to construct a crowd that looks anything else except a nervous group of broken-down paupers. At Ober-Ammergau a few village priests and representative householders who have probably never, any one of them, been inside the walls of a theatre in their lives, dealing with peasants who have walked straight upon the stage from their carving benches and milking stools, produce swaying multitudes and clamoring mobs and dignified assemblages so natural and truthful, so realistic of the originals they represent that you feel like leaping upon the stage with excitement. It shows that earnestness and effort can very easily overtake and pass mere training

THE DESCENT FROM THE CROSS.

THE DESCENT FROM THE CROSS—PASSION PLAY.

and technical skill. The object of the Ober-Ammergau supernumerary is not to earn a small fee, but to help forward the success of the sacred drama. The scene of Christ's entry into Jerusalem, surrounded by the welcoming multitude, is a wonderful reproduction of life and movement, and so also is the scene, toward the end, showing His last journey up to Calvary. All Jerusalem seems to have turned out to see Him pass and to follow Him, the many laughing, the few sad. The people fill the narrow streets to overflowing and press round the spears of the Roman guard.

They throng the steps and balconies of every house; they strain to catch a sight of Christ above each other's heads; they leap up on each other's backs to gain a better vantage ground from which to hurl jeers at Him; they jostle disrespectfully against their priests. Each individual man, woman and child on the stage acts, and acts in perfect harmony with all the rest.

Of the chief members of the cast, Anton Lang, the gentle and yet kingly Christ; Burgomaster Lang, the stern, revengeful High Priest; Anna Flunger, the sweet-faced, sweet-voiced Virgin; Rendl, the dignified, statesman-like Pilate; Peter Rendl, the beloved John, with the purest and most beautiful face I have ever seen upon a man—it would be difficult to speak in terms of too high praise. Although mere peasants, they represent some of the greatest figures in the world's history with as simple a dignity and as grand a bearing as one might expect from the originals themselves. There must be a natural, inborn nobility in the character of these highlanders. They could never assume or act that manner au grand seigneur with which they imbue their parts.

ACTS OF THE DRAMA.

At eight A. M. the orchestra in front and below the stage play an overture, while the entire corps of actors, hidden from view behind the drop curtain, kneel with the parish priest in silent prayer, invoking the blessing of God upon the sacred drama about to be enacted. The play is commenced by the appearance of the chorus. I shall never forget the first sight of this well-trained band of singers. There are eighteen in the chorus—eight men and ten women; the Choragus, who speaks the prologues, standing in the center of the proscenium, with the four men on the right and three on the left, while five female figures stand on either side of the men. Their robes and the blending of color are alone striking and beautiful; all alike wear a long white under tunic edged with gold round the neck and skirt, with a colored outer mantle edged with the Greek key pattern in gold and held together by a band across the breast. A girdle round the white robe of the color of the mantle mixed with the gold; sandals on the feet with two straps across the instep, over hose of the color of the mantle; on the head a golden diadem with a cross in the floriated center. These robes form a brilliant but harmonious chord of color. The Choragus is conspicuous by his scarlet mantle; next to him, on the right, is green, then a brownish red, green again and purple; the five women wear a bright sort of magenta, purple, a bright grey, reddish-brown and light blue. I do not think that sufficient prominence has been given to the part sustained by this admirable chorus in most of the descriptions of the "Passion Spiel," and I heard spectators say that they were wearied by it; but to me they were throughout true Schutz-Geister, as they are called, keeping the soul in tune and assisting it most truly in the long effort of mind and heart which the tremendous drama requires. The Choragus greets all who have come together, in sympathetic words, accepting them at once as friends who are like-minded with the performers and exhorting them to assist devoutly at the Mystery to be set forth, which is nothing less than the redemption of the world. He says:

"All hail! Welcome to the band of Brothers whom love Divine hath here assembled, who wish to share the sorrows of their Saviour and to follow Him step by step on the way of His sufferings to the cross and the sepulchre."

The keynote to the whole is given in this solemnly intoned prologue:

"Ich will—so spricht der Heer
Den Todd des Sunders nicht."

Which, being interpreted means, I desire not the death of a sinner, saith the Lord.

This is sustained in the lines sung as the chorus divide and retire to their side of the stage, while the curtain rises and we see the first typical tableau from the Old Testament. Adam and Eve driven from Paradise.

"Yet from afar from Calvary's height
Shines through the night the morning dawn,"

is sweetly intoned by the chorus. Nothing can be more lovely than the second tableau which follows in a few minutes. The curtain has fallen on the scene of the expulsion from Paradise, the chorus has formed again in a straight line, continuing the song of thanksgiving for redemption; and now, as they retire, the curtain rises and we behold the Tree of Life, the cross on a rocky mount. At its foot kneels a girl of about thirteen clasping it in her arms, while twelve children, clad as angels, are grouped around in attitudes of adoring thanksgiving. The grace and beauty of this picture are wonderful, and also the motionless acting of the infants, many of them with outstretched arms.

During this tableau the Schutz-Geister retires to the sides of the stage and kneels, while they sing:

"Eternal, hear Thy Children's prayer,"

and then again exhort the spectators:

"Follow the Redeemer now beside."

Now the first scene in the Passion Play begins. Often as I have read and heard of Christ's entry into Jerusalem, acted in that theatre the reality far exceeded my expectations, at least before the central figure appeared. It was to me one of the most moving and quite overcoming scenes in the whole drama, as the seemingly endless crowd flowed on, men, women and children, all swayed by one sentiment, every voice joining in:

"Hail to Thee, Hail, O David's Son!"

There is much dignity in the conception of this march chorale; it is one of the most successful pieces in the Passion music. But, of course, the opportunity is a grand one for a musician. The distance in which it is first softly heard, the waving accompaniment of arms and green branches and the onward procession add to the stateliness of the tout ensemble. The change in the spirit of the words from praise to prayer is plaintively illustrated by the music, while the surging crowd advances, their voices growing louder and the air more defined. It is an effective appeal written from the heart and powerful enough to make the listener one in sympathy with the unanimous throng. The "Volk," as they are called, come slowly on the stage, waving branches of bracken, the action of their arms and limbs full of indescribable grace, although those in front are half backing as in royal presence. We feel that every eye is fixed on One whom as yet we do not see, and that the multitude have but one soul filled with adoring homage to Him.

"Blessed is He that cometh in the name of the Lord."

THE RESURRECTION—PASSION PLAY.

Old words, old visions of childhood return to the heart. We look at the great multitude which no man can number, with palms in their hands; we hear the everlasting song of blessing and honor, glory and power to the Prince of Peace and King of Kings, and we seem to see a faint shadow of that which shall be when every discordant note has ceased and the soul is set free for the endless harmony of thanksgiving. I must acknowledge that the first appearance of the Christus was a disappointment. Perhaps because expectation had been wound up too high by the song and triumph of the multitude. At all events, my first strong feeling upon beholding Anton Lang as Christ was: "He has attempted the impossible." As the play progressed this feeling wore off and I sat amazed at the marvelous acting of this simple peasant. There is not a star or leading man on the English or American stage today that can hope to approach the superb histrionic genius of Anton Lang. It is also true that none of our popular actresses will bear comparison histrionically with gentle Anna Flunger, who played the part of Mary.

We have prepared for our readers a synopsis of the seventeen acts and the accompanying tableaux of the Passion Play, which is as follows:

First Act: CHRIST'S ENTRY INTO JERUSALEM.

Tableaux (which in each act precede the act itself, and are taken from the Old Testament):

"Expulsion of Adam and Eve from Eden" and "The Adoration of the Cross."

Second Act: THE HIGH COUNCIL OF THE SANHEDRIM.

Tableau: "Conspiracy of the Brothers of Joseph."

Third Act: CHRIST'S DEPARTURE FROM BETHANY.

Tableaux: "Tobias Departing With the Angel Gabriel," "The Lamenting Bride," "The Burden of Solomon's Song."

Fourth Act: CHRIST'S LAST JOURNEY TO JE-RUSALEM.

Tableau: "King Ahasuerus Repudiating Vashti and Elevating Esther to the Throne."

Fifth Act: THE LAST SUPPER.

Tableaux: "The Falling of the Manna in the Wilderness," "Arrival of the Grapes from Canaan."

Sixth Act: THE BETRAYAL.

Tableaux: "The Sale of Joseph."

Seventh Act: THE GARDEN OF GETHSEMANE.

Tableaux: "Adam and His Two Children Tilling the Soil," "The Treachery of Joab Towards His Rival Amasa."

Eighth Act: CHRIST BEFORE ANNAS.

Tableau: "The Prophet Micah Smitten on the Cheek by a Priest of Baal, Whom He had Denounced Before King Ahab."

Ninth Act: CHRIST BEFORE CAIAPHAS.

Tableaux: "Stoning of Naboth Under Jezebel's Orders for Refusing to Sell His Vineyard to King Ahab," "The Sufferings of Job."

Tenth Act: THE DESPAIR OF JUDAS.

Tableau: "Cain's Remorse on the Death of Abel."

Eleventh Act: CHRIST BEFORE PILATE.

Tableau: "Daniel Before King Darius."

Twelfth Act: CHRIST BEFORE HEROD.

Tableau: "Samson Pulling Down the Philistine Temple."

Thirteenth Act: THE SCOURGING AND CROWN-ING OF CHRIST.

Tableaux: "Joseph's Bloody Coat Shown to His Father, Jacob," "The Altar at Which Isaac Kneels Ready for Sacrifice."

Fourteenth Act: CHRIST SENTENCED TO DEATH.

Tableaux: "Joseph Raised to Honor by Pharaoh," "The Two Goats Presented by Aaron as His Sin Offering."

Fifteenth Act: CHRIST BEARS HIS CROSS TO CALVARY.

Tableaux: "Isaac Bearing the Altar Wood up Mount Moriah," "The Israelites Writhing in Agony From the Bites of Fiery Serpents," "The Elevation of the Brazen Serpent and the Healing of the People."

Sixteenth Act: THE CRUCIFIXION.

The chorus in this scene change their robes to the garb of mourning. Calvary is the most intense portraiture of the entire drama. The two malefactors are roughly fastened to their crosses by ropes. The central cross on which the personator of Christ is suspended is always the magnet for all eyes. The fastening of Anton Lang to the cross was startlingly real. We could see no trace of ligaments or stage illusions. He was apparently nailed to the cross. It is surmised that metal rings attached to his corset are hung upon hooks which are fastened in a groove of the cross, but we have never heard any satisfactory explanation of this realistic "business" of the play.

Sevententh Act: THE ASCENSION OF OUR LORD.

The performance lasts from 8 A. M. to 5:45 P. M., with one hour's intermission for luncheon.

Considering the length of the play, the physical endurance of the principals, chorus and supernumeraries is wonderful. The pose of this living human statuary, the facial expression, the groupings, the appropriate and splendid costumes and scenery, show excellent artistic taste and a remarkable perception of stage effect. Some of the dramatic situations and tableaux are copied with fidelity from pictures of the world's best artists. For example, the Last Supper is a minute production of the picture of the same subject by Leonardo De Vinci.

ADDITIONAL DATA.

Only one complete copy of the play is extant. The present version was written in 1850, and is retained in manuscript by the village priest, who copies for each performer his or her part. The actors are selected by him and a committee of forty-five householders. The costumes are made by the peasants themselves.

The amphitheatre is an elliptical enclosure, uncovered except in the portion most remote from the stage, and seats about six thousand people. Reserved chairs are rented for two dollars in American money, in advance for each performance, while the general admission fee costs but twenty-five cents.

Many who made the Passion Play splendid by their spiritual lives and noble acting have gone to their reward. In 1887 Tobias Flunger, one of the best players at Ammergau, died. He played Christ in 1850 and Pilate in 1860. In 1880 he was an apostle in the tableaux. His eldest daughter was the Mary in 1870 and his second daughter also appeared in the play.

We must not forget that the Passion Play is a Catholic drama produced by loving and faithful sons and daughters of our Holy Church. These village actors are educated by their church ceremonies. The scene of Christ's enry into Jerusalem is for the most part a repetition of the procession on Palm Sunday in all Roman Catholic Churches throughout the world. These Bavarian crucifix carvers dramatically display on the Passion stage very much of what they have imbibed in church. Father Daisenberger gave his whole life to the direction of his people in elevating and perfecting their performance of the Divine Tragedy. "I undertook the labor," he said, "with the best will for the love of my Divine Redeemer, and with only one object in view, namely, the edification of the world."

MOST REV. JOHN J. KEANE, D. D., ARCHBISHOP OF DUBUQUE.

DANIEL O'CONNELL.

Oration by

The Most Reverend John J. Keane, D. D.,

Archbishop of Dubuque.

INTRODUCTORY NOTE.

The praise of men of renown and of our fathers in their generation being commended even as a religious observance, the Irish National College, Rome, where the heart of O'Connell is honorably and lovingly entombed, held a solemn function in commemoration of the fiftieth anniversary of his death.

The project had the cordial approval and blessing of the Holy Father. His Holiness went even farther and deigned to express a strong desire that similar commemorations would be made all through Ireland, remarking that the soul of O'Connell being, as we trust, with God, his body is in Ireland and his heart here in Rome.

This sympathetic message was welcomed heartily and reverently by Ireland. She, only a few years before, had celebrated the first centenary of O'Connell's birth by a national demonstration which attracted the attention of the world, yet this other occasion for attesting the National esteem and love for him was warmly embraced by bishops, priests and people. In the Primatial See—Armagh—the Cardinal Archbishop presided at a Solemn Requiem and Panegyric at which the clergy and laity even from distant localities assisted in imposing numbers. The See of St. Patrick in this memorable celebration was emulated north and south, east and west. But among all, the City of Cork distinguished itself by its magnificent public procession, which in point of numbers, organization, concord, and religious devotion was an emphatic and historic tribute to the memory of O'Connell.

However, the honor of being the first to undertake the public commemoration of this fiftieth anniversary belongs not to the Irish at home or abroad; it is due to the Catholic Young Men's Society of Genoa, who, before the present year began, appealed to their fellow citizens and fellow countrymen on the motive of Catholic patriotism to join them in paying a tribute of admiration to the great Irish leader, the model champion of civil and religious freedom, on the fiftieth anniversary of the day when, having been stayed in his journey to Rome by the angel of death, he, in their own superb Genoa, bequeathed "his soul to God, his body to Ireland, and his heart to Rome." They proposed to add an artistic wreath and commemorative medallion, both in bronze, to the monumental slab which marks the mansion in which O'Connell died. The unveiling of the wreath and medallion was to take place after a solemn High Mass in the Cathedral, followed by a civic procession to the site itself. Addresses and speeches by distinguished public men were to be delivered after the newly-decorated inscription was again exposed to public view. A special public lecture upon O'Connell was to be delivered in the Grand Hall of the Association, and an extraordinary single number issue of the Society's weekly periodical, devoted exclusively to contributions from the best Catholic pens of the Peninsula upon O'Connell and bearing his name. This programme was executed with a pomp and popular concourse and general enthusiasm incredible in Ireland, and all the more honorable to Italy and to her cherished guest.

The Genoese but led the way to their compatriots in Rome, Milan and Naples. In these and other cities public lectures, numerously attended, were delivered repeatedly, even upon the character and work of O'Connell. The President of Catholic Congresses for all Italy, Count Paganuzzi, issued an address to all the Catholic organizations, exhorting all to study and follow the principles and action of O'Connell. This he declared was a great duty as the only means now left them to secure the true interests and preserve the true greatness of Italy.

Among the Irish Colony at Rome and their kinsmen from almost every nation under the sun, the very fervor of religious and patriotic devotion was excited by the commemoration at the National College. All rejoiced that in present circumstances of political discord and Non-Catholic tendencies among too many Irishmen an occasion was found to signalize their regard for O'Connell, and all felt it to be an enviable privilege to pay this tribute of admiration and gratitude in the place where his heart lies buried.

Two of the Bishops of Ireland were present. The Sacred College was associated in the persons of their Eminences the Cardinal Vicar, the Cardinal Prefect of Propaganda, the Cardinal Titular of St. Agatha, Cardinal Satolli, and Cardinal Jacobini. The Holy Father sent for the Pontifical Requiem Mass the select Vestments of the Sistine, as Pius IX had done at the time of O'Connell's death.

The preparation of the Church was undertaken by the Irish ladies with the ready and practical earnestness of the native spirit. With them their sisters in religion, their friends resident in Rome, and the College artists co-operated, and their combined taste, zeal, and union of minds and hearts easily effected such preparations as did honor to Ireland and O'Connell even amidst Roman surroundings.

A noble Celtic Cross worked in cloth of gold upon the sombre drapery of the apse indicated the spirit which inspired the celebration—the old love of religion and country hitherto unconquerable.

High up in front of the great arch uniting nave and apse appeared most conspicuously an angel of graceful design and beautifully colored upholding a grand scroll which bore the word that thrilled every spectator: Emancipation.

The monument in which the heart of O'Connell rests, draped in artistic folds of black and cloth of gold, had appended four bannerettes, two on each side bearing the shields of America and Scotland, England and Australia, upon green with gold fringe and tassels. These bannerettes represented the countries which have more signally benefited by the achievements of the Liberator, and in which his compatriots are to-day so numerous that they constitute the greater Ireland. But emblems still more eloquent were to be seen immediately in front of the monument. A large heart of roses with a cluster of shamrocks from Ireland in its centre and a scroll inscribed "To Rome I bequeath my heart," was laid in the centre of a rich green velvet carpet. This was flanked on the right by the Pontifical Arms, and on the left by the Irish Harp in mourning. Then palm branches were intertwined and carried all around the front and sides of the monument.

Other flags and banners adorned both the Church and outer portico. Among them and hanging over the central door was the large green silk banner of St. Patrick. This was once borne to battle by the Irish Potifical Brigade; now it had on one side the Papal flag, and on the other that of Ireland.

In the centre of the nave and to the height of thirty feet rose the catafalque. It was constructed in three tiers surmounted by a Celtic Cross. The panels of the second tier were adorned with the heraldic arms of the four provinces of Ireland. There were also wreaths of palm and laurel and moss from Ireland arranged with the magnificent drapery, and numerous wax lights, candelabra, &c. It was highly imposing, significant and beautiful.

Taken altogether, the preparations within the Church were worthy of the occasion. They were enhanced by the architectural perfection of the venerable Temple, so as to appear with extraordinary advantage, and leave nothing to be desired.

Outside the principal entrance from the public thoroughfare was placed the following inscription:

DANIEL O'CONNELL,
KERRY IN HIBERNIA NATO, A. MDCCLXXV.
TUM RELIGIOSAE TUM PATRIAE LIBERTATIS
STRENUO ADSERTORI ET VINDICI
QUI
ROMAM PEREGRINATUS ID MAJI MDCCCXLVII.,
GENUAE PIISIME OBIIT,
DEO ANIMAM, HIBERNIAE CORPUS, REDDENS
COR ROMAE.
COLLEGIUM HIBERNENSIUM URBANUM
LEONE XIII. P.M. PROBANTE
POST ANNOS L.
FESTA FUNEBRIA.
E.
P.

At the sacred function the Church was filled. The laity occupied the aisles and that portion of the nave which could be spared. They included several representatives of the highest ranks, and were full of most reverential piety. The students of the National College, augmented in numbers by the other Irish ecclesiastical and religious communities, and Irish contingents from the Propaganda and other colleges, together with the whole academic body of the English and Scots colleges, filled the outer choir. All were in choral habit, and amidst their beautiful and impressive files, ordered perfectly on both sides, rose the splendid and lofty catafalque described above. Dignitaries of all grades, with procurators, rectors and representative priests, were accommodated with special distinction in the inner choir. Amongst them were the Most Rev. Archbishops and Bishops Passerini, Stonor, O'Callaghan, Foley, O'Connor, &c., &c. Their Eminences Cardinals Vaughan and Satolli assisted in a special coretto, unseen according to the etiquette of the curia.

The celebrant of the Pontifical High Mass was the Most Rev. Nicholas Donnelly, Auxiliary Bishop of Dublin, an alumnus of the alma mater, in whose service and to whose great credit he was now officiating. His Lordship had as Assistant Priest the Very Rev. W. H. O'Connell, Rector of the N. American College; Deacon, the Rev. John Prior, Vice-Rector of the English College; and Sub-Deacon, the Rev. Dean of the Scots College. The singing was executed by a joint choir of all the sister colleges under the direction of the Abbate Muller, and the music was entirely Gregorian, rendered with highly devotional sweetness, tenderness and power.

Immediately after the Mass, the panegyric was delivered by the Most Reverend John Joseph Keane, Archbishop of

Damascus, one of the founders and the first Rector of the Catholic University of the United States. Born in old Donegal, richly gifted with the pious and simple devotion characteristic of the Faith of his fathers, learned, captivated by zeal for the Church, for Ireland, for every good cause, and renowned in the Old as in the New World for pre-eminence in sacred oratory, his Grace was chosen to be the preaacher on this grand occasion by general desire, voiced by the Cardinal Primate of Ireland. Speaking for a full hour, from the platform of the altar, he held the entire audience in wrapt attention. He was manifestly inspired by no other influences than the purest religion and charity. Beautiful and noble were his conceptions, starting from the very text of Scripture at the commencement which held forth the Divine mission of O'Connell, as of Moses, to deliver his nation. The statement of the facts, which for many present were hard to be heard, was a marvelous instance of skillful diction. It was straightforward, yet inoffensive, dispassionate, yet pathetic, and irresistibly powerful in effect. In every conclusion there was the cogency of correct reasoning; in every lesson there was sound wisdom. The national aspirations of Ireland and Ireland's unyielding persistence to vindicate her every just claim, civil and religious, have rarely, if ever, had advocacy more dignified, more eloquent, and more powerful. Therefore, all who were privileged to hear this panegyric long to see it published. Its benefit may so be available to greater numbers at home and abroad, and this through many generations.

His Eminence the Cardinal Archbishop of Westminster, pronounced the discourse of Archbishop Keane to rank with the masterpieces of Ventura, Lacordaire and Dupanloup, and sure to work great good among the English people.

His Eminence the Cardinal Archbishop of Sydney, having read even the succinct report of the newspapers, wrote to the Irish College, his Alma Mater: "I congratulate you on the success of your commemoration of O'Connell's demise. Monsignor Keane's discourse was excellent. I trust that Providence will soon send another leader inspired by the same religious sentiments, and gifted with the same commanding genius, to complete the good work so auspiciously begun at the time of Emancipation."

Similar comments and encomiums have been communicated by the Venerable Hierarchy of Ireland.

The panegyric was followed by the final rite of the solemn function—the absolution at the catafalque. No other ceremony harmonizes more tenderly and more soothingly with our affectionate and reverent sorrow for the departed. The invocation of Divine Mercy, the sprinkling with holy water round and round, the incensation also, and then the concluding prayers and versicles sung in solemn plaint, and responded by the united voices of all the clergy present, and all this in the circumstances described was impressive and moving beyond description. At this ceremony His Eminence the Cardinal Archibshop of Westminster officiated. No one could more appropriately or more effectively have fulfilled the office, and with the last "requiescat in pace" slowly and pathetically chanted, brought to its complete and successful accomplishment, this Catholic and international tribute to Daniel O'Connell.

O'CONNELL IN THE ETERNAL CITY.

At the celebration in memory of the fiftieth anniversary of the death of Daniel O'Connell, on May 15, in the Church of St. Agatha, in Rome, the panegyric was delivered by the Most Rev. Archbishop Keane, formerly Rector of the

Catholic University of America, at Washington, D. C. It was a splendid oration, and will probably stand as one of the eloquent Archbishop's most eloquent utterances. The Archbishop spoke as follows:

"Come, and I will send thee to Pharaoh, that thou mayst deliver My people * * * and I will be with thee." (Exodus III., 10-12.)

Fifty years ago to-day Daniel O'Connell died, leaving his body to Ireland, his heart to Rome, and his soul to God. All Christendom cried out in sorrow at the news. The Eternal City received his heart as a priceless heritage, and paid more than regal honor to his memory. Paris vied with Rome in the expression of her admiration and her grief. The two most eloquent and most learned preachers in the world declared his character and his achievements without a parallel in the history of great men, and proved that all the nations of the earth were his debtors. Heartbroken Erin covered her face in utterable, incomparable grief, giving thanks to God that she was the mother of such a son, yet feeling her bereavement, her utter desolation, great indeed and bitter and almost hopeless, now that he was gone.

The events of the half century that have since elapsed serve as a background to set forth in clearer light the features of that wonderful man, the providential meaning and purpose of that phenomenal life. Nothing is plainer in history than that ages and nations have had their providential men—men who not only towered above their generation by their superior qualities, but on whom there was manifest the impress of a divine purpose and plan—a mission from on high. Such men not only mark an epoch and give the key to its meaning, they teach a lesson—or rather the God of history teaches a lesson through them—a lesson not only for their time and their country, but which it behooves all times and all countries to study and to heed.

The student of history has no difficulty in recognizing that O'Connell was the providential man of Ireland. But he was far more than that. The Count de Montalembert, addressing him in 1845, in the name of all lovers of liberty in France, declared that they saluted him, not only as the Liberator of Ireland, not only as the man of the Irish people, but as the man of Christendom, the man of the age.

Yes, in studying O'Connell, it is a mighty lesson of God's Providence to our age that we have to study. Let us study it reverently. And that we may not mar it by any theorizing of our own, we shall simply let that wonderful life speak for itself; we shall gaze upon those majestic outlines which the hand of God has traced, praying for wisdom to appreciate it as we ought. And may the angels of peace and charity keep our hearts the while, so that studying the history of a great struggle against persecution and injustice, we may let no bitterness into our hearts, but sorrow for wrong, and love of justice and good will to all men.

The formative period in every great man's life is a time of intensest interest. Then you can see the hand of God moulding like soft clay the young mind and heart and character into their providential shape and into fitness for their providential purpose. O'Connell has himself told us most sweetly of the mould in which his life as a boy was cast. He tells us that the impressions which earliest and most powerfully acted on him were those of the Alpine scenery of his native Kerry. The fields of emerald green that stretched around his boyhood home, and reached far away in endless vistas of hill and dale, gradually developed in him an exquisite sense of the beautiful, the sweet, and gentle. The mountain slopes which, mildly starting from the meadow softness of the plain, mounted up and up, through heathery tangles and thickets of oak and fir, up to the rocky height, where St. Brendan gazed out upon the vasty deep, and where he offered up the Holy Sacrifice for the souls that might be in unknown lands beyond the waves, all this caught up the fancy of the boy and carried his imagination higher and higher, and farther and farther away, till he felt that all on earth and all in heaven was kin to him. The mountain torrent that swept and tumbled through the neighboring glen and rushed past him into the sea, filling the valley with its "eternal roar," spoke weird messages to him of the distant past, of the hidden and unseen, waking echoes of sadness and pathos in his youthful heart. He tells us how the giant waves, rolling from the illimitable ocean and flinging untiringly their masses of foam against the stupendous mountain cliffs that fenced his home, told him of the strain and strife ever going on in human things, and in which he one day should have to take so strong a part; and then the calm and exquisite beauty which, after the storm, would settle on the waves and cliffs, all bathed in the soft, pale moonlight, used to teach him that it was worth while to face the tempest and the strife which lead to betterment and to peace.

Thus was Providence moulding that young heart to sympathy with nature and with all things, moulding it in the true Celtic mould of poetry and tenderness and deep intensity of feeling, moulding it in exquisite sensitiveness to every touch of sweetness and beauty, of joy and sadness, of every mood of feeling that sweeps over the hearts of men.

And in so doing Providence was not only developing the poetry of his own nature, making it sympathetic with every human condition, fitting it unto exquisite compassion for

the sorrows, the sufferings, the needs of all the children of
Erin, but it was also making him acquainted with all the
powers of emotion that lie dormant in the hearts of others,
teaching him how to touch and rouse them, how to play
with a master hand on all the emotions of the human heart.
God destined him to enter into the inmost lives of all the
millions in Erin, to mould their minds in his own thoughts,
to move their hearts with his own emotions, to rouse their
wills to the level of his own great purpose, and hurl their
united energies in one irresistible assault against the citadel
of wrong.   Only a nature of marvelous depth and tenderness and sympathy and power could be a fit instrument in
the hand of Providence for such a work.   And it was to this
that God was silently, hiddenly, moulding his whole being
in this the first stage of his providential preparation.

Then Providence led his young mind to a higher level.
One of his favorite haunts was the old ruined abbey of
Derrynane.   The quaint old architecture, so different from
that of the houses around, charmed his fancy and made
him wonder who they were that had reared those walls and
dwelt within them long ago.   His father answered his eager
questionings and told him of the generations after genera
tions of holy and learned monks who had lived there centuries before; told him of the similar generations of saints
and sages who had made glorious the names of Ardfert,
Aghadoe, Innisfallen and Muckross in his own loved Kerry,
besides hundreds of abbeys like them all over Ireland.
These hints of a better and brighter age long gone by fired
the heart of young O'Connell with eagerness to know all
about those vanished glories.   He gathered every accessible
detail from masters and from books.   And then, he tells us,
that golden age of Erin was the favorite theme of his boy-
ish meditations.   He paused not to dwell on the devasta-

tion of Danish and Norman and Saxon invasions which had quenched that wondrous radiance. He passed beyond the storm clouds and basked in the radiances that once illumined all the land.

He says he used to like to hide in those venerable cloisters and people them in imagination with the busy throngs of masters and scholars that made them sanctuaries of religion and learning in the days of yore. He loved to live over again those marvelous three centuries when, amid the barbarian invasions that had flooded the rest of Europe, Ireland was the one secure ark of religion, the one peaceful haven of sacred and profound learning.

His young Celtic heart exulted as he dwelt on those proud and blessed days when, as Venerable Bede tells us, the gentry and nobility of England went to Ireland for divine study and to lead chaste lives, King Alfred himself being indebted to her for his education; while in England Irish masters were the instructors, under whom, he says, the English youth and their parents were imbued with learning and with sound morality; the proud and blessed days when, as Camden has recorded, "the Anglo-Saxons flocked to Ireland as to a mart of learning, and if one were away from home it was said of him, as by a sort of proverb, that he had gone to Ireland to receive his education;" the proud and blessed days when, as the Protestant historian, Dr. Prideaux, says, Ireland was the prime seat of learning in all Christendom; when she gave Charlemagne the saintly scholars who were to restore the reign of the true, the beautiful and the good, on the devastated continent of Europe; and when, as St. Bernard tells us in his "Life of St. Malachy," and many historians besides him, floods of learned and religious missionaries poured forth from the cloisters of Ireland to carry back the blessed light unto the very ends of darkened Christendom.

In later years his soul was to burn with indignation against the tyrant oppressors who had quenched this matchless radiance and robbed his country of her ancient glories. But now it sufficed him to revel in the memories that were his rightful inheritance and to drink his soul full of their inspiration. It was to be the inspiration of his life, as it had been during all these centuries the inspiration of his Erin. Faith, religion, love of God and Christ and Mother Church became the mould of his whole character, became the mainspring of all his energies, the motive power of his whole life. Every great life must be possessed by some lofty ideal, must be lifted up and broadened and ennobled by some mighty motive, must be upheld and impelled by some transcendent purpose. All this the soul of that boy was drinking in, almost unconsciously, from his charmed musings on the Christian glories of Erin's past. And while the simple, vigorous life he lived was building up in him that stalwart physical strength that he would need for the herculean labors of his future career, he was growing at the same time into the life purpose which was to give that career its direction and its greatness.

He longed to drink deep of learning. But poor, devastated Erin had no schools in which he could find it. The hand of the spoiler had swept them all away. He was too young to grasp the full meaning of the English Penal Code that ground down his country; but he had a glimpse of it when he was compelled, in order to get an education, to go seek it in foreign climes. During the four years that he spent in the colleges of Liege, Louvain, St. Omer and Douay, while plodding faithfully in the ordinary curriculum, his mind and heart were ever intent in the thoughts of his early boyhood. He loved history, because it pictured to his youthful imagination the lifelong struggle of humanity for right against might, for justice against wrong, for liberty to live, as God meant that mankind should live, in peace and welfare; for liberty to grow, as God meant that mankind should grow, unto the full stature of manly self-control and responsibility, not under the rod of pedagogues and masters forever, but in God's time, under the mighty but gentle and ennobling sway of reason, of conscience, of the law of God and of just laws made in conformity therewith. Thus side by side with his early love of religion there grew up in his soul a mighty love of justice and of liberty, and a great wrath against tyranny in any shape or in any part of the world, that would rob men of their rights, that would force on them the rule of wrong, that would shackle or restrain them from legitimate enjoyment of justice and liberty.

While he was working all this out for himself in the quiet seclusion of his classes, infuriated multitudes were working it out in bloody shape at the barricades of Paris and on the battlefields of France. At first his soul sympathized with them because they battled against manifest wrong, because they marched under the banners of justice and liberty. But ere long he saw that they had lost the great ideals which constitute justice and liberty, that Voltairean sophistry had robbed them of the principles which underlie all human welfare; that in their mad rush for liberty they were desecrating all the sanctuaries of liberty and breaking down all its safeguards; that thus they were driving on to wild extremes, and extremes must meet; that Mirabeau was preparing the way for Danton, Robespiérre and Marat, as these would logically lead on the iron despotism of Napoleon. When he left Douay for his home, in 1793, at the age of eighteen, these convictions were already clear and strong in his mind. He felt sure that his life would be spent in a struggle for his country's rights, in the mighty endeavor to wrest from English tyranny justice and liberty for Ireland. God was already whispering in his ear, "Come, and I will send thee that thou mayst deliver My people; and I will be with thee." But he saw clearly that the strife in which he was to be a leader must be totally different from the awful and bloody and godless struggle of the French Revolution. From that conviction and that resolution he never swerved for an instant.

He had left Ireland a mere boy, full of the sweet imaginings of childhood, living in fancy with his heroes in the bright glories of the past. He returned verging into manhood, his intellect developed and trained, able to look facts in the face, to estimate them rightly, and to draw practical inferences. He had read of the condition of his country, writhing under the heel of oppression, but now he saw with his own eyes what Ireland was, and the spectacle wrung his heart, nay, almost broke it. Everywhere he beheld the dire results of seven centuries of tyrannical oppression and three centuries of systematic extermination. With heart-sick avidity he studied every detail of that incomparable Penal Code, devised under Henry and Elizabeth for the extirpation of the Catholic Religion, developed and perfected under Cromwell and the rest, for the extirpation of the Catholic Irish people. He studied the exquisite minuteness with which it was detailed that if a priest were found anywhere in the island, he should be "hanged, cut down while alive, beheaded, quartered, bowelled and burned; his head to be set on a pike and exposed in a public place"; that if any one harbored a priest, he should suffer confiscation of property and death; that if any one happened to meet a

Daniel O'Connell

priest on the highway, or knew where one was hiding and did not immediately procure the priest's arrest, he should be "cast into prison, flogged through the public streets, and afterward have his ears cut off"; and that "should it appear that anyone kept up any correspondence or friendship with a priest, he is to suffer death." He learned how any Catholic sixteen years of age could be required to swear an oath of abjuration, under direst pains and penalties. He followed the ramifications of the code as it hounded Catholics through every department of civil life, shutting them out from every position of public trust or emolument, from taking any part in the political life of the country, from even teaching or being taught; so that the seven millions of Catholics had no legal right to exist, could breathe only by the tolerance of the 800,000 Protestants in Ireland, and of the British Government, which acknowledged that little Protestant minority alone. He tracked it as it entered even into the sanctuary of domestic life, offering the children every inducement to denounce their Catholic father and renounce his faith. He studied it until he saw for himself how justly the great Edmund Burke had written of it: "It was a complete system, full of coherence and consistency, and as well fitted for the oppression, impoverishment and degradation of a people, and the debasement in them of human nature itself, as ever proceeded from the perverted ingenuity of men."

He thanked God that while it had indeed succeeded in oppressing and impoverishing the Irish people and making them a race of hated aliens in their own country, it had utterly failed to degrade or debase them. The record of those three hundred years showed it amply; but no thanks for that to the Penal Code of the British Government. He saw how, during the period that immediately preceded and followed his own birth, the Government had been forced by circumstances into some relaxation of the Penal Laws. America had declared to the world that no Government had authority to encroach on the inalienable rights conferred on man by his Creator, and had made good her declaration by the glorious result of the War of Independence. France had in like manner proclaimed the inalienableness of the rights of man; she had failed to recognize the sanction of those rights in the unassailable gift of the Creator, and therefore her assertion of them had proved an awful disappointment; but the great truth which underlay the assertion was everywhere fermenting in the minds of men, and could not be gainsaid or ignored. Moreover, the conquering Napoleon had his eye on England, and England felt that in order to insure the loyalty of the Irish Catholics, who were the best material in her army, relaxations of the Penal Laws must necessarily be granted. And so, grudgingly, she yielded some concessions, and Irish Catholics could feel that, in the eye of the law, some little manhood was left in them, and some small modicum of human rights might be asserted.

O'Connell saw that now was the opportune time for the delivery of his country from slavery. Clearer and clearer God was whispering in his heart, "Come, and I will send thee that thou mayst deliver My people." Again and again, as he gazed upon the odious and intolerable persecution and felt the galling fetters in his own life and in that of his family, his blood boiled with indignation like that which fired the heart of Moses when he rose and slew the slayer of his people. But his Celtic impetuosity was wonderfully balanced and controlled by clear-sighted prudence. History had shown him how every wrathful uprising of the harassed and maddened Irish against the overwhelming odds of their armed and disciplined foes had only ended in more cruel massacre and in tightening of the fetters. Now, under his own eyes, the uprising of '98, led by the heroic Wolfe Tone, Arthur O'Connor and Lord Edward Fitzgerald, had been stamped out in the blood of more than fifty thousand vic- tims. His conclusion was drawn, positively and irrevo- cably; not by physical force was the victory to be gained, but by moral power. His plan was formed, definitely and unchangeably; he would unite into one vast army every man and woman in Ireland; he would arm them with weap- ons against which guns and bayonets would be powerless; he would fill them with clear-sighted conviction of their rights and with unflinching determination that those rights must be granted; he would teach them to declare their grievances, to protest and petition and agitate for justice, till the whole world would ring with their complaint and all mankind agree that their claim was just; he would fling the indignant public opinion of his whole country and of the whole world like an irresistible phalanx against the British Parliament, and force it to surrender, force it to do justice, force it to emancipate enslaved Erin.

To prepare himself for that task was now the one study of his life. Partial relaxation of the Penal Laws now made it possible for him to study law and be admitted to the bar. He unhesitatingly chose this career, because it would give him standing and influence, because it would make him master in all legal procedure; because it would give him opportunities to right injustice; because it would train him in perfect power of speech, the magic power by which he was to win and rouse and direct the energies of all his peo- ple and to batter down the opposition of all their foes.

Ere long, the stalwart, handsome, eloquent, hard-work- ing young lawyer attracted general attention and won general esteem in the courts. It had long been proverbial that no Irish Catholic had any justice to expect; but little by little it became known that there was now in Dublin a young barrister, openly and emphatically both Irish and Catholic, but so marvelously masterful in legal knowledge, in all the arts of debate, in grand and stormy eloquence, in withering sarcasm, in fearless and unrelenting purpose, that no one could withstand him, that prejudiced judges were powerless to resist him, and that through every iniquitous law he could "drive a coach and six." Wider and wider spread his fame, and when, on the eve of the abolition of the Irish Parliament, this young barrister of twenty-five arose in mass-meeting and thundered against the proposed iniquity, against this outrageous injustice to Ireland, the whole people felt that a great power had risen among them, a man in whose heart there was an echo to all the woes of Erin, an echo to all the patriotism that had ever armed her sons for her defense, a man of wisdom and power and nobleness of soul whom they could trust, whom they could follow and obey in the mighty struggle to which his finger was already pointing them.

On and on he pushed in his splendid career, winning fame and fortune for himself, but winning also what he prized far more, the confidence of the Irish people. It was no easy task. They had grown so used not only to tyranny but to betrayal, that it was no wonder they had grown diffident, suspicious of every would-be leader. Especially was this true of the clergy and the bishops, they had so often seen their poor flocks roused to frenzy and led out to certain slaughter by well-meaning but imprudent demagogues, that they were not to be blamed for long mistrusting this new arch-agitator who spoke in such thunder-tones against long-rooted injustice, and was beginning to stir so profoundly the hearts of the entire nation by his demand of justice for Ireland. No wonder that nearly all who were engaged in trade or possessed vested interests, feared that this agitation would disturb economic adjustments and entail pecuniary loss on themselves, and that therefore they should deprecate it with all their might. And no wonder that many a hot-headed enthusiastic patriot, whose blood was boiling with anger against British tyranny, who had lost all hope—if ever he had any—in British justice, who was full of the spirit that in '98 had risen half armed and rushed to death for Ireland, should now scoff at this lawyer patriot, scoff at his denunciation of physical force, scoff at his peaceful agitation, at his law and order campaign, scoff at his hope and his promise that through mere moral power the Irish people would wring from England what they had failed to win with guns and pikes.

All this O'Connell had to overcome ere his people could be one with him; and he overcame it all. It took him ten years and more to conquer all mistrust, to answer all objections, to remove honest prejudices, to expose and defeat self-interested opposition, to pour his own strong convictions and his own lofty purpose into every Irish heart. This resistance he had counted on, and it did not discourage him. Nay, it was all the better, hard-won allegiance would be all the more lasting and reliable. On and on he fought in this campaign of conviction, breaking down the mistrust, the hopelessness, the apathy, the prejudices of his people, till every mind in Ireland saw the truth and every heart was with him, and from end to end of the land he was acclaimed the Man of the People.

Then began the long campaign of assault upon the foe. Two great rights O'Connell was determined to wrest from British tyranny: religious liberty and civil liberty. He put religious liberty first, because it is the more sacred of the two, because the man who has not liberty of conscience has no rights that are worth the having. And so throughout the land the cry went up for Catholic Emancipation. Meetings were held in every town and on every hillside, to hear O'Connell tell them of their country's rights and their country's wrongs. Thousands and tens of thousands hung upon his words, exulting and weeping by turns, as he pictured to them Erin's Catholic glories in the blessed days of yore and Erin's piteous desolation now, as she sat wan and wasted in her ruined home, wailing over the myriads of her sons that had been slain for loving her, weeping over the down-trodden multitudes of her children that were treated as helots in their own land, despised by the Sassenach because, like their mother, they loved the religion of Jesus crucified, and found their consolation with Mary and John at the foot of the Cross. Their blood boiled as he dwelt upon the crying injustice of refusing civil rights to Catholics, as such, in a land where, in spite of centuries of persecution, nine-tenths of the people were Catholics. Outbursts of honest indignation arose as, in strains of withering invective, he repelled the lying assertion that Catholics, as such, were less fit to be loyal citizens of the empire than their Protestant neighbors. And when, in tones of matchless eloquence, he thundered forth the demand for Catholic Emancipation, those tens of thousands sent forth a shout whose echoes came with startling force to the ears of King and Parliament.

On went the agitation, till every man and woman in Ireland was in it. On it went, till it became manifest to all observers that this was not a passing outburst of enthusiasm, but a calm, strong utterance of conviction and a purpose that had "come to stay" and that must prove irresistible.

In organization is strength, and therefore, in 1823, the mighty movement was organized into the Catholic Association. Its branches were in every town and hamlet; every man and woman in Ireland swelled its membership; even the poorest of the poor gloried in paying in their monthly Emancipation penny for carrying on the warfare. Thus O'Connell found himself at the head of a well organized army of seven millions of followers, assuredly the strongest man in all the world.

Never in all these centuries of misrule was England so apprehensive as now. Favorite oft-tried methods of bribery and cajoling were used to bring disunion into the Irish ranks; but in vain. Meetings were prescribed, associations were outlawed; but the fertile brain of O'Connell found legal means to evade each condemnation and roll the movement on under other forms. Sentences of imprisonment were passed on O'Connell and his aids, and through sheer shame of their flagrant injustice, had to be cancelled. The eyes of the world were on the strife. In the mighty struggle O'Connell had grown colossal; he towered up a very Hercules in intellectual strength, in tireless labor, in matchless genius, in irreproachable integrity, while around him the whole Irish people stood in single-hearted devotedness and inflexible resolve, such an army of moral power as the world had never beheld. And the whole world burst forth in admiration and applause. The world declared that O'Connell and Ireland were right, and that England must yield. From end to end of Christendom the cry was re-echoed: "Religious liberty for Ireland!"

King and Parliament stormed and swore and vowed that it should not be. But King and Parliament were powerless against the verdict of the world. The critical moment had come. The electors of Clare sent O'Connell to Parliament.

They knew and he knew that, as a Catholic, he was ineligible. But they elected him all the same.

Such a revolution as England had never had to deal with was thundering at the very doors of the Parliament, a revolution that meant no bloodshed, but that meant victory for justice, and must have it. Foaming with rage, the Parliament surrendered; fuming and cursing, the King signed the bill. Catholic Emancipation was won, and Ireland was free from the yoke of centuries. O'Connell must be admitted to Parliament, but they will make it as hard for him as they can. When he appears before the House of Commons they offer him the old oath, which was equivalent to an abjuration of the Catholic faith. Slowly and deliberately he scans it from beginning to end, while all eyes are breathlessly fixed on him. Then, in majestic tones: "One-half of this oath I believe to be untrue, and the other half I know to be false," and he flings it from him. With ill-restrained rage he is told that since he cannot take the oath which was in force at the date of his election he must withdraw. A second time the men of Clare elected him. This time he enters triumphant, the oath of abjuration being buried, and Parliament feels that it has received its master. A few English Catholic members had preceded him, through the door of Emancipation which he had burst open. The new era of Religious Liberty had been won, not for Ireland alone, but for every spot in the wide world where the flag of England floated, and all the millions of emancipated Catholics throughout the English-speaking world joined with Ireland in hailing O'Connell by the glorious title of the Liberator. Never since the days of Constantine had the world beheld such an achievement or honored such a hero.

But there is a worse tyranny than that of coercion and

persecution; it is the tyranny of enslaving patronage. When the signs of the times began to indicate to England's far-seeing statesmen that Catholic Emancipation would have to be granted at last, they resolved that, since the chains of iron that had so long galled the enslaved Church must be thrown off, they would try to replace them with manacles of gold. They offered to grant Catholic Emancipation on conditions that the Government should have a veto in the appointment of the Bishops; and they further offered that the salaries of the priests should be paid by the State. The gilded bait was eagerly caught at by thousands, and many an unsuspecting Catholic, and many a long persecuted and impoverished priest, and many a Bishop eager for peace to the Church at almost any cost, favored the acceptance of the fair-seeming offer. Rome itself inclined to think it an advantage that ought not to be rejected. Two men, however, had the penetration to see the hook through the bait. Bishop Milner and O'Connell raised their voices in solemn warning. At first their protest was most unwelcome to the almost deluded Catholics of both England and Ireland. But they were immovable, and proved, with unanswerable eloquence, that a salaried clergy would have to be the obedient minions of the State; that, if England had the veto, then the men who ought to be Bishops would never be appointed; that in fact, the whole offer was a deliberately concocted scheme for a worse enslavement of the Church than that from which they offered to emancipate her. Better a thousand times, they exclaimed, the Penal Laws and Poverty and persecution, with honor and freedom, than the pampered and gilded slavery offered them instead. And the eyes of the people were opened and they saw that this was true. Rome also saw through the cunning device and rejected it. Like one man, the people cried out that from their very poverty they would joyfully and amply provide for the loved "Soggarth Aroon," but that he must be their father, their very own, and not the liveried servant of the Crown. And O'Connell and his mighty following spurned the offer of Emancipation at such a cost, and fought on the good fight till the boon was won without bargain and without compromise, on the sole basis of man's inalienable rights.

The British Parliament expected to find in O'Connell an uncouth "bog-trotter" and a wild demagogue. To their amazement, they found him the peer of the best of them in refinement and culture, and the master of them all in every power that makes the consummate orator. I once heard Wendell Phillips, the most polished of American orators, give his estimate of O'Connell. Lincoln Hall, in Washington, was crowded with the elite of the Capital to hear the great American agitator discourse on the world-renowned Irish Liberator. He told us how the first time he went to hear O'Connell, he expected torrents of turbulent passion, of wild, uncultured rudeness. To his amazement, he found in him the most majestic and finished orator that he had ever heard or could imagine. Nearly fifty different times he managed to hear him speak, and every time his wonder grew at the marvelous powers of the man and the equally marvelous art with which those powers had been trained and were used. He declared that in that one man he had found combined the argumentative persuasiveness of Eschines, the overwhelming force of Demosthenes, and the exquisite diction of Cicero. He was awful in attack, fearful in denouncing and repelling the wrong, sweet as a woman and gentle as a child in winsome presentation of the just, the true, the pathetic, the good.

All his great powers were consecrated to the one purpose

of winning full justice for Ireland. He had won for her religious liberty, but the victory would be incomplete till he should also win for her civil liberty. God was still whispering in his ear as in the ear of Moses: "I have sent thee that thou mayst deliver My people." Moses demanded for his people not only religious liberty to worship God ascording to the Divine behest, but also civil liberty in the Promised Land. To fulfill his mission O'Connell had to do as much. He was fifty-four years of age when Catholic Emancipation was won, and the thirty years of incomparable toil that it had cost him must have told severely even on his iron frame. But with all the energy of youth he now made for the second goal, which still lay far before him.

All his contention for civil liberty he summed up in one single demand, the demand for the repeal of the act of legislative union by which, in the year 1800, the Irish Parliament had been abolished. He insisted, in the first place, that that act was in its every feature a crime of unmitigated iniquity. He was in Dublin at the time, and had witnessed the procedure in its every detail. He knew full well that when the Parliament was granted to Ireland, under the coercion of Grattan's masterful pleading, it was deliberately constituted in such form as not to represent the Irish people, as to prove surely a curse rather than a blessing during its career, and with the deliberate purpose, too, of shortly bringing that career to an end. He related to his unwilling hearers the shameful scenes of those closing sessions, when, like a jury carefully "packed" for conviction, those false representatives of Ireland decreed the civil death of the country, voting the extinction of her Parliament. He told of the bribe that was paid for the infamous act, the million and a half pounds which they were to receive, and which was to be wrung from them from the very vitals of poor Ireland. It was a crime, and had no extenuation.

He insisted, in the second place, that all the results of the act had been unmitigated disaster to Ireland; that it had paralyzed and blasted all her hopes for industries, for commerce, for the development of her boundless natural resources, for her taking her due place among the active peoples of Christendom; that it had doomed her inevitably to inaction and poverty, to a poverty that was ever on the brink of starvation, and might at any moment tumble over into the abyss.

He insisted, in the third place, that the righting of the great wrong, the restoring to Ireland of a Parliament that would have her interests at heart, while it would be of incalculable benefit to his country, would in no way injure the Empire, but the contrary. While developing all the resources which God and nature had bestowed on Ireland, it would simply develop contentment among the people, and end forever the chafing, the discontent, the wrath, with which an injured people must necessarily regard their oppressor. Again and again he dwelt upon the manifest truth that injustice to Ireland is weakness to England; that justice to Ireland would be strength to the whole Empire. He was seeking not disunion and strife, but union and peace. But peace can rest only on justice, therefore he demanded justice that there might be peace.

But he was speaking to deaf ears. Again and again his Bill for the Repeal of the Union was rejected, as a measure which aimed at separating Ireland from the British crown. This allegation O'Connell repelled indignantly. He fearlessly averred indeed that if such were Ireland's contention, it would be but a demand for fullest justice, since it would be the undoing of what she had always denounced as the traitorous act by which suborned chieftains had in 1541 voted the crown of Ireland to Henry VIII. But he proclaimed unceasingly that Ireland no longer demanded this; that she accepted loyally the accomplished fact of three centuries standing which linked her fortunes with Great Britain; that she professed heartily and loyally her allegiane to the crown, only asking the common-sense right of self-government as to her own merely internal and domestic affairs, which English or Scotch legislators could hardly be expected to understand or deal with sympathetically, ready in all matters of general interest to co-operate cheerfully and generously with her sister nations for the common welfare of the Empire.

English good sense and English love of fair play could not but see that he was right. But English prejudice and obstinacy would not consent to being coerced even into manifest justice by the despised and hated Irish. Then O'Connell determined that, while still carrying on their agitation in Parliament and wringing from it every possible measure of justice, the great contest for the Repeal of the Union, like that for Catholic Emancipation, should be carried on in the vast arena of public opinion, on the plains of Ireland and throughout the wide world.

For seventeen years the Titanic struggle went on. The Catholic Association having dissolved when its end was accomplished, the Repeal Association took its place. The monster meetings of three hundred thousand and five hundred thousand eager patriots hanging on the almost superhuman eloquence of O'Connell, and thundering forth the demand for justice to Ireland, were a spectacle of amazement and admiration to the civilized world.

And the one man who inspired all this, moved all this, and absolutely controlled that tremendous power by a word or a gesture, stood forth unquestionably the most wonderful man of the age and was well called Ireland's uncrowned monarch. No crown did he desire, save the crown of Erin's love and her people's gratitude.

But he felt keenly the awful responsibility of such a position. He held in his hands the affections, the energies, almost the destiny of an impulsive warm-hearted, hot-blooded people. He knew how terrible would be his accountability if the forces pent up in these assembled hundreds of thousands should on any unfortunate occasion explode, if even hostile critics could find aught of violence or ill conduct to allege against them. But fortunately his appeals to the people to prove themselves worthy of freedom by self-control and blameless conduct were well heeded; his warning that whoever committed a crime gave strength to the enemy was fully appreciated.

Fortunately, too, he had with him the whole clergy of Ireland, and through them the spirit of the Prince of Peace held and controlled their flocks. But most fortunately of all, Father Mathew, the Apostle of Temperance, began just at the opportune time his wonderful crusade against the one great weakness, the potent evil, which would especially cause danger of excitement and violence. Soon the millions that marched under the banner of Repeal were equally enrolled under the banner of Temperance. Then O'Connell knew that the cause was safe. And when, in the monster temperance procession through Dublin, O'Connell, then Lord Mayor, walked side by side with Father Mathew, and when, as they parted, the cheering and heart-touched multitude saw the Liberator kneel in the street to ask the blessing of the Apostle of Temperance, then all Ireland took the lesson to heart, and saw where safety and prosperity were to be found.

But even as the great agitation went on, the Government only grew more grimly obstinate. Pharaoh's heart was hardened, and petition, argument, remonstrance, the cry for justice, only angered him the more. The peacefulness, the strict legality of the agitation, was, above all, intolerable. Those Irish multitudes must be goaded to violence.

The Repeal Association was interdicted, and the Repeal penny was made treason. O'Connell and the people instantly submitted; but the meetings went on under other names and the support came in in other ways. Police and soldiers were multiplied; but O'Connell and the people only laughed, and the "peelers" had nothing to do. The monster meetings must be stopped; the five hundred thousand assembled at Mullaghmast, the seven hundred and fifty thousand gathered on the Hill of Tara, gave assurance that O'Connell's call for a million of men at Clontarf would be more than responded to. Regiment upon regiment of soldiery rolled in, and only the afternoon before the meeting was to be held it was interdicted. Bad faith was evident. The resolution to force a breach of the peace was manifest. But O'Connell and Ireland were equal to the emergency, and on the plain of Clontarf not a man of the million appeared. Finally, O'Connell and his colleagues were tried, convicted and dragged to jail as conspirators. Even in that awful hour the genius of O'Connell was able to hold the wrath of Ireland under control. For one hundred days the venerable Liberator, then nearly seventy years of age, languished in prison. Day after day the Bishops, Clergy, the people of Ireland, Protestants as well as Catholics, came in solemn embassies to his prison, to offer him their sympathy and to protest against this gigantic injustice. The House of Lords itself was shamed into annulling the sentence against him, and it was a popular triumph, like that of

Caesar or Augustus, that he was escorted from the jail to his home.

But the end had come. O'Connell's strength was exhausted by his unparalleled labors and by his cruel imprisonment. He could lead the Irish millions no longer in their peaceful warfare for justice.

Then the popular indignation against this doggedness of tyranny began to manifest itself in acts of violence, and the Young Ireland party broke the Liberator's heart by beginning their heroic, but ill-advised, agitation for armed resistance. Then the famine, like a horrible black pall, came down on all the land. O'Connell's warnings were realized; misgovernment had forced poverty over the precipice into the abyss of starvation. Hundreds of thousands were dying of starvation in a country whose storehouses held grain enough to feed twice the population, and the starving people saw it carted away guarded by bayonets, while they were told to eat rotten potatoes and grass. The inveterate spirit of religious bigotry seized its opportunity, and the "soupers" offered the starving wretches food for themselves and their children if they would renounce popery; and they smiled, and kissed the Cross, and died martyrs. O'Connell's heart broke utterly. One last effort he made to reach Parliament, to rise and implore them, in trembling, tearful tones, to have pity on starving Ireland, to grant measures of relief, or one-fourth of the population must die of hunger.

The appeal of the venerable Liberator touched profoundly the heart of the Government and of the whole English people, and most generous efforts were made to stem the awful torrent of woe and desolation. This was the end. Then, tottering, he bade good-bye forever to Ireland and to Britain, and start to ask the blessing of the Vicar of

Christ ere he should die.   His faith had been the inspiration of his life.   His religion had been his support under the awful burdens she had had to carry.   He spoke and acted with superhuman power, because every morning he knelt with the adoring angels at the altar of the Eucharistic Sacrifice, drinking in the spirit and the power of his Saviour, and very often—it is even said, every day—receiving the Communion of the Bread of the Strong.   His rosary was his inseparable companion, and from its joyful, sorrowful, and glorious mysteries of the life of the sweet Jesus and His Blessed Mother he derived unfailing encouragement and inspiration in the God-given mission to which his life was consecrated.   And now that his work was over and his life at its close, he wished to die under the shadow of St. Peter's, in the City of the Martyrs, at the feet of Christ's Vicar.

Yes, O'Connell was dying.   Like Moses, he had led his people within sight of the Promised Land of Civil as well as Religious Liberty.   From the mountain-top of vision he saw that goodly land outstretched before him.   He knew now that he would never enter it, but he was sure that his people some day would enter in and possess it.   And we may well believe that God gave him some perception of the providential reason why the granting of full justice was delayed, some prevision of the marvelous mission which the exiled children of Erin were first to accomplish for God in all the wide world.   Forth he saw them pouring in hundreds of thousands, on and on and on, till seven millions of them had poured forth to Great Britain, to America, to Canada, to Australia, to the ends of the earth.   And in the distant perspective he saw them everywhere planting the Cross, everywhere building up the Church of Jesus Christ. Yes, and everywhere, building up the Greater Ireland, too, leavening all the English-speaking population of the world with their faith, with their hatred of tyranny and wrong, with their determination that wrong must cease and justice must be done in Ireland and everywhere.

He foresaw all this, and he knew that his life had not been in vain, that his mission had not been a failure. He had educated the people of Ireland for self-government. He had planted the seed of civil liberty throughout the land, and now the winter snows were on, it, and had hidden it out of sight, in order that the harvest of freedom might, in God's time, be surer and richer. He died content. The world enshrined his name among the greatest men of all time. The nations of the earth have made O'Connell a symbol of purest patriotism, of heroic loyalty to the cause of religious and civil liberty. Our age, misguided by Voltairean sophistry, beholds in him a living demonstration that faith, religion, devotedness to the altar and the priesthood and Mother Church, are not only compatible with love of freedom, but are its loftiest inspiration and its surest safeguard. And now, most appropriately, the heart of Ireland's Liberator lies enshrined in this venerable Church, erected, it is said, by Constantine, the Liberator of Christendom, and under the custody of Erin's chosen Levites. May they who are privileged to kneel so often close by this bravest and noblest of hearts be filled with its spirit for their own ennobling and for Ireland's good!

What hand shall reap the harvest of freedom which O'Connell planted? What hand shall yield the sword of moral power which O'Connell laid down so gloriously? Like the Heaven-bestowed sword of King Arthur, it can be wielded only by chivalrous faith, by chivalrous purity of life, by chivalrous unselfishness and disinterested patriotish. It has not, like Arthur's sword, been flung hopelessly into the lake. It has been laid in Erin's hands, and she is waiting for him who will be worthy to wear and wield it in O'Connell's place.

Meantime Erin's face and heart are turned towards freedom, waiting for freedom, sure of freedom, because it is right and just, because only in freedom and justice can there be peace. O Erin, land of my fathers, land of my birth, the hand of O'Connell still holds high uplifted before thee and thy sons, the standard of the Cross of Christ, the standard of Constantine, now made thine own, and his voice still cries to thee, as in the days gone by: "In this Sign thou shalt conquer!"

MOST REV. P. J. RYAN, D. D., LL. D., ARCHBISHOP OF PHILA.

MASTERPIECES OF THE MOST REVEREND P. J. RYAN, D. D., LL. D.,

Archbishop of Philadelphia.

THE DIVINE ORIGIN OF CHRISTIANITY.

The subject of the propagation and permanence of the Christian religion as an argument in favor of its divine origin when the fundamental truth of Christianity is often questioned is opportune. Other arguments there are of great and convincing cogency, arguments from miracles performed, prophecies fulfilled, the intrinsic excellence of Christian ethical teaching. But these arguments presuppose a belief in miracles and prophecies, and an appreciation of the ethical teaching of Christ. Alas, in our day there are too many who question these foundations of such proofs. But no rational being can question causality as a base for argumentation. No man can say that an effect must not have a cause adequate to that effect. Now, my contention is that the propagation and permanence of the Christian religion are effects which can have no other cause than the divine origin of that religion. To a keen observer in Judea, who had not the key to the Christian system, it might have appeared that Christianity was to be buried with its founder. I can well imagine a Jewish skeptic of that day thus soliloquizing: "What a marvelous man was this young Rabbi! How far above all our prophets and teachers, in personal excellence and sublime doctrine. How holy His life, how wonderful and awful His death! Was He the incarnate

Deity He claimed to be, and on account of which claim we stoned Him and finally crucified Him? If Deity ever became incarnate, could it be enshrined more appropriately than in this man? At times I have felt as if I could be His follower, and sever all connections with Judaism—take up the cross and follow Him. But now I feel relieved of this necessity. I feel He was only a man—one, indeed, above all the children of men on this earth, but still only human and erring in His judgment. He spoke of the great kingdom He was to found, the prophesied fifth kingdom of Daniel, the prophet. He told His apostles to go forth and teach all nations. He sent them as an army to conquer the forces of the triple alliance of intellectual error, moral depravity and social rebellion against God. But He has shown His weakness and unwisdom in the selection of men destined for this gigantic conquest. He has chosen the wrong men. Did He dare hope that these fools would overcome the wise, and these weaklings the strong, and these nobodies the rulers of the world? At their head, in the van of His army, is the veriest coward, who with an oath did thrice deny Him."

If, dear brethren, in spite of such weakness and ignorance on the part of the first apostles, they did still conquer, surely their power was from God alone. But when we consider some of the obstacles they had to surmount and how they overcame them, this becomes unquestionable. The first obstacle was the exclusiveness of the new religion.

Another obstacle which the new faith had to overcome was the state and individual pride of these pagan days. In the doctrine of the perfect equality of men before the Supreme Being—the equality of the master with his slave, the equality of the poor barbarian captive, who, bound in chains, followed the chariot of the conqueror in Roman triumph—this equality with the man who sat in the chariot, and to whom it was necessary to whisper at times, "Thou art a man," lest he might believe himself a god—such all-leavening doctrine seemed to menace and degrade imperial power. It is true that Christianity taught perfect obedience to the laws, and gave the Divine sanction for their observance, declaring that all power was from God, and that he that resisted the power resisted the ordinance of God, and they that resisted deserved condemnation. Still, as the position in sight of the Supreme Being was the true criterion of excellence, and, as Christianity, though it recognized the superiority of the ruler in the state, made him perfectly equal with his slave when kneeling in the Christian church, it was galling and humiliating to pagan pride. The truth is that the virtue of humility was almost unknown and unpracticed in those days. The very word in Latin generally implied lowliness and degradation. It is true that there were some great souls, "naturally Christian," like Plato, who tried to know themselves, and who felt the limitations of their natures ; but they were rare, and pride deep, intense and all-corrupting, was the characteristic of paganism. The new teacher cried out to this proud generation, "Learn of Me, for I am meek and humble of heart, and you shall find rest for your souls. Let the pride of intellect and heart bow down in subjection before Me, for I am King of both. Though My kingdom is not of this world, it is still a kingdom, and I am King, as I answered to Pontius Pilate. My dominion extends into regions beyond the sway of all earthly monarchs. They influence only the outward acts of men. But I am King in the sanctuary of the heart, where earthly monarchs dare not enter, King in the noble regions of the intellect, which are ever free from any other domination—King of kings and Lord of lords, Monarch of the kings of thought, and Lord of the lords of knowledge." To humble pride of intellect, Christianity revealed mysteries which demanded the tribute of our understanding—the royal tribute of the intellect itself to the supreme sovereignty of God. Such were some of the obstacles which Christianity had to encounter, and such the means by which they were overcome. I have already described the character of the men commissioned to effect the wonderful revolution, and how, humanly speaking, they seemed totally inadequate for this gigantic work. What, however, were the results?

Marvelous to relate, within a century, the new faith met the mighty foes which we have described, and conquered them to an extent that cannot possibly be accounted for on any human hypothesis. This wonderful progress is recorded by pagan as well as Christian writers. Thus, Tacitus, in the second book of his Annals; Pliny, in the celebrated letter to the Emperor; Lucan, in his "Pharsalia"; Juvenal, in the first book of the Satires, and Porphyry, in his five books against the Christians, confirms what was proclaimed by Christian writers.

St. Paul, writing to the Romans, twenty-five years after the death of our Lord, praises them because their faith was spoken of in the whole world. Less than sixty years after Christ, Pliny, in writing to the Emperor Trajan, informed him that in consequence of the rapid diffusion of Christianity, the temples of the gods are almost abandoned, and the sale of victims for the pagan sacrifice proportionately suspended. He asks what course he should adopt to check the further progress of the evil of Christianity. St. Justin Martyr, who died sixty-six years after St. John, the Evangelist, says that there is not any one race of men, barbarian or Christian, or of those who are nomads or shepherds in tents, amongst whom prayers and eucharists are not offered to the Father of the Universe through the name of Jesus crucified.

Tertullian, born about the year 160 of the Christian era, says in his Apologia, "We are but of yesterday, and yet we have filled every place belonging to you. Cities, islands, castles, towns, assemblies—your very camps, your tribes, companies, palaces, senate, forum—we leave you only your temples."

The force of the proof from the propagation of Christianity in favor of its divine origin is sought to be weakened or neutralized by Gibbon, the historian, by the well known arguments from the five causes which he puts forth to account for that propagation. These five causes are the zeal of the first Christians for the progress of their faith; second, their belief in the immortality of the human soul; third, the miraculous powers ascribed to the early Church; fourth, the great sanctity of the primitive Christians, and fifth, the wonderfully wise organization of the Church herself. Now, on close examination, these five causes are simply effects of the divine life of the Church, and only secondary causes of its progress. You behold the progress, like a vast river sweeping onward; these causes are like streams that flow into it from the mountain heights. But follow the streams upwards to the mountain's top from which they sprung, and you will find the mountain to be Calvary, and the five sources, the five wounds of Jesus Christ crucified.

Why were the first Christians zealous? Why was their belief in the immortality of the soul so deep and intense as to influence others to become Christians? Pagans believed in this immortality, but made few converts. If miracles were performed, they prove the divinity of Christianity; if they were not performed, then the progress of Christianity without them, as St. Augustine observes, was itself a miracle. The sanctity of the primitive Christians effected conversions, but what caused the sanctity itself? The marvelous organization of the Church attracted and kept inquiring minds within its pale, as it still does. But who fashioned that wondrous organization? It was clearly above the power of the first apostles to do so. It was, and is, a power uniting the most discordant elements into perfect unity. It has the conservatism of absolute monarchy with the liberty of republicanism. Thus we see that though these five causes were indeed causes, yet they were but effects of one great cause, and the cause of the causes was and is divine.

That was effected in the first centuries of Christian history, continued and continues to be accomplished. The obstacles are similar and the triumphs similar. Pride and passion, the enemies of the human race, continued arrayed against Christianity, and will continue so until the end. The Church, which is Christianity organized, seeks to save the children of God from these enemies. Now, how did Christianity triumph? As I have said, humanity, poor and crippled by sin, stood at the gate that was called Beautiful, and the Church, represented by Peter, its supreme head on earth, took humanity by the hand, raised it, healed it, and sent it in bounding and rejoicing through the beautiful gate, into the temple of the living God. This was effected by the name and power of Jesus Christ, as Peter fearlessly announced to the Jewish rulers concerning the crippled man narrated in my text.

To understand the philosophy of the history and triumphs of Christianity we must bear in mind that it is pre-eminently a personal religion—that the personality of its founder permeates the whole system, which we can never understand and appreciate until we shall have understood

Him. "I am with you all days until the consummation of the world." Now, who was He, who bore the glorious name which you have given to your Church—and who is alive, still working? His nature and work are described in a few sentences by St. Paul, which if we study, we have the key to the Christian religion and its conquests.

"Who being in the form of God thought it not robbery to be equal with God:

"But emptied Himself, taking the form of a servant, being made in the likeness of men, and in habit found as a man: He humbled Himself, becoming obedient unto death: even to the death of the cross.

"For which cause God hath also exalted Him, and hath given Him a name which is above all names:

"That in the name of Jesus every knee should bow of those that are in heaven, on earth and under the earth.

"And that every tongue should confess that the Lord Jesus Crist is in the glory of God the Father."

Behold in this short passage, the epitome of the nature and history of the Founder of Christianity. We see Him first in the glory which He had with the Father before the world was made; "Who being in the form of God thought it not robbery to be equal with God," and therefore was equal to God, for no being can be equal to God but God, and it would have been robbery and blasphemy and the crime of Lucifer for any created being to seek equality with the Most High. He was the same of whom the beloved disciple wrote, "In the beginning was the Word, and the Word was with God, and the Word was God. This was in the beginning. All things were made by Him and without Him was made nothing that was made." But "He had emptied Himself taking the form of a servant." He descended from Heaven, became man and did not cease to be

God. "In Him," says St. Paul, "dwelt the plentitude of the Divinity corporally." Observe you, no partial communication of the Divinity, but its plentitude. Foreseeing this incarnation and nativity, Isaias the Prophet cried out in holy rapture: "A child is born to us and a son is given to us and the government is upon His shoulder, and His name shall be called Wonderful Counsellor, God the Mighty, Father of the World to come, the Prince of Peace." And He Himself said to the Jews, "Abraham, your father, rejoiced that He might see My day. He saw it and was glad." The Jews therefore said to Him, "Thou art not yet fifty years old, and hast Thou seen Abraham?" Jesus said to them, "Amen: I say to you, before Abraham was made I am." They took up stones to cast at Him. He did not say before Abraham was made I was made, but before Abraham was made I am, giving to Himself the very name which God gave to Moses, as the name by which the Almighty should be known. Hence the Jews cast stones at Christ, as a blasphemer, because, as they said, "being man, He made Himself God."

Hence we must ever bear in mind that the Founder of Christianity was God Himself. But He was also a man, like unto one of us in all things except sin. But we must not think of Him as possessing merely a human body with the Divinity as its soul, as our souls are the lives of our bodies.

This is not true, and gives quite an erroneous idea of our Lord. Besides His Divinity and human body, He had that glorious human soul which brings Him so near to us. The soul that suffered, that was sorrowful even unto death, that naturally, like every human soul, recoiled from suffering and cried out with inconceivable anguish, "Father, if it be possible, let the chalice pass from Me." That human soul it was whose deep sympathies caused Him to weep by

Lazarus' grave, when the Jews whispered to each other, "Behold, how He loved Him." That human soul it was that caused His tears to flow at the only moment of joy and triumph which He seemed to have had during His early sojourn. Jerusalem seemed to have heard the voice of Isaias and to have risen and been enlightened, for her light was come. She sent out her children, bearing palm branches of victory to meet her King. They strew the earth with their garments and cry Hosanna to the King. But look into the pale face of the Son of Man. No light of triumph or of joy do you see illumine in it. No, His human soul is melted in pity for the people about to crucify Him. A beautiful tender, forgiving human soul, fit sanctuary for the Divinity.

But there are additional attractions and motives for love and submission to Him, the Founder of Christianity. He was "God of God, Light of Light, begotten not made consubstantial to the Father, by whom all things were made, who for us men and for our salvation came down from heaven and became incarnate by the Holy Ghost of the Virgin Mary and was made man." But to all this He added more, for He became obedient unto death, even the death of the cross, for our salvation. On account of which God also hath exalted Him and given Him a name which is above all names, for at the name of Jesus every knee shall bow, of those who are in heaven and on earth, and in hell, and every tongue shall confess that Jesus Christ is in the glory of the Father. Such was the Founder of Christianity —God, Man, Redeemer. Uniting all that is glorious in Divinity to all that is pure and noble and tender in humanity and all that can win gratitude by vicarious suffering, no wonder such a being conquered the world and holds captive such souls as really know Him. Only He can perpetuate and extend this conquest. We often hear of and pray for religious union of all the denominations of the world. How may this be approached? I can see but one way. To unite discordant elements you must first discover at least some principle on which they all agree. Now, I know of nothing on which there is such general concord of opinion and sentiment as admiration and love for the personality of Jesus Christ. In this Catholics and Protestants agree. The Mahometans regard Him as a great prophet, and now the reformed Jews join in the universal chorus, glory in the fact that He was of their nation and laud His doctrines. In the sublime sermon on the mount the outside world recognizes the morality that can save society from its own passions. Thus is Christ the central figure of the world—the hope of humanity. "And I when I shall be lifted up will draw all things to myself." If there is ever to be religious union, it will be found, first of all, and as preparation for further union, at the foot of the cross in personal admiration and love for Him who bears the name of Jesus. O let us all, dear brethren, first of all foster this love in our hearts by intense personal affection for our Lord. But perhaps some amongst you, deeply conscious of past sins and humiliated by that consciousness, may say, we can adore Him as our creator and thank Him as our Redeemer, but as to that personal intimate love of which you speak we feel unworthy of it. There was a time, perhaps, when innocent and holy, we might have presumed to feel its sacred thrill. But, now, it is only left to us to work out our salvation in fear and trembling. But, brethren, we must remember that there are two kinds of love for our dear Lord. The first and purest is the love that was never stained by acts of disloyalty—the love of the faithful angels—the love of the blessed Mother and the beloved disciple and of the many who never stained their baptismal robes. But there is another love of Christ—the great, strong, intense penitential love, the love of one who feels his disloyalty and ingratitude to his God and his Redeemer, the love of Peter after Peter's fall—the love that would sacrifice life itself to obliterate the record of its shame. This is the love which we can all possess. O let us cherish it and cause our sins of the past to act as embers to intensify its flame. Thou eternal and most sacred God, who sittest at the right hand of the Father—God, Man, Redeemer of our race, Jesus Christ, look down upon us to-day assembled in this new temple, which now bears Thy name. O vouchsafe to hear us for that namesake. Forgive our past sins; intensify our penitential love for Thee. Thy kingdom come. Extend that kingdom on earth. Draw all things to Thyself, that there may be but one fold and one shepherd, and all may enter in the end through the "beautiful gate" of Catholic unity into Thy everlasting tabernacles! Amen.

THE APPARITION OF THE SACRED HEART TO
BLESSED MARGARET MARY.

THE HOLY EUCHARIST.

Sermon by

ARCHBISHOP RYAN

of Philadelphia.

———

"I have loved, O Lord, the beauty of Thy House, and the place where Thy glory dwelleth."—Psalms 25, Verse 8.

The subject of the true, real and substantial presence of Christ on our altars in the Holy Eucharist is one of ineffable interest. To the Catholic this presence is the very life and heart of the Church. As a sacrifice, it is the continuation of that on Calvary; as a sacrament, it is the union of Divinity with humanity. Originally, man walked with God in the Garden of Paradise. Humanity had Deity present with it. When man became disloyal and disobedient he was driven from the Garden of Delights and walked no more with God. For four thousand years man, as an exile, wept at the gates of Eden, wept not merely for its lost delights, but supremely for the lost presence of his God. "O give me back my God, the Divine, original, after which my soul was fashioned—the only thing that can bless and sanctify me," he cried. His sighs are expressed in those eloquent Antiphons of Advent which are chanted in the office of the Church before Christmas: "O, Orient splendor of eternal light and sun of justice, come and illumine those who sit in darkness and shadow of death." "O, Emanuel, King and our Lawgiver, Expectation of the Nations and their Savior, come and save us, Lord, our God." "O, that Thou wouldst rend the heavens and come down." At length the new Adam came, and before Him the angelic sentinel of the gate lowered his sword of fire. Humanity entered the Garden again and not only walked with God, but was one with Him in the hypostatic union. The natures of God and man were united in Christ, but yet the personality of Christ was all Divine; the union was not perfect until the body and blood, soul and Divinity of Christ were united with the individual, by the real presence in the Eucharist. Hence, to the Catholic this presence is the very heart of religion from which flows the blood which gives continued life to the Church of God. And to the non-Catholic, whether a believer in the Christian revelation or not, the subject must prove exceedingly interesting. It is the key to the whole Catholic system. It accounts for the elaborate ceremonial of the Church, the splendor of her temples, the celibacy of her clergy and religious, and many things otherwise without a reason for their being. If this doctrine be true, as the Catholic believes, it is the most interesting and sanctifying in all revelation; if it be false, as the non-Catholic believes, even then it is not without interest, to find out how it could have originated, how the whole Christian world for fifteen hundred years believed it, how three-fourths of the Christian world still believes it most firmly, how its deniers constitute but one-fourth of Christendom during only one-sixth of the period that Christianity has existed. Thus, whether fact or fraud, truth or superstition, the subject becomes deeply interesting.

The rationalist must bear in mind that intellects far greater than his, men like St. Augustine and St. Thomas Aquinas, and the vast procession of the "kings of thought" for nearly nineteen centuries, have bowed their heads in faith and adoration before the real presence of the King of Kings in the adorable sacrament of the Eucharist. In accepting it as a truth, we believe in but one mystery; in rejecting it as false, we have several mysteries to account for. It is, of course, a mystery difficult to accept.

But God represents the human intellect, which He formed, and asks no man to believe without a reason. The reason is in proportion to the mysterious truth to be accepted. That reason is His own Divine word, communicated to man by a messenger who cannot err in its transmission from the Divine to the human intellect. Of course, if the messenger can err and deliver a false report, I cannot, without lessening the dignity of my reason, accept and believe a mystery. The Catholic Church is the unerring messenger from the infallible God, and hence I follow my reason in believing a truth delivered by such a messenger already proved to me to be infallible.

Now there is no truth of revelation more clearly revealed by God through His Church than this one, and by a logical necessity, he who rejects it would be forced to reject all revelation.

If it be so clearly revealed, some one may ask, why is it not universally accepted? But we must bear in mind how much will has to do in the matter of faith. Proofs as clear and convincing as those of mathematical science have been rejected by man. We cannot imagine anything stronger than the proofs furnished by our Lord of His Divinity and the Divinity of His Mission. Prophecy fulfilled, miracles performed, sanctity of His life and doctrines did not move men. When He raised Lazarus from the dead, His enemies sought to kill Lazarus in order to destroy the proof which His resurrection from the dead afforded. As St. Gregory says: "All nature acknowledged Christ, but the Jewish

heart would not." The firmament acknowledged Him and
sent its star to conduct the wise men of the East to the
lowly palace of the new-born King. The sun acknowledged
Him and hid his face of splendor at the crucifixion. The
sea acknowledged Him and bore Him as He walked upon
her waters; the waves and the winds acknowledged Him
and were hushed at His command. The earth acknowledged Him and trembled at His death; the rocks acknowledged Him and were rent, when men were "digging His
hands and feet and numbering all His bones." The blind
saw Him, and the deaf heard Him, and the lame followed
Him, and Death itself relaxed its grip at His command.
But the heart of man, higher in its pride than the firmament, and harder in its obstinacy than the rocks, blind to
the most dazzling evidences and deaf to the strongest
proofs, rejected Him. There is no parallel to this rejection
more perfect than that of the reformers of the sixteenth
century, who rejected Him in the holy sacrament of the
Eucharist, for these men, unlike most of their followers,
well knew the arguments in favor of this doctrine, arguments so strong that Luther himself continued a believer in
this great truth.

I do not propose here to enter on the usual dogmatic
proofs of the real presence, but simply to repeat for you the
words of its revelation, and ask you, is it possible that
anything can be more clearly revealed? The truth is,
that the Scripture proofs are so strong that the only mode
of attempting to meet them is, by saying that the doc-
rine is physically or morally impossible, and therefore,
these words must be interpreted in some other than
the literal sense. But such a position is absurd. No man
can deny that the great Creator of matter can give to one
substance the appearance of another. We must bear in

mind that the body of Christ in the Eucharist is His glorified body, the only body He possesses. It is a human body,
'tis true, but in a glorified state, in the state of which St.
Paul speaks when he says of our glorified bodies at the last
day "they were sown material bodies, they shall rise spiritual bodies." It was the body of Christ which came forth
from the sepulchre whilst the official seal was yet unbroken,
and entered the room where the disciples were assembled,
"the doors being shut." Philosophers have not yet decided
on the essential qualities of matter, even in its natural state.
Shall we limit God's power, and whilst we know so little of
matter in its natural condition and almost nothing of it in
the state of a glorified body, shall we dare, in the face of
such declarations as I have quoted for you to-day, to assert
that it is impossible that the body and blood of Christ can
appear under the forms of bread and wine? Leibnitz, the
great German philosopher, the rival of Sir Isaac Newton,
and a Protestant, declared that there was no such physical
impossibility in the doctrine of the Eucharist. Nor is there
any moral impossibility.

We are, of course, tempted, in view of the majesty of
God, to cry out, as we see Him in some poor country church
on a neglected altar, that this humiliation is too much, too
deep. O, how often are we thus tempted in regard to the
relations of God to man. The Incarnation was too much.
He came, in the language of the spouse in the Canticles,
"leaping over the mountains, skipping over the hills," rising above all impediments for the love of the creature
whom He had made to His own image and likeness. From
the dazzling height of that glory He had before the world
was made, He descended to the earth. "Whilst the night
was in the midst of her course, and silence held all things,
the Omnipotent Word leaped down from the royal throne

as a conqueror." From Bethlehem to Nazareth, and from Nazareth to Calvary, and from Calvary to Mount Olivet, and then back to the royal throne in Heaven, how many marvelous humiliations that startle and confound our human pride. The additional humiliation of the Eucharist would be too much for any but Thee, O Thou thorn-crowned King, Thou bleeding lover of the mount of crucifixion. And yet, on reflection, it is not more difficult to believe in Christ's presence in the Eucharist than in His presence on the earth during His life and passion. He is more honored now on our altars than He then was in Judea. The glorious cathedrals of the world have been erected to receive His Eucharistic presence. Processions in which royalty does honor to the King of kings pay tribute to this presence. In thousands of churches and convent and hospital chapels He is honored and loved and worshiped, and millions are ready to die for Him in this sacrament of His love. There is, therefore, no more moral possibility of His dwelling with His children of the nineteenth century than there was with His dwelling with those of the first. Therefore, because Christ, in terms the most emphatic and unmistakable, revealed this doctrine, and His unerring messenger has delivered it, because the Catholic world has believed from the beginning, because it involves no physical or moral impossibility, because we cannot reject it without undermining the whole fabric of God's revelation to man, therefore we accept it and believe and love it.

INSPIRATION OF ARCHITECTS.

The first consequence of our faith in the presence of Christ on our altars in the Holy Eucharist is that we should love the beauty of the house in which this presence rests.

RAPHAEL, BY RAPHAEL.

Every Catholic Church on earth becomes by this doctrine the House of God, a veritable palace of the King of kings in these, His earthly dominions, and it is supremely becoming that His subjects here should render it as far as possible worthy of its Divine occupant.

This thought was the inspiration of the Christian architects, that erected and the Chrisian artists that adorned our temples. San Micheli, the great architect of Verona, would never design a church until he had mass offered that God might inspire him to build a temple for His greater glory. It was the thought of God's presence in the Eucharist that caused Michael Angelo to exclaim, "I will lift the Pantheon in the air as a canopy for His altar," and he did it in the vast dome of St. Peter's. Haydn, the great composer of church music, was sometimes found on his knees beside his piano, whilst composing his masses, praying that God might move his soul that in glorious harmony he might proclaim His praises during the holy sacrifice.

A PALACE OF GOD.

This is the same thought also, that has influenced the greatest living Gothic architect who designed this beautiful temple and erected near all the great cathedrals of this country, and the thought which influenced the Christian family who contributed the means to build and adorn it. Each church is the palace of God; therefore come, O Christian painter, and deck its walls with the products of the genius which God has given to you. It is the palace of God; therefore come, O Christian sculptor, and place in its niches your all but breathing statues. It is the place of God, therefore come, O Christian singer, and chant your sweetest, holiest song within its consecrated walls.

God Himself has given to us in His temple of creation,

where He dwells in the natural order, the example of such use of the beautiful in His worship. He was the first architect who built, the first artist who adorned this magnificent temple, that "the invisible things of Him from the beginning of the world be clearly seen, being understood by the things that are visible, His eternal power also and His Divinity."

Who was it that introduced into the temple of creation the fine art, those missionaries of the beautiful, that like the spirits in the dream of sleeping Israel, bring earth and heaven into sweet communion? Who was the first sculptor that struck with his chisel the marble rocks and fashioned them as He would? Who was the first painter whose wondrous brush tinged the variegated gold and silver and purple, the clouds that hang as a veil before His eternal sanctuary? Who studded with starry gems the "milky way" and spread it, as an arch of splendor, across the concave roof of His earthy temple? Who tinged with green and blue the mighty ocean, that mystic baptismal font in whose waters a world was purified? Who cast His sacred fire into the censor of the sun, lit up the planets as everlasting sanctuary lamps to hang before the eternal altar and cause men to look upward to the Holy of Holies? Who was the first composer of glorious music? Who commanded the sons of God to shout with joy, and the morning stars to sing together over young creation? Who gave to His angels the golden harps, when earth and air and heaven celebrated His praises until the intruders-in broke the universal chorus, jarred against nature's chime, tore the angelic harp strings? And who, by conquering sin and death, has restored the lost artistic beauty and broken melody? Who, but the God whom we adore in the Eucharist? O, how at home are these glorious arts in the Catholic sanctuary before the tabernacle of the God of the Beautiful, the Creator and inspirer of them all!

But in the churches of our separated brethren, like frightened doves, they appear timidly, and only here and there. They were seen at first in stained glass symbolism, stealing, as it were, in through the windows, and they still keep near the windows, as if fearing a second excommunication which the improved aesthetic taste of the congregations can alone prevent. But in the Church of the Eucharist, in the Church of the "Corpus Christi," they are enshrined forever, because here there is a special reason for their being there to honor the present incarnate God. In a few moments you will hear music proclaiming her "Credo" in His Divinity, and then over the kneeling multitude whispering the mighty fact of his becoming man in the "Incarnatus est," "Homo factus est," and His suffering and death in the wonderful "Crucifixus" which calls out all the power and pathos of an eloquence far above that of mere speech. And when He descends on the altar at the awful moment of consecration and is lifted up for our adoration at the elevation of the Host and Chalice, then music welcomes Him in the sublime "Benedictus qui Venit." "Blessed is He that cometh in the name of the Lord. Hosanna in the Highest."

And now, what are the practical lessons which we should learn from this great occasion and the words I have spoken to you? The Catholic should become more devoted to the great doctrines of the Holy Eucharist and more zealous for the "beauty of the house of God and the place where His glory dwelleth." To the Protestant who is a disbeliever in this real presence, I have a parting word to say. It is to recall a sublime and touching incident in the life of that dear Lord in whom we both believe and love. It was the fourth watch of the night and the disciples were on the stormy sea of Galilee dashed from wave to wave. Peering through the darkness and the storm, they saw a figure as of a spirit moving over the waters. Peter, with characteristic ardor, cried out, "If it be Thou, Lord, command me to come to Thee." And the figure answered "Come," and Peter walked to Him upon the waters, but, as the tempest was high, he feared and then began to sink. But the Lord rebuked him, saying, "Why hast thou doubted, O thou of little faith?" Inspired by these words, he walked fearlessly with the Lord to the boat, and when they entered the boat Peter, falling at the feet of Christ, exclaimed, "Indeed Thou art the Son of God." After what you have seen and heard to-day, is it too much to ask you, when the Sacred Host is lifted up for the first time within these walls, to cry out in your heart, "If it be Thou Lord, command me to come to Thee." I know not if it be, but strange doubts and new emotions agitate my soul. Suppose it should be, am I to live and die in ignorance of such a benediction? O, command me to come upon the trembling waters of doubt and through the dense darkness. And Jesus will answer "Come," and you shalt walk upon the waters and enter the bark of Peter, which is the Church of God, and falling down before the tabernacle you shall exclaim, "Indeed Thou art the Son of God!"

SAINT CECELIA, BY NAUJOK.

CHURCH MUSIC.

"At last divine Cecilia came,
  Inventress of the vocal frame;
    The sweet enthusiast from her sacred store,
  Enlarged the former narrow bounds,
  And added length to solemn sounds,
    With nature's mother-wit and arts unknown before."
                                                —Dryden.

The power of music over human emotions was acknowledged long before we have any trace of its beginnings as an art. Music owes its evolution entirely to man. Painting, sculpture and poetry, apart from the media which they employ, necessarily involve a reference of nature. Music, in so far as it relates to its subject, could exist if there were no world of nature at all. It is at once sensuous and spiritual. Its direct appeal is made to the auditory nerve. But it has certain qualities which penetrate beyond and reach an aesthetic faculty which we have every right to call the soul. Beethoven wrote on the Mass in D, "From the heart it has come, and to the heart it shall penetrate," and all true music may take those words for its maximum.

The Bible itself bears frequent witness to the power of music exerted by even so imperfect an instrument as David's harp. "When the evil spirit was upon Saul, David took an harp, and played so Saul was refreshed, and the evil spirit departed from him." The most patient of men speaks of those "who take the timbrel and harp and rejoice at the sound of the organ." The early Fathers of the Church also frequently testify to the emotional power and value of music.

St. John Chrysostom said of it: "It hath a sweetness and utility, and glorifieth God, purifieth our hearts, elevateth our contemplations and helpeth to make us wise unto salvation." St. Augustine speaks of the "way music has of soothing whatever passions hurt the soul, repressing sensuality and moving to holy contrition and godly sobriety." St. Basil, after describing the power of music to repel demons and lure the ministry of angels, further says: "It hath pleased him to borrow from melody that pleasure which, being mingled with heavenly truths, conveys them as by stealth into our minds." The most striking testimony to the ethical influence of music is to be found in the writings of the Greek philosophers. The forms of music in ancient Greece were known by national or tribal names, which are called modes. Of these four were more commonly used, namely, the Dorian, Phrygian, Ionian and Lydian. Each of these was regarded as capable of arousing particular emotions and of acting on the mind in a way to exert an important influence on the formation of character. Both Socrates and Plato mention it as a serious consideration to choose wisely those musical forms to be used in state education. Socrates says: "Give me the mode which will imitate the accents of a brave man enduring danger and distress, and fighting with constancy against misfortune."

There was a Te Deum Dante thought he heard in accents blended with sweet melody; the strains came over his ear even as the sound of choral voices that mingle with the organ in solemn chants. The delight in music is universal. It is discovered in all races and in all ages. It even anticipates terrestrial history, for in the Book of Job, the oldest in the world, we read that God Himself said: "Where wast thou when I laid the foundations of the earth, when the morning stars sang together?" Music has been rightly called the "language of heaven." The modern church organ is the development probably of the shepherd's pipe, corresponding to the pipe of Pan in the Greek mythology. Consisting at first of only one or two, it afterwards comprised seven pipes made of reeds and differing from each other in length. If music is the expression of human emotion, does it not follow naturally that sacred music should be the expression of purely religious emotion? We are, therefore, not content that certain tunes should have been written for the Church; we contend further that the composers should be those who in their souls have experienced the emotions they musically express so as to arouse similar emotions in others.

"If you wish to touch my heart," writes Horace to the poets, "you must begin by showing me that you have touched your own." It can hardly be doubted that religious feeling was one of the earliest motives for calling music into existence. Love, ecstacy and devotion are states of mind most liable to foster a musical utterance. One of the features which distinguishes the Christian religion from all others is its quietness. The early Christians discouraged all outward signs of excitement, and from the very beginning, in the music they used, reproduced the spirit of their religion—an inward quietude. All the music employed in their early services was vocal, and the rhythmic element and all gesticulation were forbidden.

The Christian Church first took up the antiphonal method of singing of a melody by men an octave lower than it is sung at the same time by boys; the process has been miscalled by us, "singing in unison." Among the Christians it meant the responsive singing by two choirs. It is to St. Ambrose, Bishop of Milan, that the credit belongs of having made the first arrangement of sacred music. St. Ambrose adopted the responsive singing between two choirs of the verses of the Psalms and he also rearranged the hymns for the regular services of the Church. St. Augustine tells us in his "Confessions" that he was moved to tears as he heard these hymns sung by the great congregation in the Church of Milan. The next improvement in church music was instituted by the Pope, St. Gregory. He rearranged the Ambrosian hymns, with their melodies, and his style is known as the Gregorian, from its author's name. One of the latest inventions in the development of harmony was counterpoint. In general, counterpoint means a new voice-part added to one already existing; this voice is an individual, distinct and independent part, not merely a natural bass. Palestrina produced a mass which has been the model of sacred composition ever since its first rendition. It is called the "Missa Papae Macelli." The presence of a soul within it immortalized Palestrina's work. It was his work to breathe into music the breath of life; to lift it from the dry formulae which stifled it and give it an aesthetic beauty. To his work Palestrina brought the qualities of heart and mind which are a sine qua non in the composition of sacred music. Notwithstanding the beauties of the Palestrina school, the Gregorian chant still remains one of the most perfect in the expression of religious feeling.

History records numerous instances of the power of this devout and solemn music; as how worldly, sensual and wicked men, happening to hear this chant as it poured forth from cloistered walls, have then and there resolved to change their lives. The conversion of St. Augustine was attributed to just such a chance hearing of this wonderful song of the monks.

There always seems to have been in the minds of the really great composers a deep conviction of the dignity of their labor whenever they attempted to express the solemn truths of sacred subjects. Handel, in commenting on the Hallelujah Chorus, said: "I did think I did see all heaven before me, and the great God Himself." At the head of his scores Haydn inscribed the words, "In Nomine Domini," and at the end of them, "Laus Deo."

It was in the middle of the sixteenth century that the class of composition now ranked as the highest was originated. The oratorio dates its existence and its name from the meetings held by St. Philip Neri in the oratory of his church in Rome, at first in 1556, for religious exercise and pious edification. Originally this consisted of laudi or short hymns, the extent of which was afterward enlarged. By and by the spoken matter was replaced by singing, and ultimately the class of work took the form in which it is cast by present composers. Such is the source of the didactic oratorio. The dramatic oratorio is an offshoot of the same, but is distinguished by its representation of personal characters and their involvement in a course of action. History now steps on to the great name of Mozart, who wrote forty-eight symphonies, some of them in the tenderest years of childhood. It is related of Mozart, that one day a stranger called and requested him to compose a requiem, and offered to pay for it in advance. The composer began the work under the influence of superstitious fear, believing that the messenger had been sent from the other world to warn him of his own approaching death. Meanwhile he received a commission to compose an opera for the coronation of the Emperor at Prague. He worked incessantly and far beyond his strength. The coronation took place and its splendors threw the opera very much in the shade. The "Magic Flute" was produced within the same month and had a successful run. But the requiem still remained unfinished.

The stranger therefore made another appointment, paying a further sum in advance. Mozart worked at it unremittently, hoping to make it his greatest work. His sacred music, though less florid than Haydn's, was even more voluptuously beautiful, perfect in its kind, though showing no trace of the stern grandeur of Handel or the devotional purity of Palestrina. In the requiem he surpassed himself, but he was not permitted to finish it. When the stranger called the third time the composer was no more. We are not yet prepared to judge of the latest and perhaps most radical revolutionist in music, Richard Wagner. As he devoted himself to dramatic compositions intended for the theater, a consideration of his music dramas has no place in this essay. We are concerned here with music and musical composers dedicated to Almighty God. We cannot close a consideration on this subject without paying a tribute to the special patroness of music and musicians, St. Cecilia. Half the musical societies in Europe are named after her, and her love for music has led the votaries of a sister art to find subjects for their works in episodes of her life. The painting reproduced in this volume of the "Masterpieces" shows St. Cecilia, wrapped in an ecstacy of devotion, seated at that most kingly of all musical instruments, the church organ. The Church, ever mindful of humanity and knowing the shortest and most direct avenues to our hearts and souls, has ever encouraged the evolution of music. In its sublime ritual the Church employs the world's masterpieces with this limitation, that the musical composition used must be of a devotional and elevating nature.

> Borne on the swelling notes our souls aspire;
> While solemn airs improve the sacred fire,
> And angels lean from heav'n to hear.

JAQUES BENIGNE BOSSUET.

SELECTIONS FROM BOSSUET.

Jacques Benigne Bossuet, sacred orator, historian, theologian and controversalist, was born in Dijon, France, on September 27, 1627. Unquestionably he is one of the greatest Catholic divines France ever knew, and some do not hesitate to name him as the greatest of all French pulpit orators. Bossuet was a most prolific writer. In the best edition, that of Abbe Caron, his writings fill not less than forty-one volumes. The most important of Bossuet's works are the "Sermons" and the "Discourse Upon Universal History." The sermons were undoubtedly among his most perfect productions. He was a born orator; his majestic bearing, his melodious voice, his noble gestures and his matchless style made the magnificent sentences, the beautiful and striking imagery of his speeches doubly impressive. Unfortunately, with only a few exceptions, Bossuet's sermons have reached us in a very imperfect form. He did not, as a rule, fully write them, and the art of taking down verbatim the utterances of public speakers had not in his time been invented. Bossuet's funeral orations were prepared with great care. They were delivered, as a rule, several months after the death of the person to be eulogized. In the funeral oration on the Princess Henrietta, the preacher shows his marvelous power as an orator to the best advantage. Only two or three hours before her death, when fully conscious of her desperate position, the unfortunate Princess had directed that an emerald ring of hers should be, after her death, handed to the great preacher. "What a pity," some one remarked, "that such an incident cannot find place in a funeral oration!" "Why not?" asked Bossuet. When he delivered the oration the emerald ring was on one of the fingers of his right hand; and when speaking of the Princess' virtues and charming qualities, he alluded to the art of giving, in which she excelled. "And this art," he went on, "never deserted her, not even, I know it, in the throes of death," at the same time raising his right hand and placing the precious jewel in full view of the audience. With the funeral orations one might mention another series of religious discourses, not strikingly different from them—the panegyrics of saints, of which twenty have been preserved, that on St. Paul being indisputably the best.

We submit in this volume the opening of the funeral oration on Henrietta of France and a selection from the "Discourse Upon Universal History," as illustrations of the genius of Bossuet.

OPENING OF THE FUNERAL ORATION ON HENRIETTA OF FRANCE.

He who reigns and who is the Lord of all the empires, to whom alone majesty, glory and independence belongs, is also the only One who glories in dictating laws to kings, and in giving them, when it so pleases Him, great and terrible lessons. Whether He raises or lowers thrones; whether He communicates His own power to princes, or reclaims it all and leaves them nothing but their own weakness, He teaches them their duties in a manner both sovereign and worthy of Him; for when giving them His power, He commands them to use it as He does, for the good of the world; and He shows them in withdrawing it that all their majesty is borrowed, and that, though seated on the throne, they are nevertheless under His hand and supreme authority. Thus does He teach princes, not only by deeds and examples. "Et nunc, regis, intelligente; erudimini, qui judicatis terram." Christians, ye who have been called from all sides to this ceremony by the memory of a great Queen —daughter, wife, mother of powerful kings and of sovereigns of three kingdoms—this speech will bring before you one of those conspicuous examples which spread before the eyes of the world its absolutely vanity. You will see in a single life all the extremes of human affairs: boundless felicity and boundless misery; a long and peaceful possession of one of the world's noblest crowns; all that can be given of the glories of birth and rank gathered upon a head which is afterwards exposed to all the insults of fortune; the good cause at first rewarded by success, then met by sudden turns and unheard-of changes; rebellion long restrained, at last overriding everything; unbridled licentiousness; destruction of all laws; royal majesty insulted by crimes before unknown; usurpation and tyranny under the name of liberty; a queen pursued by her enemies and finding no refuge in either of her kingdoms; her own native land become a melancholy place of exile; many voyages across the sea undertaken by a Princess in spite of the tempest; the ocean surprised at being crossed so often, in such different ways, and for so different causes; a throne shamefully destroyed and miraculously restored. Those are the lessons which are given by God to the kings. Thus does He show to the world the emptiness of its pomps and splendors. If I lack words, if expression is unable to do justice to a subject of such magnitude and loftiness, things alone will speak sufficiently; the heart of a great Queen, formerly raised by long years of prosperity and suddenly plunged into an abyss of bitterness will speak loudly enough. And if private characters are not allowed to give lessons to princes upon such strange occurrences a King lends me His voice to tell them. "Et nunc, reges, intelligente; erudimini, qui judicatis terram": "Understand now, ye kings of the earth; learn, ye who judge the world."

But the wise and religious Princess who is the subject of this discourse was not simply a spectacle presented to them that they may study therein the counsels of Divine Providence and the fatal revolutions of dynasties. She was her own instructor, while God instructed all princes through her example. I have said already that the Divine Lord teaches them both by giving and by taking away their powers. The Queen of whom I speak understood one of these lessons as well as the other, contrary as they are, which means that in good as well as in evil fortune she behaved as a Christian.

In the one she was charitable, in the other invincible. While prosperous she made her power felt by the world through infinite blessings; when fortune forsook her she enlarged her own treasure of virtues, so that she lost for her own good this royal power which she had had for the good of others. And if her subjects, if her allies, if the Church Universal were gainers by her greatness, she gained by her misfortunes and humiliations more than she had done by all her glory.

SELECTED FROM BOSSUET'S DISCOURSE UPON UNIVERSAL HISTORY.

Even were history useless to other men, it would still be necessary to have it read by princes. There is no better way of making them discover what can be brought about by passions and interests, by times and circumstances, by good and bad advice. The books of historians are filled with actions that occupy them, and everything therein seems to have been done for their use. If experience is necessary to them for acquiring that prudence which enables them to become good rulers, nothing is more useful to their instruction than to add to the example of past centuries the experiences with which they meet every day. While usually they learn to judge of the dangerous circumstances that surround them only at the expense of their subjects and of their own glory, by the help of history they form their judgment upon the events of the past without risking anything. While they see even the most completely hidden vices of princes exposed to the eyes of all men, in spite of the insincere praise which they receive while alive, they feel ashamed of the empty joy which flattery gives them and acknowledge that true glory cannot obtain without real merit.

Moreover it would be disgraceful—I do not say for a prince, but in general for any educated man—not to know the human kind and the memorable changes which took place in the world through the lapse of ages. If we do not learn from history to distinguish the times we shall represent men under the law of nature or under civil law the same as under the sway of the Gospel; we shall speak of the Persians conquered under Alexander in the same way as of Persians victorious under Cyrus; we shall represent Greece as free in the time of Philip as in the time of Themistocles or Miltiades; the Roman people as proud under the Emperors as under the Consuls; the Church as quiet under Diocletian as under Constantine; and France disturbed by civil wars under Charles IX and Henri III as powerful as in the time of Louis XIV, when, united under such a great King, alone she triumphs over the whole of Europe.

MOST REV. PAUL BRUCHESI, D. D., MONTREAL.

ORATION ON SAINT PATRICK.

By

His Grace Archbishop Paul Bruchesi,
of Montreal.

The Most Rev. Paul Bruchesi, D. D., Archbishop of Montreal, who delivered the splendid oration on St. Patrick, which follows, was raised to the archiepiscopal dignity August 8, 1897. His Grace is considered by many scholars the greatest master of the French language on this Continent. The Archbishop is dearly beloved by the Irish people of Montreal, and his high regard for the sons and daughters of Erin doubtless led to his selecting the oration printed here for his contribution to "The Masterpieces of Catholic Literature, Oratory and Art." The editor is pleased to acknowledge gracious assistance from the Rev. Luke Callaghan, D. D., Vice Chancellor of the Archdiocese of Montreal.

SAINT PATRICK.

By

Most Reverend Paul Bruchesi, D. D.

"I have kept the faith." Words of St. Paul in his second Epistle to Timothy, fourth chapter, fourth verse.
Dearly Beloved Brethren:
In October last I was in Dublin, the far-famed metropolis of the capital of Ireland, your native land, or the home of

your noble ancestors. I went there not as a mere tourist. On my way to Rome to kneel at the tomb of the Apostles for the first time as Archbishop, I felt in duty bound to stop over in France, the mother country of this Canada of ours. A thought came to my mind. Did not God entrust to my pastoral care and solicitude a large number who claim Erin for the land of their birth, or whose forefathers hailed from that Island of Saints? If so, I should not pass by without treading a soil sanctified by the prayers, the tears and the labors of their national Apostle. I thought of the majestic churches that your ancestors erected to the glory of God, to the honor of the Saints; the monuments which your nationality inspired and which your generosity achieved; the love of country embodied in the poetic lines of a Moore, a Mangan, a Griffin; the heaven-born principles of an O'Connell and of other eminent statesmen in the arena of political and constitutional warfare, in the outspoken and dauntless cause of your national rights and religious liberties. Full of the warmest enthusiasm at the magnificent sight that met my gaze, I penned a few lines to your much revered pastor, claiming the privilege and joy of Pontificating on the coming celebration of your illustrious Patron's national festival and of addressing you on that solemn occasion. The hopes I then entertained are now realized. I do not believe that I could, in any other way, offer you a better pledge of the sincerity of my kindly feelings towards you. Year after year orators of your own nationality, deeply versed in sacred eloquence, have ascended this pulpit to laud your patriotism and revive your nation's glorious deeds, to rehearse the transcendent virtues and the imperishable achievements of your saintly Patron. It would be presumption on my part to rise to their level, but, nevertheless, my foreign accent will not fail to impart to you all what it cannot disguise, that

LACORDAIRE.

there beats within my breast a fatherly and friendly heart in perfect touch with yours and in perfect keeping with your own sentiments and aspirations.

LACORDAIRE'S TRIBUTE.

With your kind indulgence I may, I believe, recall the remembrance of my youthful days. I was in the act of perusing for the first time the sublime panegyric of the Liberator of Ireland by Lacordaire, a prince among the orators of France. I came across the following: "Look at the map of the world. At both extremities lie two groups of islands, the Japanese and the British. Along the line for three thousand leagues you may read the names of Japan, China, Russia, Sweden, Prussia, Denmark, Hanover, England, Ireland. In none of those kingdoms or empires does the Church of God enjoy her inalienable rights. Her voice her sacraments, her gatherings are proscribed. What! So many nations deprived of the sacred freedom of the children of God! What! Among the two hundred millions who people those lands, have none been bold enough to stand up and assert their rights of conscience, their dignity as Christians? No, no, gentlemen. God has never left the truth without martyrs; that is to say, without witnesses to seal it in their blood, and, as in Ireland, so widespread, so enduring, so rigorous was the spirit of oppression that God, on His part, wrought a new miracle in the history of martyrdom. Men, nay, whole families, have shed their blood in testimony of their faith and left after them only their mangled remains and an imperishable name, but nowhere does history record that an entire nation handed down to posterity persecution and death as precious heirlooms. God willed it, however, and it was done. He willed it in our times and in our times it came to pass. Among the above mentioned nations, bound to one another by their geographical positions and by a kind of spiritual slavery, one alone never accepted the yoke. Brute force might subdue her body; trammel her soul, never; I shall not mention the name of that dear, saintly nation, that nation which outlived death itself. My lips are not pure, they are not fervid enough to pronounce its name. Heaven knows it. Earth blesses it. Generous hearts have offered her a home, an asylum, together with their love. Heaven, thou who seest her; earth, thou who knowest her. All ye who are better, worthier, than I speak out, tell her name, say, Ireland."

These words deeply moved me, and I felt as if I should look more inquiringly into the motive that prompted a eulogy so much like to the most enthusiastic song of the prophets of old.

WHAT MADE IRELAND SO GREAT,

so loveable, so deserving of admiration that none but angelic lips could utter her name? Could it be the fertility of her soil, the agricultural ascendancy of her inhabitants? No, for other lands are equally favored as she, and may be regarded as her superior in their fields with their golden harvests, their orange groves, their trees and their flowers. Could it be wealth? No, for her children, by the thousands, have been for centuries groaning in poverty. Could it be the inspiration of her bards, the genius of her artists, the productions of her writers? No, they are to be met with elsewhere, and rivals and masters in the arts and sciences, too. No, no, the reason lies in the fact that Ireland, favored by God and taught the revealed truths by her priests, has preserved intact the sacred deposit. Religion, in her onward march from land to land, has indeed found disciples and defenders, but has it not likewise been thwarted on many a battlefield and weakened in many an encounter? Nations as well as individuals have apostatized and denied the faith in which they were cradled, nursed and fostered. Doubtless, a nation may recover. For my part, I do believe in the possibility of their resurrection. Nevertheless, the sight of a whole nation steeped in apostacy cannot but sadden us. Ireland has kept the faith, but not without the greatest sacrifice. She may well apply to herself the words of St. Paul, "I have fought the good fight, I have kept the faith." From out the deep darkness of paganism,

IRELAND STEPPED FORTH INTO THE FULL LIGHT OF CHRISTIANITY.

She renounced her once cherished idolatrous practices, so flattering to fallen nature, and generously embraced the stern principles of Christian morality.

St. Patrick, a child of France, was the ambassador of Christ who, by the preaching of the pure doctrine of Rome, by his wise counsels and the example of every Christian virtue achievéd over their minds and hearts a complete conquest. He converted both subjects and rulers, established convents and monasteries all over the land, founded schools and universities, whither young men flocked from all parts of Europe, and thus built up a generation of enlightened Catholics, who became competent to spread the truth in every part of the world. Every country has its golden period; Greece had its age of Pericles, Rome its Augustan era, Italy its age of Leo X, France its period of Louis XIV, and Ireland its golden days from the middle of the sixth to the middle of the eighth century. When the so-called Reformation dawned upon the horizon, Ireland met it with contempt. She heeded not its teachings, but clung tenaciously to the old Faith, though all human favors were offered her to reject it. She professed the Roman tenets in prison, in exile and upon the scaffold, "in spite of dungeon, fire and sword." She was unconquerable. Her temples were confiscated by the plunderers, and when her fearless sons and daughters could not adore therein, because they were polluted by a false worship, they built themselves altars on the mountain slope or in caves, even at the cost of their mortal existence, and when, last of all, they

WERE DRIVEN FROM THEIR HIDING PLACES, they adored their God in the sanctuary of their own souls, but never would they consent to frequent the church once theirs, and they preferred to die of famine than to accept a morsel of food from the hands of the tempter who sought to win them over under the cloak of charity. Heresy had flattered herself with the prospect of an easy conquest; she was doomed to disappointment. Apostatize, she cried out, and whatever I can bestow, you shall obtain. You are poor; apostatize, and I will enrich you. You are despised; apostatize, and you will be esteemed and honored. You are slaves; apostatize, and I will break your chains asunder and restore you to the blessings of freedom. But no, your noble ancestors preferred the bread of heaven to the bread of earth, the faith taught by St. Patrick to the tempter's gold and silver. Earth they cared not for. Heaven alone was their home, the height of their ambition, the goal of their aspirations. The eloquent Macaulay has fittingly remarked: "We have used the sword for centuries against the Catholic Irish—we have tried famine—we have tried extermination—we have had recourse to all the severity of the law. What have we done? Have we succeeded? We have neither been able to exterminate nor enfeeble them. I confess my incapacity to solve the problem. If I could find myself beneath the dome of St. Peter's, and read, with the faith of a Catholic, the inscription around it, 'Thou art Peter, and upon this rock I will build My church, and the gates of hell shall not prevail against it,' then could I solve the problem of Ireland's story."

What he could not do, we can. We can read that inscription with Catholic faith. It is the key to explain

THE ALLEGIANCE OF ERIN'S SONS

to him who struck off the shackles which held their ancestors in a spiritual bondage. On the very day I reached Dublin hundreds of your fellow-countrymen knelt at the feet of Leo XIII to speak their sentiments of filial love and attachment. The Vicar of Jesus Christ greeted them in these terms: "The most Catholic people in the whole world are the Irish." Greater praise than this could not be tendered to a nation, and it is a pleasure for me to repeat his words on this solemn occasion, which has led you to the foot of God's altar to give expression to the sentiments that filled the souls of your countrymen in presence of the Sovereign Pontiff. Your forefathers have bequeathed to you the priceless inheritance of example. Be like them, men of faith; that is, love and cherish your holy religion. Accept submissively her teachings, practice them unflinchingly, defend them on every occasion. Faith is the foundation of the supernatural order, the root of justification, for "without it," writes the Apostle St. Paul, "it is impossible to please God." Without supernatural truth it is but an empty sound. The Catholic Church alone has it. She is "the pillar and ground of truth." Her doctrines are but the utterances of Christ Himself. A poet has said, "To err is human." She cannot err because she is not a human, but a Divine institution. To preserve her from error Christ Himself set in her bright diadem

THE PEERLESS GEM OF INFALLIBILITY,

thereby imparting to His own earthly spouse a share in His divinity. Religion to be Divine must contain mysteries or incomprehensible truths. This announcement ought not to startle any thinking or observing mind, for is not nature veiled in impenetrable mystery? And if, the world over, all admit the existence of mystery in the natural order, without, however, being capable of comprehending it, they ought, if consistent, yield absolute assent to the incomprehensible in the supernatural order. The doctrines inculcated by the Catholic Church, though beyond the comprehension of a finite intellect, merit, therefore, your unreserved assent. Promulgated by a Divine, infallible Doctor nigh two thousand years ago, they are proposed to your belief by a Church which, like her Divine Founder, is today, yesterday and forever; by a Church which alone lays claim to inerrancy in matters of faith and morals. Belief alone is not sufficient. "Faith without works is dead," remarks St. James. The test of one's belief lies in its exercise or in a conformity and continuity of action in keeping with it. To act differently is universally regarded as a moral weakness and branded as such. A man of sound principles is a man of character, and to act against those principles is, in a word, practically their denial. The faith of your predecessors was a living faith; that is, accompanied by good works. They confessed Christ by word and deed. Consult the history of your fatherland. Every page of it is marked with the

SEAL OF LOYALTY AND ATTACHMENT TO THE DIVINE AND ECCLESIASTICAL PRECEPTS.

The law of God was written on the tablets of their minds and enshrined on the altar of their hearts. To them may be applied the words of the Royal Psalmist: "Blessed are the undefiled in the way, who walk in the law of the Lord." To complete your glory you must add the dignity of the apostle to the character of the practical Christian. Defend your religion. Be conversant with its teachings so as to be ever ready to "give an account of the faith that is in you." Has Divine Providence entrusted you with an important office, are the interests of your fellowmen, the welfare of society or of your beloved country in your hands? Never swerve from the path of duty. Be on all occasions the fearless, outspoken champions of the rights of your Church and of Catholic principles. Never suffer party spirit to betray the dictates of conscience or prove untrue to the memory of your sainted ancestors. Love your children. Set them an example of every Christian virtue. Send them to schools where the poison of indifference or error will not be instilled into their youthful minds. See that they comply faithfully with the laws of God and of the Church. Thus they will become the bulwarks of religion. Cherish with predilection the home of your forefathers, the home of the Popes, two spots on earth ever dear to the Irish heart. Before expiring in Genoa, the immortal O'Connell bequeathed his body to Ireland. It was meet that the hero's mortal remains should rest in the bosom of the land for which he had lived and died. His heart he left to Rome. A stronger pledge of filial love and submission towards the See of Peter he could not have given. His soul he consigned to his Maker.

A threefold love that should glow in the breast of all, love of country, love of Rome, love of God. I know you love your country, and it seems I hear you repeating with the bard:

"Forget Ireland! no, while there's life in this heart,
It shall never forget thee, all lone as thou art.
More dear in thy sorrow, thy gloom and thy showers
Than the rest of the world in its sunniest hours."

Let your fervent petitions ascend to the throne of the
Most High that peace, prosperity and happiness may smile
on poor Erin. But, above all, cling to her faith. Remember, you are the descendants of heroes, children of the Isle
of Saints, and, by your exemplary lives, prove yourselves
worthy of the title you bear. Amen.

ST. BERNARD.

PREFATORY NOTE

ST. BERNARD.

St. Bernard, of Clairvaux, one of the prodigies and ornaments of the Middle Ages, was born at Fontaine, near Dijon, in Burgundy, 1091, became a monk of Citeaux in 1113, founded a new branch of that order at Clairvaux, in Champagne, and became its first abbot in 1115, died Aug. 20, 1153, and was canonized by Alexander III., 1174. His ascetic life, solitary studies and stirring eloquence made him, during his lifetime, the oracle of Christendom. He was honored with the title of the "mellifluous doctor," and his writings were termed "a river of paradise." In the course of his life he founded 160 monasteries. His writings are exceedingly numerous. They consist of epistles, sermons and theological treatises. Of the first we possess 439, of the second, 340, and of the third, 12. They are all instinct with genius. Notwithstanding St. Bernard's love of retirement, obedience and zeal for the divine honor frequently drew him from his beloved cell; and so great was the reputation of his learning and piety, that all potentates desired to have their differences determined by him; bishops regarded his decisions as oracles or indispensable laws, and referred to him the most important affairs of their churches. The Popes looked upon his advice as the greatest support of the Holy See, and all people had a very profound respect, and an extraordinary veneration for his person and sanctity. It may be said of him that even in his solitude he governed all the churches of the West. But he knew how to join the love of silence and interior recollection of soul with so many occupations and employ, and a profound humility with so great an elevation.

LETTERS AND SERMONS OF SAINT BERNARD.

Abbot of Clairvaux.

Translated by

SAMUEL J. EALES, M. A., D. C. L.

LETTER CDXII (A new letter).

To T., a young man, who had vowed to enter the monastic life.

To his very dear son, T., Bernard, Abbot of Clairvaux, health and that he may go forth to meet the Bridegroom and the Bride.

1.   I will speak to you in simple words: Man is a being rational and mortal: the one of these qualities he owes to the grace of his Creator; the other is the consequence of sin. In the one we are companions of the dignity of the angels; in the other of the weakness of the brute creation. Yet each ought to be a motive to us to seek the Lord; both the dignity of reason and the fear of death. Be thou mindful of the promise that thou hast given me, and in which I repose full confidence. I ask its performance; the time to redeem it approaches; have no fear where there is nothing to fear. It is not a burden but an honor to serve the Lord in joy and gladness. I cannot grant to you a long delay: for while nothing is more certain than death, nothing is more uncertain than the hour of death. Your tender age is no safeguard against early death. The fruit is often torn

from the tree by the hand or by a tempest, even while it is still green. Why do you rely upon your health and your comeliness?

"O beautiful youth, trust not overmuch to your bloom. The flowers of the white privet fall, the dusky hyacinths are gathered." (Virgil, Ecl. ii. vv. 17, 18.)

Come forth, come forth with Joseph from the house of Pharaoh and leave your mantle, that is, the glory of the world, in the hand of the Egyptian mistress; come forth from your country and your kindred; forget your own people and your father's house; and the King shall be charmed with your beauty. The Child Jesus is not found among relations and acquaintances. Come forth from your father's house to seek Him, for He came forth on your account from the house of His Father. His coming forth is from the height of heaven. Deservedly was He found of the Syro-Phoenician woman, who came forth from her own land and cried to Him, saying: "Have mercy upon me, O Son of David!" For He, upon whose lips is grace found, quickly replied to her: "O woman, great is thy faith; be it unto thee even as thou wilt." (St. Matt. xv. 22-28.)

2. Satan perhaps may be hostile to Satan; but can the Spirit of truth possibly be contrary to Himself? It was He, I fully believe, who spoke to me by your mouth to tell me of your conversion. See then that you do not turn aside to the right hand or to the left, but you come to Clairvaux according to your promise. This I have written to you briefly and in private, and send it by my dear son Gerard, your friend. Do not put forward any excuse. If your earnest desire is in the matter, if you still wish to be taught and to be under a master; the Master is come and calleth for thee; He, I mean, in whom all the treasures of wisdom are hidden. It is He who teacheth man knowledge, who makes

the tongues of infants eloquent, who openeth and no man shutteth, and who shutteth and no man openeth.

LETTER CCCXCIII.   (A new letter.)

To W., Patriarch of Jerusalem.
Bernard Exhorts Him to Humility.

To the venerable Lord and beloved Father, W., by the grace of God Patriarch of Jerusalem, Bernard, Abbot of Clairvaux, wishes health and the Spirit of truth, who proceedeth from the Father.

1.   Having an opportunity of sending by a trustworthy man, a friend of yours, who is the bearer of this, I, although busied about many things, write a few words to you, who art also busy.   If indeed it seem to any presumptuous and I be judged for this, yet it is a light presumption that proceeds from affection.   But that I may not write much when I promised little, let me come to the point.   When it pleased the Creator of the universe to make known the depth of the wisdom of His plan for the salvation of the human race He so loved the world that He gave His only begotten Son, who was made for men, and He called to Himself those of the sons of men whom He would, both chosen out of the rest and beloved above the rest.   And again one of these, as if elected from the elect, and beloved beyond the beloved, He separated for the special favor of His love, to whom, when lifted up from the earth, He offered with outstretched hands His evening sacrifice before He commended His spirit into His Father's hands; He, like a Brother to a brother, a virgin Himself, committed His virgin Mother to a virgin in His stead.   To what end such a beginning?   Listen carefully.

2.   The Lord has chosen many, and made them princes among His people that they might have the dignity of the Episcopate; but thee, by a special grace, He placed in the

house of His servant David. To thee also, of all the bishops in the whole world, has been committed that land whence sprang the green herb, and the fruit of the earth after its kind; from which sprang also the Rose of Sharon and the Lily of the Valley. Thee alone, I say, the Lord chose above thy fellows to be to Him, as it were, a bishop for His household, day by day to enter into His Tabernacle and to adore Him in the very place where His feet once stood. We read that it was said to holy Moses when he received a command from the Lord to make known to the sons of Israel: "Loose thy shoe from off thy feet, for the place whereon thou standest is holy ground." (Exodus iii. 5.) That place is also holy, but it was sanctified by type and figure, while this has been hallowed by the very Truth Himself. That spot was holy, but this is holier. What comparison is there between the figure of the truth, which is seen only as in a glass and darkly, and that glory which shall be revealed when the veil is at length taken away? And yet when all these things were shown in figure and as still future, it was said to Moses: "Loose thy shoe from off thy feet, for the place whereon thou standest is holy ground." And I say to you: Loose thy shoe from off thy feet, for the place where thou standest is holy ground. If hitherto your affections have been in any degree set on dead works, give them up quickly, for the place whereon thou standest is holy ground. O how fearful is that place in which first, through the mercy of our God, the Dayspring from on high hath visited us! O how fearful is that place in which first the Father met the Son returning from a region so little worthy of Him ,and, falling upon His neck, clothed Him with a robe of glory! O how fearful is that place in which the sweet and righteous Lord poured into our wounds both oil and wine, in which the Father of mercies and the God of all consolation made with us a covenant of peace! Thanks to Thee, O Lord, thanks to Thee, because Thou hast worked a good work in the midst of the earth, in the midst of the years, making this a mark of law and grace. For when Thou wert very angry Thou didst remember pity. Behold a place far more sacred than that on which Moses stood, and far more noble, for it is the place of the Lord, the place, I say, of Him who came by Water and Blood; not only by water, as Moses, but by Water and Blood. Behold the place where they laid Him. Who shall ascend into the hill of the Lord, or who shall stand in His holy place? He alone ought to ascend who has learnt from the Lord Jesus Christ to be meek and lowly of heart.

3. The humble can alone ascend securely, because humility has no exaltation from whence it can fall; the proud, although he climb, yet cannot stand for long, like one who wishes not to stand on his own feet, but has taken to himself that of another, like him of whom the Prophet says in detestation: "Let not the foot of pride come against me." (Ps. xxxvi. 11.) For my pride has only one foot, the love of its own excellence. And so the proud cannot stand for long, like one who only leans on one foot. For who can stand on that foot, on which have fallen those who worked iniquity as an angel in heaven and a man in Paradise? If God spared not the natural branches; the man, I mean, whom He crowned with glory and honor, and set over all the works of His hands; nor an angel, who was the beginning of His works, full of wisdom and of perfect beauty; much more is it to be feared lest He spare not me when I boast myself, being no longer in the garden of pleasure nor in the realm of heaven, but in the vale of tears. Therefore, that you may stand firm, stand in humility; stand not on the one foot of pride, but on the feet of humility that your footsteps be not

shaken. For humility has two feet, the consideration of Divine power and of its own weakness. O beautiful feet and firm, neither wrapped in the darkness of ignorance, nor stained with the slippery soil of luxury! Do you, then, who are placed on high, refrain from high thoughts, but fear; and humble yourself under the powerful hand of Him who will bow down in His strength the necks of the proud and lofty. Think of the church committed to your hands, not as a servant into those of a master, but, to go back to the beginning of my letter, as a mother to the care of a son, as Mary to John, so that of thee also it may be said to her, "Mother, behold thy son." And of her to thee, "Behold thy mother." For so shalt thou be safe in thy coming in and in thy going out; and in thy approach to His majesty, who, although He be high and inhabiteth eternity, yet has regard to the humble both in heaven and in earth.

LETTER CDLXXXII.

To David, King of Scotland.

To the Lord David, the most illustrious King of Scotland, whom he embraces in the bowels of Christ, (Bernard), called Abbot of Clairvaux, health and eternal life.

Long since, O most illustrious sovereign, have I been drawn by your high reputation to regard you with affection and to desire to see you face to face. I desire it, I repeat, and I know that it is written: "The Lord hath heard the desire of the poor: Thine ear, O Lord, hath heard the preparation of their heart." (Ps. x. 17.) Fortified with this confidence, then, I trust in the Lord that I shall some time behold you even in the body, and even now I view you in mind and spirit with satisfaction, and often recall the memory with sweetness and joy. Our brethren who are at Rievaulx had felt the bowels of your first kindness, and to them you opened the treasure of your good will; you have cherished them with the anointing of your mercy and pity, and the palace of the Heavenly King was filled with the fragrance of the ointment. I am not ungrateful for these kindnesses, which are as welcome to me as if they had been bestowed upon me in my own person. But there are still others of our brethren who have lately become neighbors of yours. I think you are not ignorant of the manner in which (some of the monks) of St. Mary's Abbey at York, where they had lived too carelessly, received an inspiration from on high and went forth into a solitary place; how they endured persecutions and injuries inflicted on them both by guile and by open force; how when they were rich and abounded in the things of this world, they became poor religious for the love of Christ, true seekers after the apostolic life and holiness. The world would love them, according to the saying of the Lord, if they were of the world. But now, because they are not of the world, it persecutes them as strangers and aliens. And they, indeed, by the help of God, bear patiently whatever the world attempts against them. But we and whosoever fears God ought to assist the servants of God in their tribulation. To you, then, most compassionate King, I commend these servants of Christ of whom I speak. I supplicate you on their behalf that you would afford to them some solace in their poverty. And I hope that you will receive for your reward an everlasting kingdom from Christ, the King of kings, in the day of the recompense of the righteous. Amen.

LETTER CCCXCVIII. (Formerly No. 312.)

To Guy Abbot of Montier-Ramey, and the Religious of that Abbey.

Bernard having been requested by the Abbot and monks to compose an Office for the festival of their patron, St.

Victor, pleads the difficulty of the task and his own scanty qualification for it; he expounds the qualities needed in forms intended for public worship and traces the rules of the Ecclesiastical Chant.

To the venerable Guy of Montier-Ramey, and to his holy community, Bernard, the servant of their Holiness, health and the power to serve God in holiness.

1.　You ask me, my dear Abbot Guy, in company with all your good brethren, to write for an Office to be solemnly said or sung on the Festival of St. Victor, whose sacred body rests among you. You urge me to do this in spite of my reluctance and feeling of insufficiency, which you overrule, though it is so well founded. And as if there could be any more powerful motive to me to comply with your wish than the wish itself, you employ also the intercessions of others with me. But it seems to me that you ought to have consulted your own judgment, to have reflected, not merely on you affection for me, but on my (obscure) position in the church. For a task of that importance needs not merely a friend, but a learned and able man, whose greater authority, sanctity and more polished style would both adorn the work and befit its holiness.

2.　Who am I, the humblest among Christian people, that my compositions should be read in churches? And how little eloquence or faculty of invention have I that I should be called upon to produce a chant suitable to be used and listened to on a festival? What! can I begin anew to sing on earth the praises of that Saint, who is now being praised, and that worthily, in heaven?

To wish to add anything to the celestial praises is to detract from them. Not that men may not praise here below those whom the angles glorify above, but because, on a solemn festival, the praises of the church ought to have nothing of novelty or of lightness, but to be authentic and serious, redolent of hoary antiquity, of grave and church-like character.

But if there was a desire, and an occasion, for the composition of an Office, I should have thought (as I have already said) that it should have been intrusted to some one whose reputation and whose eloquence would have enabled him to treat it both more agreeably to the ears of the worshippers and more profitably to their hearts.

The author's aim should certainly be to glorify the truth, to inculcate righteousness, to recommend humility, to teach justice; it should enlighten the mind, elevate the heart, mortify the passions, discipline the senses, crucify evil desires and inspire devotion. The chant, if one is used, should be full of solemnity, and equally distant from rusticity and luscious sweetness.

Yet let it be sweet so that it be not trifling; and let it so please the ear that it may touch the heart.

Let it be such as to lighten sadness, to lower the fire of anger, and let it not obscure, but heighten, the sense of the words. It is of no small detriment to the spiritual sense to have the attention withdrawn from the intention of the words by the levity of the chants and to be more attracted by the flexibility of the voices than by the sense of the words they dwell upon.

Such are the qualities which, it seems to me, are needed in the offices of the church, and such the ability which those require who undertake to compose them. Am I such as this, or are these qualities to be found in what I have written for you? 'And yet, out of my poverty, as you continued to knock and to call upon me, I felt constrained to rise up, and, according to the word of the Saviour, not because you were my friends, but because of your importunity, to give you that which you asked. I send you then, at your earnest request, if not what you wished, at least such as my hand was able to compose. I have made use of facts from ancient writers, which you have sent to me, and have written two discourses on the life of the Saint, as well as I was able, avoiding, on the one hand, such brevity as to make them obscure, and, on the other, a tiresome prolixity. Then, as regards the musical part of the Office, I have composed a hymn, taking more heed of the meaning of the words than of the rules of the metre. I have arranged in their proper places twelve Responsories[2] with twenty-seven Antiphons, adding one Antiphon for the first Vespers, and two others to be sung according to your rule upon the Festival itself, the one at Laud, the other at Vespers.

Now, for all these things, I expect a return; I ask payment. What then do I expect? Whether you are pleased with them or no, it matters not, because I have given you what I could. And the price I ask for it is your prayers for me.

The sentiment which Bernard expresses here with his usual elegance merits serious attention. It would be easy to supplement it with those of other Fathers, and to show what they have thought respecting church music, did the length of a note permit. Nevertheless, as the rule here laid down may seem somewhat severe and rigorous to the opinions and tastes of the present age, I may be permitted to quote the opinion on this subject of a man confessedly pious and religious, who has treated, in a style full of elegance and charm, of subjects important equally to piety and virtue. To musicians he writes thus: "Here permit me to observe to you that a new kind of singing rules in our churches, unusual in character, rapid and dancing in time, and in no way suitable for religious purposes, but rather fitting for the theatre or the concert room.

"In the search for artifice we lose the ancient manner of praying and singing; we follow a secular taste and neglect the interests of piety. What else is this novel and dancing kind of chant, in which the singers are made, like actors, to take now solos, now duets and anon choruses; or that in which they reply to each other as in a dialogue, then leaving all of a sudden the field to one who expatiates alone, the others speedily joining in?"

A little farther the same author continues: "In the last age there were musicians of surpassing genius, as you yourselves allow, who have composed a kind of music very different from yours, and (if I may say so) much more religious But your disdain has long since buried their books of music. Restore to us, I entreat, somewhat of the ancient religiousness in our sacred music; take to heart and spend your care upon the addition of beauty to Divine worship by composing chants more in harmony with the meaning of the words which they are to interpret. What is the use to me in church of varied airs and harmonies in many parts, if there be no unity in the chant and if I am unable even to distinguish the words which the music ought to make an entrance for into the heart?" (Jerome Drexelius Rhetor, Celest. B. i. C. 5.)

[2]A Responsory was a versicle sung by the choir in answer to the priest or other officiant, or as a refrain between the verses of a Psalm or Lection; also before or after a Lection.

An Antiphon was of a similar character, but before or after a Psalm. Generally only a few words were said before, and the whole after, the Psalm in question; but on great festivals this was altered. (E.)

LETTER CCCLXXXVIII.   (Formerly No. 353, the former No. 388 is now 348.)   (Circa A. D. 1150.)

Letter of Peter the Venerable to Bernard, Abbot of Clairvaux.

He rejects titles and praises and declares how much he values Bernard and his friendship.

He freely accepts his apology for the tone of his letter.

Brother Peter, the humble Abbot of the Cluniacs, to the venerable Bernard, Abbot of Clairvaux, a man renowned among the members of Christ, loved after God and in God.

1. What shall I say? I am accustomed to speak, but now I am stricken dumb. Why so? you ask. Because your letter, which would ordinarily have made me eloquent, has made me dumb. Wherefore? I read so much in it, although it was so brief, that if I should try to pour myself out in answer I should seem rather taciturn than talkative. But I am speaking to a serious and religious man. Therefore, we must act as gravity demands; as your profession, if not mine, directs. What, is not this true? The letter is short, but contains much to be answered. Pardon me, I pray, if I have said other than was befitting. For it is the part of true friendship not only to endure the amenities of a friend, but also to hide or tolerate even words that are unsuitable. I have received, as I said, from you a most excellent letter, a letter breathing most tender love and honor more than I deserve. You call me "Most Reverend," you address me as "Father," you call me "Dearest friend." I rejoice at it; but in respect to truth, which has passed from Christ into your soul, I am unable to accept the two first, but I say nothing against the third. For I know not that I am most reverend; I cannot be styled father with regard

to you. But to be dearest friend to you I gladly assent with lips and heart.

2. So now I may be silent about the names of most reverend and dearest friend, of which, as I said before, the one does not befit me, but the other I gladly accept. About the name of father, O reverend brother, I say to you what Dom Guigo, Prior of the Grand Chartreuse, a man renowned in his generation and a most illustrious flower of the religious of his day, once wrote to me. I used often to write to him, and often, in conversation or in familiar correspondence, used to call him father. He bore this at first, thinking I was about to make an end of writing. But after he saw me to persist in it, and in frequent letters to reiterate the name of father, the good man at length broke out into these words, for he wrote me a letter in which, amongst other things, he inserted this: "I entreat you by that love with which your heart is filled for me all unworthy of it, that when your Serenity deigns to write to my humble self you would so think of my spiritual interest as not to puff up my weakness with dangerous complacency." And presently: "This I seek above and before all things, and entreat you with bended knees not to honor my unworthy self with the name of father. Enough and more than enough if he is called brother, friend and son, who is not worthy even of the name of servant." Thus he wrote to me; and I write the very same to you. Let it suffice if I enjoy the name of brother, dear or dearest friend, from you; or whatever name like those befits you to send or me to receive. So much about your salutation.

3. But what about that which follows? "I would," you say, "I could send my mind to you to read as I do this present letter." And further on: "I am sure you would

read very clearly the affection for you which the finger of God has written in my heart and in my whole being."

These words in truth, setting aside the deeper and mystical meaning of the words (of the Scripture), are as the ointment upon the head, which descended from Aaron's beard, even to the skirts of his clothing; they are like the dew of Hermon, which fell on Mount Sion. Even thus do the mountains pour forth sweetness and the hills flow with milk and honey. Do not wonder that I so carefully ponder and weigh your words; for I know they are not uttered from a careless mouth, but from his who knows not how to speak except from a pure heart, a good conscience and an unfeigned affection. I know, I say, and all the world knows with me, that you are not of the number of those who, according to the Psalm, "Have spoken vanity to each to his neighbor;" you are not of those "whose lips are deceitful; they have spoken from a deceitful heart." (Ps. xii. 2.) Therefore, as often as it pleases your Holiness to write to me, I receive and read and welcome your letters, not negligently or carelessly, but eagerly and gladly. For who would not read carefully? Who would not receive with much affection the words I have before cited and those which follow? "Now, indeed," you say, "my soul is joined fast to yours and the equality of love has made equal souls in differing persons. For what was there in common between your Highness and my humility, if your worthiness had not waived your worth? And so it has come to pass that your greatness and my humility have been united in reciprocal affection; so that neither I am humble without you, neither can you be exalted without me." Can words of this kind be negligently read? Ought they not to hold fixed the eyes of the reader, to seize his heart, to unite our souls? You see, dearest friend, what you have written, what you felt about this? I cannot do otherwise than take the letter in the simple and literal sense and accept what so great, so truthful, so holy a man has been pleased to say. Neither, as you yourself have said, do I begin again to commend myself to you. While yet young men we began to love in Christ. Shall we now, when we are old men, begin to doubt about so sacred, so lasting a love? Far be it from me (trust one who loves you) so to use your words, for it has never occurred to my heart, nor gone forth from my mouth, to doubt words which you have uttered so seriously. So I embrace, I keep and guard all that you have written in the letter of which we speak. Far rather would I be deprived of a thousand talents of gold than have these words by any means torn from my heart. But enough of this.

4. As concerning the matter about which your prudence thought me hurt. The fact was this. In respect to the matter, which is well known to you, of a certain English Abbot, your letter said: "They speak as if judgment was overturned, and justice had perished from the earth, and there were none to snatch the weak from the hand of the strong, the needy and poor from those who oppress them."

But, believe me, I was moved at this as the Prophet says of himself, although I am no prophet: "I as one deaf did not hear, and as one dumb that openeth not his mouth." And again: "I am become as a man that heareth not and as one that has not an answer in his mouth." (Ps. xxxviii. 13, 14.) I was not offended, indeed, at this, but if I had been, full satisfaction was made when you said: "My excess of business is to blame; for when my secretaries do not quite catch my meaning, they of their own accord are apt to sharpen the expressions, nor am I able to read over what I have directed to be written. For this once pardon me. Henceforth I will read over whatever I shall write to you by the hand of others, and will trust only to my own eyes and ears." Therefore I forgive and easily grant pardon. For it is no great labor to me (I speak humbly) even in great offences to forgive one who asks, to give pardon when entreated; and if it be no trouble to forgive in grave matters, how much less, rather, none at all, can it be in light ones?"

5.   Concerning the will of Dom Baroni, the Roman subdeacon, which, when at the point of death, he is said to have made in favor of your Abbeys at Clairvaux and Citeaux, those things which he had left with us. I was made aware of this by certain persons who said that this was enjoined upon them by him. Yet I wish you to know that, according to the opinion of persons worthy of credit, you will find that you owe those things more to the kindness of the Abbot of Cluny than to the will of Baroni. I know, indeed, I am not so unskilled in Divine or human law as to be ignorant how, by a will, both legacies and trusts are binding at death. But yet I read elsewhere: "Nothing is so agreeable to natural law as to hold as a binding disposition the act of a professor who himself transfers his property to another person." I say this because, as the before-mentioned witnesses confess, whatever he had deposited at Cluny he intended to leave to Cluny unless he removed it in his lifetime. Yet I was unwilling to use this privilege; and that which, according to their testimony, I believed to be mine I gave up to you and yours. What I think about the election at Grenoble, which our friends the Carthusians oppose, I have confided to my dear friend, your faithful Nicholas, to be related to you. You may believe what he tells you from me to be my opinion. If any requests have escaped my mind, when I remember them, I will ask them of my dear friend in Christ. To conclude, I ask as much as is possible and desire what I have already requested of

certain of your Order, that in this great body of holy men who have assembled at Citeaux, you will make mention of me as your sincere friend, and that you will commend earnestly me and the whole congregation at Cluny to their prayers.

SELECTED SERMONS OF SAINT BERNARD.

Now appearing for the first time in the English Language.

THE THREE SPIRITUAL PERFUMES.

I have neither such depth of knowledge, nor such brilliancy of genius, so as to discover of myself anything new. But the mouth of St. Paul is a great and unfailing fountain which is open to us. From Him I draw what I am about to say on the subject of the bosom of the Bride, as indeed, I am accustomed frequently to do. Rejoice, he says, with them that do rejoice, and weep with them that weep. He here expresses, in a few words, the affections of a mother's heart, because little children cannot either be in pain and grief, or in health and gladness, without the close sympathy of their mother in either case, nor can she fail to feel with them. Thus, following the opinion of St. Paul, I shall assign those two affections to the breasts of the Bride—to the one compassion, to the other congratulation. If it were otherwise, if she had not these as yet—that is, if she had not learned to be quick in congratulating others, or to be ready to condole with them in their grief—she would be but a child, and not of a marriageable age. If a person of such character as this is taken to discharge the oversight of souls, or to preach, he does not profit others, and to himself he does very great harm. 'And if he should thrust himself into these ministries, what a shameless action is that!

But let us return to these thus typified, to the differences between them, and to the graces they yield. Congratulation pours forth the milk of exhortation, and compassion that of consolation.

Our spiritual mother feels her pious bosom abundantly supplied from above with both the one and the other of these as often as she is fulfilled with the love of God. You see her occupied in nourishing her little children out of her abundance; to one she gives consolation, to another exhortation, according as each seems to have need. For instance, if she sees that one of her children in the Gospel has been taken unawares by some violent temptation so that he is rendered troubled and sorrowful, doubting and fearful, and is no longer able to bear up against the force of the temptation, how she condoles with him and soothes him! How she sorrows for him and gives him comfort, and finds many a pious reason to enable him to rise out of his state of depression! If, on the contrary, she sees one active, energetic, and making good progress in the spiritual life she rejoices greatly, she plies him with beneficial advice, she animates him to advance still further, instructs him in that which is requisite to perseverance, and exhorts him so that he may go on from strength to strength. To all she adapts herself, in her own heart she reflects the feelings and the dispositions of all, and lastly, she allows herself the mother no less of the feeble and failing soul than of the strong and progressive.

How many are there at the present day—I mean of those who have taken upon them the cure of souls—who are animated by sentiments the very reverse of these? It is a fact not to be spoken of without groaning and tears; they forge, so to speak, in the furnace of avarice, and make merchandise of, the very instrument of Christ's Passion—the scourge, the spitting, the nails, the lance, and, in fine, the Cross and the Death of Christ. They squander all these things for the making of shameful gains; they hasten to huddle into their own pouches the price of the Redemption of the world. The only difference which distinguishes them from Judas Iscariot is that he, for the price of all these things, received but, comparatively speaking, a few pence; while they, with a greed much more insatiable, exact uncounted sums of money as their gains. They have for riches a thirst which is insatiable; well-nigh their sole fear is lest they may lose these; and if they should do so they grieve. Upon the love of them they look in satisfaction, if, perchance, there be a moment left free from the task of keeping what they have or of gaining more. As for the salvation of souls, or their loss, they think of it not at all. No maternal care for souls have they who, being too well nourished, have fattened and grown great upon the patrimony of the Crucified. They are not grieved for the affliction of Joseph. A true mother is unmistakably to be known; she is never void of nourishment for her children. She ceases not to rejoice with them that do rejoice, and to weep with them that weep; to press from her bosom the life-giving milk—from that of congratulation the milk of exhortation; from that of compassion, of consolation. I need not say more of these, and of these, and of what they contain.

I have also to point out what are the perfumes with which the same are fragrant, provided that I am assisted by your prayers, so that by their means that which is given me to think may also be spoken worthily, and to the profit of my hearers. The perfumes of the Bride differ from those of the

Bridegroom, as they are different the one from the other. What was to be said of those of the Bridegroom is contained in another discourse. Let us consider just now only the perfumes of the Bride; and that with the greater care, because Scripture commends them particularly to our attention in calling them not only good, but best of all. I mention several kinds, so that out of many those most befitting the Bride may be chosen. There is the perfume of contrition, the perfume of devotion, and that of piety. The first is pungent, and causes pain; the second is soothing, and relieves pain; the third is curative, and removes disease. Now we will speak of these separately.

There is, then, a perfume or unguent which the soul—that is, if it be ensnared and entangled with many crimes—compounds for itself, and if when it begins to reflect upon its ways, it collects, heaps together and pounds in the mortar of conscience its sins of many different kinds, and putting them into the caldron, as it were, of a heart that heaves and boils with distress, cooks them together over a kind of fire of grief and repentance, so that the man may be able to say, with the Psalmist: "My heart was hot within me; while I was musing the fire burned." Here, then, is one unguent which the sinful soul ought to prepare for itself at the commencement of its conversion, and to apply to its still fresh wounds; for the first sacrifice to be made to God is a troubled and contrite heart. Although the sinner is poor and needy, and therefore unable to compound for himself an unguent better and more valuable, yet let him not neglect to prepare this, though of poor materials and of no value, for a broken and contrite heart God will not despise; and it shall appear so much the less vile in the sight of God as by the remembrance of his sins it becomes the more so to the sinner himself.

Yet if we say that this invisible and spiritual unguent was designated in type by that visible ointment wherewith the feet of God manifest in the flesh were anointed by the woman who was a sinner, we shall not be able to regard it as altogether worthless. For what do we read of it in the Scripture? That the house was filled with the odor of the ointment. It was poured by the hands of a sinful woman, and poured upon the extremities of the body—that is, upon the feet; yet it was not so vile and so contemptible that the power and the sweetness of its perfume could not fill the whole house. And if we consider with what fragrance the Church is perfumed by the conversion of one sinner, and how powerful an odor of life unto life each penitent becomes if his repentance is perfect and public, we shall be able to pronounce, without the least doubt, that the house was filled with the odor of the ointment. Assuredly the odor of penitence extends even as far as the mansions of the blessed in heaven, so that as the Truth Himself declares, there is joy among the angels of God over one sinner that repented. Rejoice, O penitents; be strengthened, ye that are weak of heart. To you I speak who are but lately converted from the world and from your evil ways, who are feeling the bitterness and confusion of a mind touched with repentance, and in whom the excessive pains of wounds, as it were, yet recent, still throbs and torments. Your hands may with safety drop the bitterness of myrrh into this salutary ointment, for a broken and contrite heart God will not despise. Nor is such ointment as this to be despised or counted vile, of which the odor not only draws men to conversion but moves the angels to joy.

Yet there is a perfume as much more precious than this, as the materials of which it is composed are of more excellent kinds. For the materials of the former do not require to be sought from far; we find them without difficulty within ourselves, and in our own little garden plots gather them easily in great plenty, as often as necessity requires. For who is there who does not know himself to have sins and iniquities of his own, enough and too many, always at his hand, unless he desires to deceive himself upon this point? But these are, as you recognize, the materials of the former ointment, which I have described. But as for the sweet spices which compose the second, our earth does not produce them at all; we must seek them in a land very far off. For is not every good gift, and every perfect gift from above, and does it not come down from the Father of Lights? For this perfume is compounded which Divine goodness has bestowed upon the human race. Happy is he who with care and pains collects them for himself, and sets them before the eyes of his mind with acts of thanksgiving proportioned to their greatness. Assuredly when these shall have been bruised and pounded in the mortar of our breast, with the pestle of frequent meditation, then boiled together on the fire of holy desire, and finally enriched with the oil of joy, there will be as the result a perfume far more precious and more excellent than the former. Sufficient as proof of this is the testimony of Him who says: "Whoso offereth praise glorifieth Me." Nor can we doubt that the remembrance of benefits is an excitement to praise of our benefactor.

Furthermore, while Scripture, when speaking of the former, testifies only that it is not despised by God, of this latter it is plain that it is the more commended, in that it is said to glorify God. Besides, the former is poured upon the Lord's feet; the latter upon His head. For if in Christ the head is to be referred to His Divinity, as St. Paul declares the head of Christ is God, then, without doubt, he anoints the head who renders thanks; for this is addressed to God, not to man. Not that He who is God is not Man also, for God and Man is one, Christ, but because every good gift, even that which is ministered through man, comes from God, not from man. For it is the Siprit which quickeneth; the flesh profiteth nothing. And we know that cursed is the man that trusteth in man; although all our hope rests rightly upon Him who is the God-Man, yet this is not because He is Man, but because He is God. Therefore, the former perfume is poured upon His feet; but this upon His head, because the humiliation of a contrite heart is befitting to the humility of the flesh, but praise and glory to the Divine Majesty. See then of what a nature is this perfume which I have been describing to you, with which that head, so august even to the principalities and powers of heaven, does not disdain to be touched; nay, rather regards it as an honor to Him, as He Himself declares: "Whoso offereth praise glorifieth Me."

Wherefore it does not belong to Him who is poor and needy and of small courage to compound such a perfume as this, inasmuch as it is confidence alone which commands the sweet spices which are its materials, but a confidence which is born of freedom of spirit and purity of heart. For the soul which is of small courage and of little faith is hampered by the consciousness of the little which it possesses; its poverty does not permit it to occupy itself in the praises of God, or in the contemplation of those benefits which produce the praises. And if ever it has the wish to rise to that point, immediately it is recalled to the consciousness of its cares and uneasiness about its necessities at home, and is straitened in itself by the miseries which press it hard. If you ask of me the cause of that misery, I reply that you are, or have been, conscious in your own selves of that which I refer to. It seems to me that this depression of mind and want of joyful trust usually comes from one of two causes. Either, that is to say, it is from newness of conversion, or especially, if the conversion is not recent, from lukewarmness of conduct. Both the one and the other cause humiliates and casts down the conscience, and throws it into trouble and inquietude, since it feels that its former passions are not yet dead in it, either because of the shortness of the time since its conversion or because of the feebleness and want of zeal in its efforts, and thus it is obliged to occupy itself entirely with rooting up from the garden of the heart the thorns of iniquity and briers of evil desires, nor is it able to divert any thoughts from itself. What then? How can one, who is wearily occupied in sighing and groaning over such a task as this, at the same time rejoice in the praises of God? How can thanksgiving and the voice of melody, to borrow from the phrase of the Prophet Isaiah, sound forth from the mouth of one that is groaning and lamenting? For, as the Wise Man teaches us, Music in mourning is a tale out of season. And the giving of thanks follows the benefit, not precedes it. But the soul that is still in sadness needs to receive the benefit, and does not rejoice in having obtained it. It has a great reason to offer its prayers, but not to offer its thanksgiving. How is it to acknowledge a blessing which it has not in fact received? It was correct, therefore, for me to say that it was not the privilege of a soul that is poor and needy and of small courage to compound this precious perfume, which requires to be composed of remembered benefits of God; nor is such one able to behold the light, as long as its gaze is fixed upon the darkness. For it is in bitterness—the sorrowful remembrance of past sins occupies it; nor can it admit any thought of joy. It is to such that the prophetic spirit bears testimony saying: "It is vain of you to rise up early"; as if he would remind them: It is vain for you to rise up that you may behold bounties to be a delight to your soul, unless you have first received the light which shall comfort it with regard to the stains of sin which trouble it. This perfume, therefore, is not for the soul which is in a state of spiritual poverty.

But see who they are who may rightly take the glory of having it in abundance. The Apostles departed from the presence of the council, rejoicing that they were counted worthy to suffer shame for the name of Jesus. Assuredly these men were well filled with that unction of the Spirit, whose cheerfulness did not abandon them, I do not say, because of words, but even because of blows. They were indeed rich in charity, in whom it was exhausted by no spending, and who were enabled to offer themselves as a complete and worthy burnt sacrifice to God. Their hearts poured forth everywhere that holy unction with which they had been imbued in plenitude, when they spake in various tongues the wonderful works of God as the Spirit gave them utterance. Nor can it be doubted that they abounded in the same perfumes of whom the apostle thus speaks: "I thank my God always on your behalf, for the grace of God which is given you by Jesus Christ: that in everything ye are enriched by Him in all utterance and in all knowledge; even as the testimony of Christ was confirmed in you, so that we come behind in no gift." Would that I too might be able to render the same thanksgivings on your account, and to see you rich in virtue, ready and prompt to praise God, and superabounding in this spiritual fatness in Jesus Christ our Lord.

SERMON No. 2.

Text: "He shall be great, and shall be called the Son of
the Highest."—S. Luke I. 32.

We celebrate today, brethren, the commencement of Advent. The name, like that of other seasons of the Church,
is well known and familiar to all; but the reason of the name
is not perhaps so familiar. For the children of Adam are
so unwise as to neglect the truths which belong to their
salvation, and devote themselves in preference to vain and
transitory things. To whom shall we liken the men of this
generation, whom we see unable to separate themselves, or
to be separated, from worldly and fleshly pleasures? They
are like people plunged into deep waters and struggling for
life. See how they catch at everything that comes near
them, though it be but a stick or a straw, and hold it fast,
though it cannot be of the least use to them; and if anyone
swims to their help, they will frequently seize them in
such a grasp as to drown them with themselves. So the
children of Adam perish in the vast and deep sea of the
world; snatching at perishable things, and neglecting those
abiding realities which they may grasp, and thus be able
to keep afloat and to have their souls. For it is not of
vanity, but of the truth, that it is said: Ye shall know it,
and it shall make you free. Do you then, brethren, to
whom as little children, God has revealed those things
which are hidden from the wise and prudent, meditate with
care on those precious things. Consider now the reason
of this Advent; who He is Who comes, whence He came,
to whom He came, and why. Curiosity upon these points
is praiseworthy and salutary; for the Church universal would
not celebrate Advent with so great devotion, if it did not
enshrine some great mystery.

CHRIST RAISING JARIUS' DAUGHTER—BY RICHTER.

2. First consider with the same wonder and admiration the greatness of Him who comes. He is, according to the testimony of the Angel Gabriel, the Son of the Highest, and He himself is therefore the Most High. We dare not think the Son of God degenerate: He is of necessity of equal greatness and glory. The sons of Kings are themselves kings, and the sons of Princes of princely rank. But wherefore is it that to the Three Persons in the Supreme Trinity, whom we believe in, confess and adore, it is not the Father, not the Holy Spirit who comes to us, but the Son? There is doubtless some deep cause why this was so. But who has penetrated the design of the Lord? Or who has been His counsellor? Yet it was not without some deep purpose of the Holy Trinity that it was predestined that the Son should come into the world: and if we consider the cause of our exile, we may perhaps be able to understand in some degree how fitting it was that it should be the Son who should come to save us. For that Lucifer who was the Morning Star, having striven to make himself equal to the Most High, and by an outrage assumed that he was equal with God (which is the right of the Son), was therefore hurled headlong from heaven. The Father defended the glory of His Son and declared as it were by his action: Vengeance is mine, and I will repay. Then I saw Satan fall from heaven as lightning. What right then hast thou to pride, thou who art dust and ashes? If God spared not the angels in their pride, how much less shall He spare thee, who art but corruption and a worm. Lucifer himself did nothing, effected nothing; only of a thought of pride was he guilty; and in a moment, in the glance of an eye, he was flung down without remedy into the abyss, because, according to the evangelist, he abode not in the truth.

3. Fly then from pride, my brethren, I pray you. Pride is the beginning of every kind of sin. It was that which so swiftly plunged into the everlasting darkness that Lucifer, who shone the brightest among the stars. It changed him from being, not only an angel, but the first of angels, into a demon. Then envying the happiness of man in his heart, he contrived to bring to light the iniquity which he had conceived in his own; persuading him that by eating of the forbidden tree he would become as God, knowing good and evil. O, unhappy one! What dost thou promise, what hope dost thou give to the man; when it is only the Son of the Most High who has the key of knowledge, yea, the Key to David, which shuts and none can open. In Him are all the treasures hidden of wisdom and knowledge. Wilt thou then steal them, to impart them to the man? You see how, according to the saying of the Lord, he is a liar and the father of a lie. For he was a liar when he said I will be like unto the Most High. And was he not the father of a lie when he poured into the heart of man the poisoned germ of his own falsehood, we shall be as God. And thou also, O man, when thou sawest a thief consentedst unto him; for you heard, my brethren, what was read from Isaiah this night, when the Lord said: "Thy princes shall be unbelievers," or, as another translation has it: "disobedient and companions of thieves."

4. Thus then our first parents (principles), Adam and Eve, the founders of our race, are disobedient and companions of thieves; since they attempt, by the counsel of the serpent, or rather of the devil who used the serpent as his instrument, to snatch at that which is the right of the Son of God only. Nor did the Father pass over the injury to His Son, for the Father loveth the Son, but on the instant visited the man with just judgment; and His Hand weighs heavy upon

us still. For in Adam have we all sinned and in him have
been condemned. What shall be the part of the Son, seeing
that the Father visits with judgment on His account, and
will spare no created being? Behold, He says, because of
Me My Father loves the creature He has made. The first
of the angels desired to usurp the greatness which was Mine,
and had found adherents among his fellows: but instantly
the justice of My Father has stricken him, and his followers
with dreadful punishment, with an incurable wound. The
knowledge also which pertained to Me man wished to steal,
and My Father has had no pity upon him, nor has His eye
spared him. Doth God take care for oxen? Yet He had
made two noble creatures to whom He had equally imparted
reason, and had made them capable of blessedness, namely,
the Angel and Man. But behold, He has lost because of
Me a multitude of angels and all men. But that they may
know that I love My Father, let Him recover by means of
Me those whom on My account He seems to have lost. If
because of me this tempest has arisen, said Jonah, take me
up and cast me forth into the sea. All look upon Me with
envy. Lo, I come, I will show myself to them in such a
condition that whosover envies Me, whosoever takes in
hand to imitate me, their envy shall become salutary consolation, their endeavor shall turn to their good. But I
know that the angels have deserted the right path, have
done so through gratuitous malice and wickedness, and
have not sinned through any ignorance or weakness. They
therefore as refusing to repent, must of necessity perish.
For the love of the Father, and the honor of the supreme
Sovereign require justice.

5. This is why He also created men in the beginning that
they might supply the place of those and restore the ruins
of Jerusalem. For he knew that for the angels no way of

return lay open. He knew the pride of Moab that he is very proud; and pride does not admit of the remedy of penitence and consequently not of pardon. But in the place of man God has created no other creature, wishing to show by this that man is still capable of restoration. He was ruined by the malice of another, and therefore the love of another was able to do him service. So, O my God, I entreat that it may please Thee to raise me up, because I am powerless of myself; and because I have been cast down by fraud from my first state and although innocent have been cast into this place. Innocent indeed I was not altogether: but in comparison of him who seduced me I was well-nigh innocent, I was made to believe a lie. O Lord, let the Truth come that falsehood may be taken away, that I may know the truth and the truth make me free: if only I shall renounce the falsehood when it is made clear to me, if I shall cling to the truth when it is made known. Otherwise it will not be a human temptation nor a human sin, but a diabolic obstinacy. For to persevere in evil is a thing diabolic, and whosoever continue in their sin, like the devil, are worth to perish with him.

6.   You have heard, brethren, who it is that comes. Consider now whence He comes, and to whom. He comes, that is to say, from the right Hand of His Father into the bosom of the Virgin Mother; He comes from the highest heaven into the lower parts of the earth. But why? Is it not because we human beings had our life appointed upon the earth? Yes, but on condition that He remained there. For where could it be otherwise than well where He is? Whom have I in heaven but Thee? and there is none upon earth that I desire in comparison of thee. God is the strength of my heart and my portion forever. Though I walk through the valley of the shadow

of death, I will fear no evil, if only Thou art with me. Well, we see today that He has descended, not only into the earth, but also into the place of departed spirits itself; not as a captive bound, but as free among the dead; as the Light which shined in the darkness, though the darkness comprehended it not. Wherefore, His soul was not left in hell, nor did His holy body see corruption in the earth. For Christ, who descended, is He who also ascended upon high that He might fill all things; of whom it is written: He went about doing good, and healing all who were oppressed of the devil and in another place. He rejoiced as a giant to run his course; his going forth is from the height of heaven, and his circuit even unto its height again. Rightly therefore does the Apostle proclaim: See those things which are above, where Christ sitteth at the right hand of God. It would be in vain that He strove to raise our hearts on high, if He did not show us that the Author of our salvation was there. But let us proceed; for although the matter we have to treat is abundant and fruitful, the shortness of our time does not admit a corresponding length of discourse. Thus when we have considered Who He is that comes? we have found that He is a Guest of great and unspeakable majesty. When we have looked up to see Whence does He come? a prospect has unrolled before our eyes extending into the far distance, according to that which was testified beforehand by the prophetic Spirit, "Behold the name of the Lord comes from far." Finally, if we enquire to whom He comes? we recognize the honor inestimable, and almost inconceivable, which He has deigned to do to us in descending from so high into the horror of this prison-house.

7. Now who can doubt that it must have been for some great cause that one of so great Majesty should deign to

ascend from so far into a place so unworthy of Him? Unquestionably the motive must have been entirely great, because it is nothing less than a great mercy, a grand compassion, an overflowing charity. To what end it is to believe that He came? It is that which we have now to examine. Nor is there need of much search in this respect, since His words and His actions declare aloud what was the motive of His coming. It was to seek the hundredth sheep which had wandered that He hastened to descend from the celestial mountains; it was on our account and that His mercies might make known the Lord more clearly to His people, and His wonders to the sons of men, that He came. Wonderful the condescension of God in seeking man, great the dignity of man to be thus sought! If anyone should desire to boast of this, assuredly he would not be wrong in so doing; not because He would appear to be anything in His own self, but because He who has done this is one of rank so exalted. All the riches and all the glory of the world and whatever can seem desirable to us here below, all this is little, or rather it is absolutely nothing, in comparison with this honor and with the worth of man himself. Lord, what is a man, that Thou glorifiest him? Or why does Thy heart yearn towards him?

8. And yet I ask of myself why He has willed that He should come to us, rather than that we should have gone to Him. For ours was the necessity; but it is not the custom of the rich to come to the poor, even if they wish to do them good. It is true, brethren, that it would have been more proper for us to go to Him, but there was a double hindrance in our way. In the first place, our eyes were darkened that they could not see and He, He dwelt in the light that no man can approach unto: while we, lying

paralyzed upon our couch, were entirely unable to draw
near to that Divine brightness. Because of this, our most
kind Saviour and Physician of our souls descended from
His high place and softened His glory, to suit our weak
eyes. He clad Himself, as it were, with a lantern, with that
Body glorious and most pure from every stain which He
took unto Him. This is indeed that light and effulgent
cloud, upon which the Prophet had predicted that the Lord
should mount in order to go down into Egypt.

9. We must now also consider the time at which the
Saviour came. This was, as you know, not at the beginning, or in the middle, but at the end of time. Nor was it
determined without reason, but on the contrary, with abundant reason, by the Supreme wisdom, that it would bring
help to men only when their necessity was at the greatest,
as not being ignorant of the proneness to ingratitude in the
Sons of Adam. It may be truly said that already the day
was far spent and the evening was drawing near, the Sun
of Righteousness had declined in some degree towards the
horizon, and diffused over the earth only lessened warmth
and enfeebled brightness. For the light of the knowledge
of God had become very feeble, at the same time that, as iniquity abounded, the fervor of mutual charity had grown
cold. No angel any longer appeared, no prophet raised
his voice, it seemed as if, overcome by the excessive hardness and obstinacy of men, they had ceased to appear or to
speak: but then spake the Son: I said, Lo I come. Thus,
while all things were sunk in deep silence, and night proceeded on her course, Thy Almighty Word, O Lord, came
from Thy royal throne as in the same sense said the Apostle:
When the fulness of the time was come, God sent forth His
Son. Without doubt, the fulness and abundance of temporal
things had produced a forgetfulness of and scarcity in things

eternal. For to pass over other things, temporal peace itself was at that time so widespread, that at the bidding of one man a census of the whole world was carried out.

10. You have now considered who He is that comes, and to what place: also the cause and the time of His coming. One thing remains to consider, the road by which He came; and this also we must diligently inquire into, that we may be able to go to meet Him, as it is right we should do. But as He came once upon the earth in visible flesh to work out our salvation, so He comes daily in the Spirit and invisibly to save our souls. As it is written: "Christ our Lord is a Spirit before our eyes." And in order that you may know that this spiritual coming is secret, it is said: "In His shadow shall we live among the heathen. On this account it is suitable that even if the sick man is not able to go very far to meet the coming of so great a Physician, he should at least make an effort to lift his head and raise himself up a little towards Him who comes. It is not needful for thee, O man, to sail across the seas, to rise up into the clouds, to cross the mountains, in order to meet thy God. The way that is shown to thee is, I say, not long; thou hast but to enter into thy own soul to meet Him. For His word is very nigh thee: it is in thy mouth and in thy heart. Go then to meet Him even as far as the repentance of the heart and confession of the mouth, so that at least thou mayest come forth from the dunghill of thy defiled conscience; for it were an unworthy thing that the Author of purity should enter there. And let these few words suffce concerning the Advent in which He deigns to enlighten the mind of each of us by His invisible presence.

11. But it is needful also to consider the way of His visible Advent, since His ways are ways of pleasantness and all His paths are peace. Behold, says the Spouse, my beloved

comes leaping upon the mountains, bounding over the hills. You see Him, O beautiful one, when He comes, but you were not able to behold Him before, when He was reposing. For then thou didst cry out: Tell me, O thou whom my soul loveth, where thou feedest thy flocks, where thou liest down. While He rests, they are the angels whom He feeds throughout endless eternities, whom he satiates with the vision of His eternal and unchangeable existence. But do not slight thyself, O beautiful one, for that marvelous vision is produced from thee, and by thee it is strengthened and yet thou art not able to reach it. Yet behold, He has come forth from His holy place, and He who while resting, nourished the angels, begins a new work and applies Himself to cure our ills. He shall be seen coming and strengthened, who before when resting and nourishing the angels could not be seen. For he comes leaping upon the mountains, bounding over the hills. By mountains and hills understand patriarchs and prophets; and in the book of the genealogy you may see how He has come leaping upon the one and bounding upon the other: Abraham begot Isaac, Isaac begot Jacob, etc. You will find that from those mountains came forth the root of Jesse, from whence, according to the prophet, came forth the shoot, and from it uprose the flower upon which rested the sevenfold Spirit. It is that which the same prophet explains to us in another place, saying: Behold a Virgin shall conceive and bear a Son, and His name shall be called Emmanuel, which being interpreted is, "God with us." Thus, what in the former he called a shoot, he explains in the latter by calling a virgin. But it is needful to reserve to another day a consideration of this very deep mystery; it is a subject very worthy of a separate sermon, especially as the discourse of to-day has extended to a considerable length.

SERMON No. 3.

Text: "Ask thee a sign of the Lord my God; ask it either in the depth or in the height above. But Ahaz said, I will not ask, neither will I tempt the Lord."—Is. VII. 2.

1.   We have in this, the prophet Isaiah advising King Ahaz to ask a sign from the Lord, either in the depth below or the height above.   We hear also his reply, having, indeed, a form of piety, but not the power of it and because of this he deserved to be reproved of Him who reads the heart, and to whom the thoughts of man lie open.   Ahaz was filled with pride because he was exalted upon a throne, and his words show the astuteness of human wisdom. Isaiah then had heard from the Lord: "Go, say to that fox that he seek from the Lord a sign in the depth."   For a fox has his burrow, but even if he shall descend into the depth of hell, He is there who taketh the wise in their own craftiness: also Go, saith the Lord, say to that bird that he seek a sign in the height above.   For the bird hath his nest, but even if he shall climb up into heaven, He is there who resisting the proud, tramples under foot by His strength the necks of the proud and exalted ones.   But he pretended not to wish at all to ask of God a sign of His power in the heavens, or of His incomprehensible wisdom in the depth: because of this the Lord Himself promises a sign of His goodness and love for the house of David, so that those whom neither power nor wisdom strike with terror, the display of his love may win over.   It is possible also I allow, that in the phrase "in the depth" He may have wished to speak of that love that no one has ever exceeded, which made Him die for His friends and descend from them into the depth of Hades: so that King Ahaz might be taught to tremble at the Majesty of Him who reigns on High, or to embrace the love of Him who descends into

the depth. Whosoever then has no impulse to tremble at the Majesty of God, nor thinks with gratitude upon His love, is insupportable, not only to man, but also to God. Therefore He says, the Lord Himself shall give you a sign, in which both His Majesty and His glory shall be plainly set forth. Behold, a Virgin shall conceive and bear a Son and call his name Emmanuel, which being interpreted, is, God with us. Do not seek to fly, O Adam, because it is God who is with us. Do not fear, O man, nor tremble at hearing the name of God: because He is with us, though He is God. With us in likeness of flesh, with us in unity of nature. He comes on our account, He comes as one of us, like us in appearance and equally subject to pain.

2. He says finally: Butter and honey shall He eat. As if he said: He shall be an infant, and eat infant's food. That He may know to refuse the evil and choose the good. Here also we are told of the good and the evil, as before of the forbidden tree, the tree of disobedience. But He, the second Adam, made a far better choice than the first; choosing the good, He rejected the evil, not like him who delighted in cursing and it came unto him, who delighted not in blessing and it was far from him. In the words which precede, "Butter and honey shall He eat," we may understand the choice of this Child. Now His grace comes to our aid and enables us (which is a matter of great importance) to think rightly of Him, and to bring His words suitably to our understanding. There are two things in milk, butter and cheese; butter is soft and rich; cheese, on the contrary, is hard and dry. Wisely then does this child know how to choose, when he prefers the first and leaves the second. Who then is the hundredth sheep who wandered and who speaks in the Psalm: I have gone astray as a sheep that is lost? Even the human race:

which the Good Shepherd seeks, while the other ninety-nine are left upon the mountains.   In this sheep then are found two things also: one nature sweet and good, even very good; that is the butter: and the corruption of sin, that is the cheese.   Notice then how excellently our Child has chosen, in that He has taken our nature without any corruption of sin.   For it is said concerning sinners under the Law: Their heart has been curdled like milk inasmuch as the ferment of malice, the curd of iniquity, has corrupted the purity of the milk.

3.   So also with regard to the bee: if it possesses sweet honey, it has also a sharp sting.   But it is the bee which feeds among the lilies, which dwells in the flowery land of the Angels.   There it took its flight towards the village of Nazareth (which means a flower) it reached and remained upon the sweetly-perfumed blossom of perpetual virginity.   Of its honey and its sting he is not ignorant who sings with the prophet of mercy and judgment.   And yet when coming to us, he brings the honey and not the sting, that is mercy and not judgment: for when His disciples begged that the city which would not receive Him, should be destroyed with fire from heaven, He replied, "The Son of man has not come to judge the world, but to save it." Our bee had not then a sting, he was, as it were, disarmed, when enduring such unworthy treatment.   He responded with mercy only, not with judgment.   But do not rest your hope on iniquity, do not commit iniquity in that hope. For there shall be a time when our bee shall retake his sting and plunge it deep into the marrow of sinners: since the Father does not judge any, but hath committed all judgment unto the Son.   But at the present the Holy Child eats butter and honey, since He unites in His own Person all that is good in human nature with the mercy

which is in God, that He might be truly Man, yet without
sin: God merciful and gracious, and not yet showing Himself in judgment.

4. From all this it is clear, what is the stem proceeding
from the root of Jesse, what is the Flower upon which rests
the Holy Spirit. The Virgin, the Genitrix Dei, is the stem,
her Son the Flower. Yes, the Son of the Virgin is
that Flower white and glowing red, chiefest among ten
thousand; the Flower upon which the Angels come to gaze,
of which the perfume restores life to the dead; and as He
Himself declares, a flower of the field, not of the garden.
For the field blooms with flowers without human help;
it is not sown nor tilled, nor enriched with nourishment.
Thus it was with the womb of the Virgin: inviolate, un-
touched, it brought forth, as a prairie of living green, this
Flower of immortal fairness, whose glory shall never fade.
O, Virgin, lofty stem, to what an exalted height dost thou
attain! even to Him who sitteth upon the throne, unto the
Lord of Glory. Nor is this strange, since thou sendest
deeply into the ground the roots of humility.

O plant truly heavenly, more precious and pure than all
others, truly the tree of life, which was found worthy to
bear the fruit of salvation! Thy cunning, O malignant
serpent, has overreached itself; thy falseness is made evident. Two charges thou hadst brought against the Creator; of untruth, and of envy; and in each thou hast been
shown to have lied. He, to whom thou didst say, Thou
shalt by no means die, dies from the beginning; and the
truth of the Lord endureth forever. Tell me, if thou canst,
what tree there is whose fruit can be an object of envy
to him, to whom God has not denied this chosen stem and
its lofty fruit? He who spared not His own Son, how
shall He not with Him also freely give us all things?

5.   You have understood, I think, that the Virgin is that royal way, by which the Saviour came to us; proceeding from her womb, as a bridegroom from his chamber.   Pursuing them the way, which we began to investigate, if you remember, in my former sermon, let us endeavor, brethren, to ascend to Him by it, as by it He descended to us: and by it to come into His grace, who by it descended to share our unhappiness.   By thee let us have access to thy Son, O thou who wast blessed in finding grace, and becoming the mother of the Life and the Salvation.   May He who was given to us by thee, by thee receive us also.   May thy holiness excuse with Him the fault of our corruption, and thy humility, pleasing to God, plead for pardon of our vanity.   May thy abundant charity conceal the multitude of our sins, and thy fulness make us fruitful also in good works.   Our Lady, our mediatrix, our advocate, reconcile us, commend us, represent us to thy Son.   Do so, O blessed one, by the grace which thou hast found, by the prerogative which thou hast merited, by the mercy of which thou art mother; so that He who has deigned to become, by thy means, a sharer of our weakness and our misery, Jesus Christ, thy Son, Our Lord, may at thy intercession, make us sharers of His glory and blessedness, who is above all, God blessed forever.   Amen.

SERMON No. 4.

OF THE THREEFOLD COMING OF THE LORD, AND OF WHICH THE SEVEN COLUMNS WHICH WE OUGHT TO RAISE UP IN OURSELVES.

Text: "He was in the world, and the world was made by Him, and the world knew him not."—S. John I. 10.

In the Advent of the Lord which we are celebrating, if I

look on the Person of Him who comes, I cannot grasp the excellence of His Majesty; and if I regard those to whom He came, I tremble at the greatness of His condescension.

Certainly the angels themselves are astonished at the newness of the prodigy, as they see below themselves Him, who being above them, they continually adore, and as they ascend and descend to the Son of Man. If I consider for what reason He came, I embrace to the utmost of my poor powers, the wide reach of His priceless charity. If I regard the manner of His coming, I am struck with the ennoblement it effected in the human condition. In fact, He who is the Creator and Lord of the universe, comes to men, comes on account of men, comes as Man. But someone will say: "In what way can He be said to have come, who has always been everywhere?" It is very true that He was in the world, and the world was made by Him, and the world knew Him not. He did not then come into the world as if He had ever been out of the world, but He became visible there who had before been invisible. That is why He took upon Him a human form in which he might be known by others, since He dwelt in the Divine Light which none can approach unto. Nor was it altogether inglorious to the Majesty of God, to show Himself in His own likeness which He had made in the beginning, nor unworthy of God to allow Himself to be beheld in a bodily form by those who were not able to behold Him in His substance. So that He who had made man in His own image and likeness, should Himself when become man, be made manifest to man.

It is then the Advent of so exalted a Majesty, an Advent of so profound condescension, of so great charity, and also of a glory so great for us, that the whole Church solemnly celebrates the remembrance of, once each year. But would that it were so celebrated now, as it will be always in eternity. That would be more worthy of it. For how great a folly is it, that after the coming of so great a thing men should wish or should dare to busy themselves with other things; and not rather to lay other things aside and employ themselves wholly in His worship, so as not to bear in mind anything else in his presence? But all men are not of those of whom the prophet says: They shall abundantly utter the meaning of Thy great goodness. Nor do all bear this in memory, for no one speaks of that which he has not tasted, or has only just tasted; and the mouth exhales the odor of that only with which the man is filled and satiated. Those whose mind and whose life is entirely of this world, never exhale the sweet odor of these spiritual truths, even although they recall them to memory; and they observe such days as these without devotion or affection, by the force of lifeless custom. Lastly, the very memory of this inestimable condescension is taken (which is most shocking) for an occasion to the flesh, so that men may be seen on these solemn days full of anxiety about the splendor of vestments, and preparing more delicate food, as if Christ sought these things, or things of this kind, in His nativity, and as if it were more worthily commemorated, the more things of this kind were carefully prepared. But hear what He Himself says: He who hath a proud look and a greedy heart, with him I will not eat. Why do you prepare vestures with such ambition for the day of My birth? I detest pride, I will not endure it. Why do you lay up with such anxious care, stores of dainties for that time? I condemn and will not accept the delights of the flesh. Evidently you are insatiable in heart, to procure for yourself so many things and from so great a distance: since the body would be satisfied with fewer, and those more easy to be procured.

Though, then, you are celebrating My Advent, you are honoring Me only with your lips, and your heart is far from Me. It is not I whom you worship ,but your god is your belly, and your glory is your shame. Altogether unhappy is he who seeks for the pleasures of the senses, and honors the vanity of this present world. Blessed is the people whose God is the Lord.

Brethren, fret not yourselves because of evil doers, nor be envious against the workers of iniquity. Rather look to the end which awaits them, pity them in your heart, and pray for those who are surprised into some transgression. Those unhappy ones act thus because they are ignorant of God. If they had known Him, they would not so madly provoke against themselves the Lord of glory. But we, dear brethren, have no excuse on the score of ignorance. It is certain that you, whosoever you are, have come to know Him, and if you should say, I know Him not, you would be like worldly people, deceitful. For if you have not known Him; who brought thee hither or why art thou here? If you do not know Him at all, how have you been brought to renounce spontaneously the affection of your friends, the pleasures of the flesh, the vanities of the world, and to devote all your thoughts to God, to lay every care that you have upon Him, if your conscience bears you witness that you have deserved nothing good, or rather so much evil, at his hands? Who could have persuaded you (I ask again) if indeed you knew Him not, how good the Lord is to those who trust in Him, to the soul that seeks Him; and if you had not known for yourself how sweet and gentle is the Lord, how full of mercy and truth? But whence have you come to know this, if not because He has come, not only to you but also within you?

4. The coming of Christ is in fact threefold; to men, within men, against men. He has come to all men without distinction; but not so within all men or against all men. The first and the third kind of coming are well known, since they are open to all eyes, as to the second, which is secret and spiritual, listen to what He himself says: If a man love Me, he will keep my words, and my Father will love him, and We will come unto him and make our abode with him. Blessed is he, O Lord Jesus, in whom Thou makest Thy abode. Blessed is he in whom Wisdom builds for herself a house and hews her out seven columns. Blessed is the soul which is the abode of Wisdom. But what is that soul? It is the soul of the righteous. How should it be otherwise, since it is justice and judgment which prepare for Wisdom her seat? Who is there among you, brethren, who desires earnestly to prepare in his soul a habitation for Christ? Behold what silken hangings, what rich carpets, what a softly cushioned couch it is needful to prepare for Him.

Justice, He says, and judgment are the habitation of thy seat. Justice, because it is the virtue which renders to each that which is his own. Render therefore to three sorts of persons that which is theirs, and that which is their due from you; to your superiors, to your inferiors, and to your equals; and then you will celebrate worthily the Advent of Christ and prepare for Him His seat in justice. Render, I say, the reverence due to him who is set over you, and obedience of which the former is a virtue of the heart, the latter of the body. It is not sufficient to yield to our elders in action only, unless in the depth of our hearts we have feelings of respect for them. If it should happen that the life of a superior should be so manifestly unworthy, as not to admit of being passed over, nor of being excused;

even then, because of Him, from whom comes all power, we ought to have respect even for such a superior; if not because he merits it Himself, at least by consideration for the order established by God, and for the dignity of the charge which he bears.

5. So, also, we owe to the brethren among whom we live, our counsel and our help, by the double claim of human association and of brotherhood. For these we, on our side, desire that they should bestow upon us: advise to instruct our inexperience, and help to supply our weakness. But perhaps there is someone among you who will silently reply to this: What advice can I give to my brother, when I am not permitted to say a simple word to him without license? Or what help can I render to him, not being able to do the least thing beyond the law of obedience? To which I reply: You will always find something to do for your brother, if you have a feeling of brotherly kindness for him. No advice, I suppose, could be better for him that you should study to instruct him by your good example, what he ought to do and what he ought to avoid: animating him to better things, and advising him not by tongue or by word; but by deed and in truth. Can any help be more useful and efficacious than to pray earnestly for him, not to neglect to reprove his faults, and not merely to avoid putting in his way any occasion of falling, but to remove such out of his way to the utmost of your power, as an angel of peace; taking away scandals from the Kingdom of God, and also the occasions of such? If you afford to your brother such assistance and such counsels, you will discharge your debt in his behalf, nor will he have any right to complain of you.

6. But are you placed over others? Then, indeed, you owe to them the duty of a fuller solicitude; and they re-

quire of you vigilance and discipline. Vigilance, that offences may be prevented; discipline, that whoever offends, may not escape unpunished. But if you have none other under your authority, you have at all events yourself, and towards yourself you ought to exercise both vigilance and discipline. Without doubt, it is the appointed task of your soul to direct your body; you ought then to be vigilant over it, so that in it sin may not reign, nor make your members instruments of iniquity. You ought to discipline it, that it may be mortified and rendered obedient, and bring forth worthy fruits of penitence. Yet the debt of those who have to answer for many souls is more weighty and perilous. Miserable man that I am, whither shall I go, if I am too careless in guiding so great a treasure, so precious a deposit as (a soul) for which Christ thought good to shed His blood! If it had been permitted to collect at the foot of the cross the blood of Jesus as it dropped from His wounds, and if it were stored in a vase of crystal that it behooved me to carry about wherever I went; what apprehensions should I not feel for the danger I ran? And it is certain that I have received into my charge such a treasure, for which a wise merchant, indeed Wisdom Himself, gave His own blood. More than this, the treasure is in fragile vases, exposed to many more dangers than those of glass. It adds to the burden of my care and the weight of my anxiety, that although I have the charge of my neighbor's conscience as well as my own, I have no certain knowledge either of the one or the other. Each of them is an unfathomable abyss, a dark mystery, to me, nevertheless the safe custody of each is required of me, and I hear a voice which calls to me: "Watchman, what of the night? Watchman, what of the night?" It is not for me to reply with Cain, Am I my brother's keeper? but to confess humbly with the prophet:

"Unless the Lord keep the city, the watchman waketh but in vain." I am to be held excused in this, only by the care with which I have discharged the duty which, as I have said before, I owe, equally, of vigilance and of discipline. If these four things are not wanting: reverence and due obedience to superiors, counsel and help to equals, all of which justice requires, then Wisdom will not find her seat unprepared.

7. We may perhaps call these six out of the seven columns which she hews out in the house which she has built for herself: let us now consider what is the seventh, if Wisdom will deign to enable us to find it. As, then, the six were found in justice, why should not the seventh be understood of judgment. For not justice alone, but justice, it is said, and judgment are the preparation of thy seat. Finally, if we render to our superiors, to our equals, to our inferiors that which is due to them, shall we render nothing to God? But of a certainty, no one can repay unto Him the whole of our obligations, because He has heaped upon us the treasures of His mercy; so great is the multitude of our faults, so weak and insignificant are we, while He is great and sufficient to Himself, and needs nothing that we can give, yet I have heard one to whom He had revealed the secrets and the mysteries of His wisdom say, that the honor of the King loveth justice. He asks for nothing from us which He does not find in Himself: only let us confess our iniquities and He will justify us freely, so that His grace may be made manifest. He loves the soul which considers and judges its own condition constantly and without pretense, as in His sight. This judgment He demands of us for our own sake: because, if we judge our own selves, we shall not be judged. Therefore, he who is wise, suspects his own doings, examines and weighs them with care, and

judges them without prejudice. That man honors the truth who acknowledges without reserve and confesses in all humility that which he finds himself to be. If you would be convinced that God demands of us all judgment according to justice, hear what He says: When you shall have done all that is commanded to you, say, we are unprofitable servants. This is, as far as a man is concerned, a worthy preparation for the Lord, of His throne of majesty; that he should both study to observe the commandments of righteousness and should acknowledge his endeavor and himself to be imperfect and unprofitable.

SERMON No. 5.

OF HIS TWOFOLD ADVENT, AND OF THE ZEAL WE OUGHT TO HAVE FOR TRUE VIRTUE.

Text: "The foolish said unto the wise, Give us of your oil, for our lamps are gone out."—S. Matt. XXV. 8.

1. It is proper, brethren, that you should celebrate the Advent of the Lord with all possible devotion, that you should be cheered by so great a consolation, should realize so vast a condescension, and be moved to gratitude by such Divine love.

But be not content to think only of the first Advent, in which He came to seek and to save that which was lost, but think also of the second, in which He shall come and take us to be with Him. Would that you were unceasingly occupied in meditating upon those two Advents, in making yourselves familiar in thought with all He has done in the first, and all that He promises in the second. Would that you slept as it were between these two heritages. For these are the two arms of the Bridegroom, of which the bride reposing said: His left hand shall be under my head, and

His right hand shall embrace me. For indeed, as we read elsewhere, In His left hand are riches and glory, and in His right, length of days ˙ O sons of Adam, ambitious and greedy race, listen to this: In His left hand are riches and glory. Why do you strive for earthly and temporal glory, which are not really what they claim, nor belong to you at all? What are gold and silver but red earth and white earth, which only the error of men makes to be, or rather thinks to be precious? Again, if these things were truly yours, you could take them away with you when you die. But no, when man perishes, he takes with him none of those things, nor shall his glory follow him into the tomb.

2. The true riches do not consist in treasures, but in virtues; which the conscience of a man bears with him and renders him rich forever. As for glory, the apostle says of it: Our glory is this, the testimony of a good conscience. This is indeed true glory, which is from the Spirit of truth. For the Spirit Himself beareth witness with our spirit that we are the sons of God. But the glory which they who seek not the glory which comes from God alone, receive from each other in turn, is vain; since the children of men are themselves foolish. O foolish man, who storest thy merchandise in a sack full of holes, who makest the mouth of another thy treasure house! Dost thou not know that that chest cannot be made fast, and has no bolts? How much wiser are they who themselves guard their treasure and do not confide it to others: Will they indeed keep it safe always? Will they hold it always hidden? A day shall come when the secrets of the heart shall be revealed, and those things which have been merely pretended shall vanish altogether. Hence it is that when the Lord is coming, the lamps of the foolish virgins are gone out and those are not owned by the Lord who have received their reward in this

world. Wherefore, I say to you, dear brethren, that if we make anything precious, it is better to hide it than to make a show of it. We must do as beggars when they ask alms: they do not display costly garments, but limbs half naked, or ulcers if they have them, so that compassion may be more excited in the mind of the sepctator. The observance of this rule of conduct the publican in the Gospel followed much better than the Pharisee: therefore he returned to his house justified rather than the other, that is, in preference to him.

3. It is time, brethren, that judgment should begin at the house of God. What shall be the end of those who do not obey the Gospel of Christ? What judgment for those who do not rise up in this judgment? Those who have no wish to have part in this judgment, which is now, in which the prince of this world is cast out, have reason to expect, or rather have reason greatly to fear, the Judge who will cast them out themselves with their prince. But as for us, if we are perfectly judged now, we may await with entire security the coming of the Lord Jesus Christ, who will change the body of our humility and make it like to the body of His glory. Then shall the righteous shine, the unlearned equally with the learned; they shall shine forth as the sun in the kingdom of their Father. And then the brightness of the sun shall be sevenfold, that is, as the light of seven days.

4. The Saviour then, when He comes, shall transform the body of our humility, and make it like unto the body of His glory, provided that our heart has been previously transformed and made like unto the humility of His heart. Therefore He said: Learn of Me, for I am meek and lowly in heart. Remark on this subject that there are two kinds of humility, as the words of the Saviour indicate; the one

of conviction, the other of feeling, or, as it is here called, of the heart. By the first we are enabled to recognize our nothingness; and this we can learn by ourselves alone, and even in our own weakness; by the second we are enabled to trample under foot the glory of the world; and this we learn from Him who emptied Himself and took upon Him the form of a servant, Who, when he was sought for to be made a king, fled; and when He was sought for to endure the shameful, ignominious punishment of the cross, presented Himself of His own accord. If, then, we wish to sleep between the two heritages, that is to say, between the two Advents of Christ, we need to have the wings, covered with silver, of a dove, that is to say, that we should hold fast the model virtues which Christ, when He was in the flesh, taught by word and by example. For we may not improperly understand by those words "covered with silver," His Humility, and by "Gold" His Divinity.

5. Thus then all our virtue is as far from true virtue as it is different from that model of virtue shown us in Christ; and (so to speak) the wing is of no value if it be not "covered with silver." A wing of great power is that of poverty, by which we fly so quickly into the kingdom of heaven. For to all the other virtues which come after it, promises are only made for the future; but to poverty it is not promises for the future that are given, but an actual gift in the present. He says: Blessed are the poor in spirit, for theirs is the kingdom of heaven, whilst in speaking of the other virtues it is said, "They shall inherit, they shall be comforted, etc.," and similar words. For there are some poor people who, if they had a true poverty, would not be so sorrowful and fearful, since the kingdom of heaven would be their portion. Such are they who are willingly poor, provided that they want for nothing: and who love poverty on the express con-

dition that they are called upon to endure no privation. Such are those also who are gentle, but only as long as nothing is said and nothing is done contrary to their will; for it will soon appear how far they are from true gentleness, if a slight provocation should occur. How could such gentleness as this have part in a heritage, which fails before the heritage appears? I see others also who have the gift of tears; but if these tears proceeded from the heart, they would not so easily give place to laughter. But now when thoughtless and abusive words flow more abundantly from their lips than tears did before from their eyes; I cannot conclude, that it is to tears of this kind that Divine consolation is promised, since they are so easily dried by weak and silly consolations. Others inveigh so violently against the offences of others that one might believe that they have truly a hunger and thirst for righteousness but they are far from regarding their own faults with the same severity: now divers weights are an abomination unto the Lord. Again there are those who abuse others with a violence as impudent as it is useless, while they flatter themselves with as much folly as falseness.

6. There are some persons who are benevolent with goods which do not belong to themselves, who are scandalized if abundant charity is not distributed to all, provided that they do not themselves suffer in the smallest degree. If they were truly benevolent, it would be from their own goods that they would give alms; and if they were not able to bestow temporal goods, they would at least give with goodwill their forgiveness to those who perhaps are thought to have offended them. They would at all events bestow a sign of goodwill, a kind word, which is worth more than the best present, in order to excite the minds of those offending them to regret. In short, they would pour out willingly

compassion and prayer both upon these and upon all whom
they knew to be in sin. Otherwise their pity is of no value,
and they attain unto no true pity. Also those who so confess their sins, as to make it appear that they are actuated
by the desire of making their conscience clear (since all
faults are washed away by confession of them), yet are not
able to hear with patience the avowal by others of similar
offences to those they themselves confess. These, if they
truly wished to be purified, as they seem to do, would not
treat those harshly who avow to them their failings, but
forgive them. There are those also who will take great
pain to appease any one who is angry and irritated, even
about a small thing, and so many pass for true peacemak-
ers; yet if anything is said or done against themselves, are
very slow and reluctant to forgive it. But if they truly cared
for peace, they would seek it also for themselves.

7.   Let us then cover (as it were) our wings with silver
by communion with Christ, as the holy Martyrs made their
robes white by union with His Passion. Let us imitate as
far as we are able, Him who so loved poverty that when the
whole earth was in His power, He had not where to lay His
head; Him whose disciples, as we read, were obliged to
rub the ears of corn between their hands to satisfy their
hunger, as they went through the cornfields; Who was led
as a lamb to the slaughter, and as a sheep is dumb before
the shearer, so He opened not His mouth; Who wept, as
we read, over Lazarus and over Jerusalem, and Who passed
whole nights in prayer. Who is never recorded to have
either laughed or jested; Who so hungered for righteousness
that though He had no sins of His own to atone for, He
made so great a satisfaction to expiate ours. Even upon the
Cross He thirsted for nothing else than righteousness; He
did not hesitate to die for His enemies, and prayed even

for His executioners; He did no sin, and bore patiently the sins of others which were laid upon Him; Who endured so great sufferings, that he might reconcile sinners to Himself.

SERMON No. 6.

OF THAT COMING OF THE LORD WHICH IS BETWEEN HIS FIRST ADVENT AND HIS LAST; AND OF THE THREEFOLD RENEWAL.

Text: "All flesh shall see the salvation of God."—S. Luke, III. 6.

I have already said that the two inheritances between which those are to rest, who have covered their wings with silver, signify the two Advents of Jesus Christ: But I have not yet said where is the place of their rest. For there is a third coming which is midway between the other two, and in this they who know him may rest with gladness. The two others are visible, the third is not. In the first Advent Jesus showed Himself upon the earth and went about among men; when, as He himself bears witness, they both saw Him and hated. And in the last all flesh shall see the salvation of our God, and they shall behold Him whom they have pierced. But there is a coming between these, in which only the elect behold the Saviour, in their own souls, and are saved. Thus in the first Advent He came in our flesh and in our weakness; in the second in the spirit and in power; in the last in glory and majesty. By power He attains to glory; for the Lord of Power He is the King of Glory. And again that I may see Thy power and Thy glory. The second coming then is, as it were, the way which conducts from the first to the last. In the first Christ was our Redemption; in the last He shall appear as our Life; in the second, that we may rest between these two heritages,

He is our rest and our consolation. That you may not suppose that what I say of this second coming is an invention of my own; listen to His own words. If any man love Me he will keep My words: and My Father will love him and We will come to him. But what does He mean by these words? For I read elsewhere, "He that feareth the Lord will do good;" but I think that something more is said of him who loves God, viz., that he will keep the words of God. But where are they to be kept? In the heart, without doubt, as says the prophet: "Thy word have I hid in my heart that I might not sin against Thee." But how are they to be preserved in the heart? Or is it sufficient to preserve them only in the memory? But the apostle says to those who thus preserve them, "Knowledge puffeth up." And besides, that which is committed only to the memory is easily forgotten. We ought, then, so to keep the word of God as we are able to keep the food of the body, and we can do this more easily, as that word is itself the Bread of Life, the food of the soul. Earthly bread, whilst it is in the chest, may be stolen by a thief, may be gnawed by the mice, may be corrupted by age. But when you have eaten it, you need fear none of these dangers. In this way, then, keep the Word of God: For blessed are they who hear it and keep it. Let it be deposited in the inmost parts of your soul, let it pass into your affections and into your character. Feed upon this good food to the full, and your soul shall delight itself in fatness. Do not forget to feed upon this your bread, that your heart may not become exhausted; but let your soul be filled with its fatness.

2. If you keep the word of God thus, without doubt you will be kept by it. For the Son shall come to you with the Father, that Great Prophet shall come who will rebuild Jerusalem and will make all things new. His coming will

work this effect upon us, that as we have borne the image of the earthly we shall also bear the image of the heavenly. And just as the old Adam was spread through the entire man and occupied him wholly, so Christ shall possess us wholly, as He created us wholly, redeemed us wholly, and shall glorify and save the whole man in the great Sabbath of the world. Once the old man was in us, that deceiver was in us, so that he acted by our hands, spoke by our mouths and felt in our hearts. With our hands doubly, by sin and by shame; by our mouth also, by pride and by envy. And in our hearts also, by the desires of the flesh and the desires of worldly glory. But now, if we have become a new creature in Christ, the old things have passed away, and instead of sin and shame we have innocence and purity. In our mouth, in place of pride, we have humble confession, and words of edification have taken the place of detraction. In our hearts, instead of the desires of the flesh, there is charity; and humility instead of the thirst for worldly glory.

See now in these three renewals the way in which each one among the elect receives Christ the Word of God. To them He says: "Set Me as a seal upon thy heart, as a signet upon thy arm." And in another place: "The word is near thee, in thy mouth and in thy heart."

SERMON No. 7.

OF THE THREEFOLD COMING OF THE LORD, AND OF THE RESURRECTION OF THE BODY.

Text: "We look for the Saviour, the Lord Jesus Christ, who shall change the body of our humiliation, that it may be made like to the body of His Glory."—Phil. III 20-21.

1. I am unwilling, brethren, that you should be ignorant of the time of your visitation, and especially of the object

THE ASCENSION—BY BIERMAN.

with which God visits us in this time of our probation. Our souls, not our bodies, supply the reason for this visitation: for the soul being far more worthy than the body, claims by the very excellence of its nature to be the first object of care. And since it appears to have been the first to fall, it is also the first to be raised up again. For the soul commenced to be corrupted when it fell into sin; and it was the cause why the body also was made liable to corruption as a penalty. So then, if we wish to be found true members of Christ, we must without doubt follow Him our Head: and must have it chiefly at heart to make good the injuries of our souls, for which He has already come into the world, and whose disease He first devoted Himself to heal. But as for the care of our body, we must put it off, and reserve it to that day when the Saviour shall come, and shall Himself take up the task of transforming it, as the apostle declares: "We look for the Saviour, the Lord Jesus Christ, who shall change the body of our humiliation that it may be made like the body of His glory." At the head of His first Advent, St. John Baptist, being truly His herald and forerunner, cried unto men: "Behold the lamb of God, who taketh away the sin of the world." He does not say, the diseases of the body; not the infirmities of the flesh; but sin; and sin is the disease of the soul, the corruption of the mind. This He takes away from the hands, from the eyes, from the neck, and in short from the whole of our flesh, in which it is deeply rooted.

2. He takes away sin from the hands, blotting out the sins they have committed: from the eyes, purifying the intention of the mind: He takes it from the neck, by destroying the tyrannical yoke which weighed upon it, according as it is written: "Thou hast broken the sceptre of his oppressor, as in the days of Midian," and also: The yoke

shall be destroyed because of the anointing." The apostle also well says: "Let not sin reign in your mortal body." And the same in another place: "I know that in me (that is in my flesh) dwelleth no good thing." And again: "O wretched man that I am, who shall deliver me from the body of this death?" For he knew that he would not be delivered from that calamitous germ of sin, which was deeply rooted in his flesh, as long as he was not freed from the body himself. Wherefore he desired to be released and to be with Christ, knowing that sin, which separates between us and God cannot altogether be done away, until we are freed from the body. You have heard of that man whom the Lord delivered from the demon, who tore and tortured him grievously before he came out at the bidding of the Lord. Therefore, I say to you that the particular kind of sin which so often destroys the peace of our souls (I mean concupiscence and evil desire) can be and ought to be, by the grace of God, overcome in us, so that it should not reign in us any longer, nor make our members to be weapons of iniquity unto sin; but it cannot be altogether done away except by death, when we are so torn asunder, that our soul is separated from our body.

3. You know for what purpose Christ has come, and that the Christian ought to endeavor to attain that same purpose. Therefore do not, O my body, preoccupy my time: for you may well hinder the salvation of my soul, but your own salvation you cannot accomplish. For all things there is a time. Let the soul strive now on its own behalf, and do you become even its fellow laborer: since if you suffer with it with it you shall also reign. Insomuch as you hinder its salvation, in the same degree you hinder your own; for not until the image of God is restored in it, can you be restored to your original excellency. You have a noble guest, O

body, a noble guest indeed, and all your well-being depends upon it. Give honor then to so great a guest. You dwell in your own land: but your soul is a stranger and a foreigner, to which you have given shelter. What peasant is there let me ask you, who, if some powerful and noble seigneur wished to take up his abode in his cottage, would not most willingly receive him, and himself lie down to sleep in some corner of his house, under the stairs or on the very hearth, in order to yield his place of rest, as was proper, to his illustrious guest? Do you then do likewise: count for nothing your privations and your sufferings; think of only one thing, that your guest should be treated honorably as long as he remains in your house. It is an honor to you to expose yourself to discomfort, as long as he shall remain with you.

4. And in order that you may not despise the guest you are sheltering, or think less of it than it deserves, precisely because it is a stranger and an exile; notice carefully, of how great advantage to you its presence is the cause. For it is because this living soul is present with you, that sight is given to your eyes; it is this inmate who supplies speech to your tongue, taste to your palate, motion to all your limbs. If there is any life, any sensibility, any beauty in you, remember that you owe it all to the presence of this your guest. In short, its departure gives proof of the benefits that its presence bestowed. For when the soul departs, instantly the tongue will become silent; the eyes will no longer see, the ears will no longer hear, the countenance will grow pale, and the whole body rigid. Then in a short space of time there will be only a corpse falling into offensive corruption, and your beauty will be changed into foulness.

Why then do you distress and wound by your carnal delights, this your guest, when you would not be able even to feel anything except by its means? When this exile, driven from the face of God because of enmity, is restored to it by reconciliation, of how great service will it be to you! Do not hinder, O body, that reconciliation, because a great glory is being prepared from thence for you. Suffer all things patiently and gladly: and do not shrink from anything that may help on the reconciliation. Say to your guest: When the Lord shall remember you, and restore you to your former place, remember me, I pray you.

5. If you will serve it well, it will certainly remember you for good: and when the guest shall have reached the presence of its Lord, he will plead for you for good, in gratitude for the good he has received from you, saying: When your servant was in exile for his fault, a certain poor man with whom I lodged had mercy upon me: would that my Lord would reward him for it. In the first place, he put himself and all that he had at my disposition, not sparing himself on my account, in frequent facts, in labors and watchings beyond measure, in hunger and thirst, in cold and nakedness. What then? The Scripture tells us truly: He will fulfill the desire of them that fear Him. He will hear their cry and will help them. O my body, if you could only taste of that sweetness; if you could only form an idea of that glory! What I am about to say, will perhaps surprise you; yet there is nothing more certain, nothing less doubtful to those who are faithful. The God of Hosts, the Lord of Power, the King of Glory, shall Himself come from the height of heaven, to change our bodies, and to render them like unto the body of His glory. What shall be that glory, that ineffable joy, when the Creator of the world, who was hidden under a humble exterior, when He came to save souls, shall appear manifest in all His glory and His majesty, and no longer in weakness, in order to glorify thee, O

miserable flesh! Who can think (without gladness) of the day of His Advent, when He shall come down in the fulness of light, preceded by angels, and with such a sound of trumpets as shall summon from the dust our bodies, and we shall be caught up to meet Christ in the clouds?

6. How long, then, will the unhappy flesh, foolish, blind, thoughtless and almost insane, seek transitory and failing delights which ought rather to be called desolations, so as to cause it to be rejected, and judged unworthy of this glory, or rather I should say, to be exposed to unspeakable torment forever? Let it not be so with you, I pray you, brethren; but rather let our soul delight itself in these Advent thoughts; let our flesh rest in this hope, and wait for our Saviour, the Lord Jesus Christ, who shall change it, make it like to the body of His glory; for thus says the prophet: My soul thirsteth for Thee, my flesh longeth for Thee. The soul of the prophet longed for the first Advent, by which it was to be redeemed, but much more still did his flesh long for the latter Advent, to be glorified. Then our desires shall be fulfilled, and all the earth be filled with the glory of the Lord. To that glory, to that felicity, to that peace which passes all understanding, may He in His mercy bring us; and may the Saviour for whom we wait, Jesus Christ our Lord, who is blessed above all forever, let us not be disappointed in our hope.

SERMON No. 8.

OF THE THREEFOLD FRUIT OF THE ADVENT OF CHRIST.

Text: "If God be for us, who can be against us?"—Rom. VIII. 31.

1. If we celebrate with devotion the Advent of the Lord, we only do that which we are bound to do: since He who

needs nothing of us, has come, not only to us, but on our account. The greatness of His condescension shows clearly the greatness of our need. For as the peril of a disease is indicated by the costliness of the cure, so the number of diseases is shown by the multitude of the remedies to which recourse is had. For why such a diversity of graces, if there was not a corresponding diversity of needs? It is difficult to pass in review in a single discourse all the needs which we experience: but at present three occur to my mind which are common to all, and may be regarded as the chief needs. For there is no one among us who has no need sometimes of guidance, of aid, and of protection; and this may be called the threefold need of all human beings. Whosoever we are, who walk in this valley of the shadow of death, in weakness of body, and in constant liability to temptation, if we reflect seriously, we shall see that we are unhappily liable to this threefold trouble. For we are easily open to be led into evil, we are weak in doing good, and have little power to resist temptation. If we try to distinguish between good and evil, we make mistakes; if we try to do good, we fail; if we try to resist evil, we are cast down and overcome.

On that account the coming of the Saviour was needful; and the presence of Christ is still needful, because of the condition of men. May God grant that He may not only come to us in the fulness of His Grace, but dwelling in our hearts of faith, may enlighten our darkness, **may** help our weakness, and casting the shield of His protection over us, may supply our need of strength. If He is in us, who will be able to lead us in error? If He is with us, of what shall we men not be capable, in Him who strengtheneth us? If He is for us, who can be against us? He is a faithful counsellor, who cannot be deceived, nor is able to deceive:

THE MARRIAGE OF THE BLESSED VIRGIN. (BY PROF. FUERSTEIN)
GERMANY.

He is a strong helper who does not know fatigue; He is a prevailing protector, who is able to tread Satan himself under our feet, and to bring to nothing all his devices. For He is the very Wisdom of God, who is able to make the ignorant wise: He is the Power of God, who is able both to succor the fainting and rescue those involved in danger. Therefore, brethren, in every time of doubt, let us have recourse to this wise counsellor: let us commit our souls in every time of struggle to this faithful defender. For this very purpose He came into the world, that He might dwell in men, with men and for men; that He might enlighten our darkness, that He might relieve our troubles, and might protect us against the dangers by which we are threatened.

SERMON No. 9.

Text: "The Angel Gabriel was sent from God unto a city of Galilee, named Nazareth, to a virgin espoused to a man whose name was Joseph, of the house of David; and the Virgin's name was Mary."—S. Luke I. 26, 27.

With what intention did the evangelist in this place enter so significantly into the enumeration of so many proper names? Without doubt, it was in order that we might give to his recital a degree of attention equal to the care which he himself showed in making it. You see that he mentions the name of the messenger who was sent of the Lord, by whom he was sent, of the virgin to whom he was sent, and of the betrothed of that virgin: and furthermore he mentions the name of their nation, their village and their province. And are we to suppose that all this was done without special purpose? By no means. For if not a leaf falls from a tree without permission of our Heavenly Father, I cannot suppose that a single word flowed uselessly from the mouth of a holy evangelist, especially in the sacred history of the Word; I cannot, I repeat, believe it. All these details are full of heavenly mysteries, and exhale a celestial sweetness, if they have a diligent reader who knows how to suck honey from the rock, and collect oil from the flinty stone. For in that day the mountains dropped sweetness, and the hills flowed with milk and honey; it was the day when the skies dropped dew from above, and the clouds gave the Just One to descend like a refreshing shower; when the earth opened and brought forth the Saviour; when the Lord gave His blessing and our land yielded her increase; when mercy and truth met together on the lofty and fertile mountains, and righteousness and peace kissed each other. At that time also a chief one among these mountains (I mean this holy evangelist) relates to us sweetly and eloquently the long desired commencement of our salvation, as with the breath of the south wind, and under the shining beams of the Sun of righteousness pouring forth spiritual odors. May God now send forth His Word and cause them to fall around us; may He breathe upon us with His Spirit, and cause us to comprehend the words of the Gospel: may He render them sweeter than honey and the honeycomb, more longed for by our hearts than gold and precious stones.

He says then: The Angel Gabriel was sent from God. I suppose that this angel was not one of those of lesser dignity, who are sent frequently upon the earth to discharge ordinary missions: his name is given, as it is said to mean, Strength of God; also he does not come, as is usual, at the order of a spirit of higher rank than himself, but it is said to be sent by God himself. And we must understand by these words by God, that the counsel of God was revealed to no other of the blessed spirits, before the Virgin, except-

THE ANNUNCIATION—BY RENI.

ing only the Archangel Gabriel, who was alone found worthy among the rest of the angels of a similar rank, of the same which he received, and of the mission which was intrusted to him. Nor is the name without relation to the mission. For what angel did it better befit to announce the coming of Christ, who is the Power of God, than he whose very name signifies Strength of God? For what else is power than strength? Nor let it seem unbecoming or unsuitable that the Lord and the messenger should bear the same name; since although they are similarly named, that is not for similar reasons. For Christ is called the strength or the power of God in one sense, and the angel is another. It is only a matter of appointment (nuncupative) that the angel is so called, but Christ is called so, according to His nature (substantive); He both is and is called the Power of God; He is the stronger man armed spoken of in the Gospel, who has overthrown by His own power the armed man who kept his house in peace, and has taken from him his spoils. But the angel is called the Strength of God, either because he had been honored by the office to announce the Advent of that same Strength, or because it was needful that he should strengthen a Virgin naturally timid, simple and retiring, and whom the novelty of a miracle might cause to tremble. And this he did, saying: "Fear not, Mary, for thou hast found favor with God." And the same angel is not unreasonably believed to have strengthened also her betrothed, a man no less humble and apprehensive, although his name is not in that instance mentioned by the evangelist. "Joseph, son of David, fear not to take unto thee Mary, thy wife." Most fittingly, therefore, Gabriel was chosen for the work which he had to fulfill, or, rather, it was because he had it to fulfill, that he was called Gabriel.

The angel Gabriel then was sent by God. Whither? To a city of Galilee named Nazareth. Let us see, as Nathaniel said, whether anything good can come out of Nazareth. Nazareth is interpreted a flower. It seems to me that there is a certain germ of the Divine thought cast as it were from heaven upon the earth in the addresses and promises made from on high to the fathers, Abraham, Isaac and Jacob; of which germ it is written: "If the Lord of Sabbath had not left us a germ, we should have been a Sodom, and we should have been made like unto Gomorrah. This germ shot forth in the marvellous deeds which were shown when Israel went out of Egypt in the figures and emblems of their journey over the desert and unto the promised land, and after that in the visions and predictions of the prophets, in the establishment of the monarchy and the priesthood until Christ.

But Christ is rightfully regarded as the fruit of the germ of these flowers, according to the word of David: "The Lord shall give His benediction, and our land shall give her increase," and that other: "Of the fruit of Thy body will I set upon Thy throne." Christ, then is declared by the angel to be about to be born in Nazareth, because to the flower, it may be hoped, that the fruit will succeed. When the fruit appears, the flower falls. So also when the Truth appears in the flesh, the type passes away. Wherefore Nazareth is called a city of Galilee, that is to say (mystically), of transmigration. In fact, at the birth of Christ, all of which I have spoken above, and of which the Apostle said, "All these things happened to them in a figure," passed away. And we, who now enjoy the fruit, see that these flowers have passed; and even while they still seem to be in vigorous life, it was foreseen that they would one day pass away. So David says: "As the grass which passeth away, in the morning it flourishes, in the evening it withers, falls and is dried up." Now, by the evening, we are to understand the fullness of time in which God sent His only-begotten Son, made of woman, made under the law, saying: "Behold, I make all things new." Old things have passed away and disappeared, even as flowers fall and dry up when the fruit begins to grow. Also it is said in another place: "The grass withereth, the flower fadeth, but the Word of our God shall endure eternally." There can be no doubt that by the "Word" is meant the fruit; but the Word is Christ.

Thus the good fruit is Christ, who shall endure eternally. But where is the grass that withereth? Where is the flower that fadeth? Let the prophet reply: "All flesh is grass and all its glory as the flower of grass." If all flesh is as grass, then the carnal people of the Jews would necessarily be consumed as the flower of the field, and is this not, in fact, the case? Is not that same people deprived of all the fatness of the Spirit, so that they hold to the dryness of the letter? Has not the flower of the nation fallen, while their glorifying, which they had in their law, has passed away? If their flower has not fallen, where is their monarchy, their priesthood, their prophets, their temple, and all those great and wonderful things of which they were wont to boast and say: "How great things have we heard and known, and our fathers have declared to us!" and again: "How great things did He command our fathers, that they should make them known unto their children." Such are the reflections which are suggested to me by these words: "Unto Nazareth, a city of Galilee."

To that city, then, was sent the Angel Gabriel by God. But to whom was he sent? To a virgin, espoused to a man whose name was Joseph. Who is this virgin so worthy of reverence as to be saluted by an angel, yet so humble as to be betrothed to a carpenter? A beautiful combination is that of virginity with humility: and that soul singularly pleases God in which humility gives worth to virginity, and virginity throws a new lustre on humility. But of how great respect must she be thought worthy in whom maternity consecrates virginity, and the splendor of a birth exalts humility? You hear her, a virgin, and humble. If you are not able to imitate the virginity of that humble soul, imitate at least her humility; virginity is a praise worthy virtue, but humility is more necessary. If the one is counseled, the other is commanded; and if you are invited to keep the one, you are commanded to practice the other. Of the one it is said: "He who is able to receive it, let him receive it"; but of the other: "Except ye become as this little child, ye shall not enter into the Kingdom of Heaven." The one, then, is rewarded; but the other is absolutely required. You can be saved without virginity, but not without humility. The humility, I say, which mourns over the loss of virginity is pleasing to God; but without humility, I am bold to say, not even the virginity of Mary would have been so. Upon whom, he says, shall my spirit rest but upon one that is of an humble and quiet spirit? Upon one that is humble. He says not upon one that is a virgin. If Mary had not been humble, the Holy Ghost would not have rested upon her. It is then evident that she conceived by the Holy Ghost just because, as she herself declares: God regarded the humility of His handmaiden, rather than her virginity. And I conclude, without doubt, that it was rather by her humility than by her virginity, where both were pleasing, that she pleased God and was chosen by Him.

What say you to this, O virgin, who art proud? Mary forgets her virginity and dwells only on her humility: and you think only of flattering yourself about your virginity, while neglecting humility. "The Lord," she said, "has had regard to the humility of His handmaiden." Who was she who speaks thus? A virgin holy, prudent and pious. Would you claim to be more chaste, more pious than she? Or do you think that your modesty is more acceptable than the purity of Mary, since you think that you are able by it to please God without humility, whilst she was not able! The more honorable you are by the singular gift of chastity, the greater is the injury you do yourself by staining it with an admixture of pride. It were better for you not to be a virgin than to grow haughty about your virginity. It is not granted to all to live in virginity; but to fewer to do so with humility. If, then, you are only able to admire, not to imitate, the virginity of Mary, study to admire her humility, and it suffices for you. But if you are a virgin and are also humble, then you are truly great.

There is something still more admirable in Mary, namely, her maternity joined with virginity. For from the beginning was never such a thing heard as that one should be at the same time mother and virgin. If you consider also of whom she was mother, to what degree will not your admiration of such a marvellous advancement soar? Will you not feel that you can hardly admire it enough? Will not your judgment, or, rather that of the truth, be that she whose Son is God, is exalted even above the choirs of angels? Is it not Mary who says boldly to God, the Lord of angels, "Son, why hast Thou thus dealt with us?" Who of the angels would dare to speak thus? It is sufficient for them, and they count if for a great thing, that they are spirits by nature, that they were made and called angels by His grace, as David testifies. "Who makes His angels spirits." But Mary, knowing herself to be mother, with confidence names

Him Son whom they obey with reverence. Nor does God disdain to be called by the name which He has deigned to assume. For a little after the evangelist adds: "And He was subject unto them." Who, and to whom? God, to human beings; God, I say, to whom the angels are subject, whom principalities and powers obey, was subject unto Mary, and to Joseph also for her sake. Admire, then, both the benign condescension of the Son and the most excellent dignity of the Mother, and choose whether of the two is the more admirable. Each is a wonder; each is a miracle. God is obedient to a woman, an unexampled humility! A woman is in the place of ancestor to God, a distinction without a sharer! When the praises of virgins are sung, it is said that they follow the Lamb whithersoever He goeth, and of what praise shall she be thought worthy who even goes before Him?

Learn, O man, to obey; learn, O dust and ashes, to abase thyself and submit. The evangelist, speaking of thy Creator, says: "He was obedient to them"; that is, to Mary and Joseph. Blush then, O ashes, that darest to be proud! God humbles Himself, and dost thou raise thyself up? God submits Himself unto men, and dost thou lord it over thy fellow-creatures and prefer thyself to thy Creator? Would that God, if ever I should nourish such an inclination, would deign to reply to me as He once reproached His apostle: "Get thee behind me, Satan, for thou savorest not the things which be of God." For as often as I desire to raise myself above my God, and then most truly I do not savor the things which are of God; for of Him it was said: "He was subject unto them." If thou disdainest, O man, to imitate the example of man, at least it will not be unworthy of thee to follow in the steps of thy Creator. If thou are not able to follow Him wheresoever He goeth, at all events deign

to follow Him where He condescends to thy littleness.
That is, if you are not able to tread the lofty path of virginity, at least follow thy God by the perfectly safe way of humility, from the strict following of which not even virgins
can deviate, I say emphatically, if they would follow the
Lamb whithersoever He goeth. Without doubt even a sinner,
if he be humble, follows the Lamb; and a virgin, though she
be proud, follows Him also; but neither follows Him
whithersoever He goeth, because neither is the one able to
attain to the purity of the Lamb, who is without spot, and
the other does not know how to descend to the humility
and gentleness of Him who was silent, not before the
shearer but before the murderer. Certainly the sinner has
taken a surer path to follow His steps, in tracing the foot-
paths of humility, than the soul which prides itself upon its
virginity, since while the humble penitence of the one puri-
fies its uncleanness, the pride of the other defiles its purity.

But happy was Mary: to her neither humility was wanting, nor virginity. And what a virginity was that which
maternity did not violate, but honored. And what an
incomparable maternity which both virginity and humility
accompanied. Is there anything here which is not admirable, incomparable and unique? Will not any one hesitate
in deciding which is the more wonderful, the birth from a
virgin or virginity in a mother; the exalted rank of the Son,
or the great humility in exaltation; except that, without
doubt, the whole is to be preferred to any of its parts, and
that it is incomparably more excellent and more happy to
obtain the whole, than any part of it. And what wonder
is there if God, who is wonderful in His saints, has shown
Himself still more wonderful in His mother? Reverence
then, O you who are married, the purity of the flesh in corruptible flesh; you also, holy virgins, admire the mother-

hood in a virgin; and all ye who are men, imitate the humility of the mother of God. Holy angels, honor the mother of your King, ye who adore the Son of a virgin of our race, who is at once our King and yours, the Restorer of our race and the Founder of your state. To Him, among you so exalted, among us so humble, be given equally by you and by us, the reverence which is His due, the honor and glory for His great condescension for ever and ever. Amen.

SERMON No. 10.

OF THE CAUTION AND MODESTY BECOMING TO THE SOUL SEEKING THE WORD, AND OF THE PRAISE OF MODESTY.

I believe that nothing more will be expected of me upon the subject of the soul's reasons for seeking the Word, for I have already sufficiently stated them. Come, then, let us continue to expound what remains of the verse before us, as far only as relates to morals. Notice then, in the first place, the modesty of the bride. I know not whether there is any virtue which man can attain more beautiful than this. This before all I would desire to take, so to speak, in my hands and to gather it as a fair flower to present to those who are young among us. Not that those who are more advanced in it ought not to preserve it with every care, but because the grace of a tender modesty shines out more fairly and becomingly in those who are of a more tender age. What is there more amiable than a young man who is modest? How fair, and even splendid, does this jewel of virtues show on the countenance and in the life of the young! What a certain and unmistakeable mark it is of goodness of character, and of that which may be one day hoped for from them! It is, as it were, a rod of correction to such an one, which is constantly present before his mind, which chastens the affections and the thoughtless actions of an age which is wont to be artful and deceptive, and which restrains its light or insolent actions. What is there more contrary than it to coarse speech or to any kind of impurity? It is the sister of continence. There is no mark so plain and unmistakeable as this, of dove-like simplicity; and, therefore, it is the proof of innocence. It is a lamp which burns without ceasing in a modest soul, so that nothing impure or unbecoming can attempt to enter there without being instantly discovered. Thus it acts as the destroyer of vices and promotor of inward purity, the special glory of conscience, the guardian of good fame, the ornament of life, the seat and the first-fruits of virtue, the glory of nature and the token or ensign of everything honorable. What grace and beauty the very color in the cheeks called up by modesty imparts to the countenance!

Modesty is an excellence so natural to the soul that even those who do not fear to act wrongly are ashamed to let it be perceived, as the Lord Himself declares: "Every one that doeth evil hateth the light." And again St. Paul says: "They that sleep, sleep in the night; and they that be drunken are drunken in the night"; that is to say, the works of darkness which are deserving of darkness everlasting, shroud themselves in darkness of their own accord. It is, however, important to distinguish here between the modesty of men who are not ashamed to do such actions, but blush to have them discovered, and, therefore, conceal them, and that of the bride, who does not merely conceal them, but rejects them absolutely and drives them away. Thus the wise man declares: "There is a shame which bringeth sin: and there is a shame which is glory and grace." The bride seeks the Word; seeks Him at night, and on her couch, but modestly and timidly; and this modesty is glorious, not sinful. She seeks to find Him for the purifying of her conscience, for the obtaining of the testimony, that she may say: "Our glory is this, the testimony of our conscience. By night on my bed I sought Him whom I loveth." Her modesty, if you notice, is indicated to you both by the place and the time. What is there so congenial to a modest man as secrecy? Now the night and the couch ensure that her prayer is secret. And, in fact, we are bidden, when we desire to pray, to enter into our bedchamber, no doubt for the sake of secrecy. That is indeed to be done as a measure of precaution, lest if we pray in the sight of men human praise may hinder the effect of our prayer and deprive us of its fruit. But we learn from it also a lesson of modesty; for what course is so appropriate to modesty as to avoid even the praises which are due to it and to fly from vainglory? It is then clear that the Son, who is the teacher and pattern of modesty, has expressly bidden us to seek for secrecy in our prayers so as to promote modesty. What can be so unbecoming, especially in a young man, as an ostentation of sanctity? It is to be borne in mind also that at that age it is particularly needful to make a beginning of religious obedience, according to the saying of Jeremiah: "It is good for a man that he bear the yoke in his youth." The prayer which you are about to offer will be well recommended if you cause it to be preceded by modesty, saying: "I am very young and despised: but I forget not Thy justifications."

It is needful that he who desires to offer acceptable prayer should observe not only the right place, but also the right time to do so. A time of leisure is the fittest and most convenient, and especially during the deep silence which night brings; for then prayer arises most freely and is most pure.

"Arise," says a prophet, "cry out in the night; in the beginning of the watches pour out thine heart like water before the face of the Lord. How securely during the night does prayer arise to heaven, unwitnessed save by God alone, and by the holy angel, who receives that prayer to present it before the altar of heaven. How acceptable and clear it is being rendered translucent by humility and modesty! How serene and peaceful, since it is troubled by no sound or interruption! And, lastly, how pure and sincere, as being free from the soiling dust of earthly care, or deflected by the praise and flattery of human witnesses! For these reasons it was that the bride, who is modest as she is prudent, sought the silence of the night and the retirement of her chamber to pray, that is, to occupy herself in seeking the Word. For these two objects are one. Otherwise you do not pray aright, if in prayer you seek some other object than the Word, or seek it otherwise than on account of the Word, since in Him are all things that you ought to seek. In him are the remedies for the wounds of your soul, in Him the help for necessities, supplies for all defects, abundance for the soul's progress in holiness, and, in a word, all things that man ought to have or to desire, all things that he needs of things that are good for him. It is, then, wholly without cause that anything but the Word is asked of Him in prayer, for He Himself is all things. For, although we sometimes seem to ask those temporal good things of which we have need, if it is for the sake of the Word that we ask them (as indeed it is fit and right we should do), it is not properly those good things themselves for which we are making petition, but for Him on whose account and for whose service we are asking them. Those whose rule of conduct it is to make use of all things so as to endeavor to deserve well of the Word, know the truth of what I say.

We shall not regret examining still farther the mysteries indicated by this mention of the bed and of the night, to see if there be some spiritual truth concealed in it, which will be for our benefit to discover. If, for example, by the bed we understand the weakness of our human nature, and by the night its ignorance, then we shall be thus taught that it is not without good cause that the bride seeks with such touching and painful earnestness the Word, who is the Power of God and the Wisdom of God, that she may be fortified by His presence against each of these evils, which are to be attributed to the fault of origin. What can be more fitting than that power should be opposed to weakness and wisdom to ignorance? And that no doubt may linger in the hearts of the simple regarding this interpretation, let them hear what is said in a Psalm: "The Lord will strengthen him upon the bed of languishing; Thou wilt make all his bed in his sickness." This is as relates to the bed. And as to the night of ignorance, what can be plainer than the statement in another Psalm: "They know not, neither will they understand; they walk on in darkness." Which expresses with preciseness that state of ignorance into which the whole human race are born. It was this, as I think, that the blessed Apostle St. Paul both confesses that he was born and glories that he has been delivered from it, saying: "Who hath delivered us from the power of darkness?" And on this account he says also: "We are not children of the night, nor of darkness"; and also he says to all those who are elect: "Walk as children of light."

SERMON No. 11.

_____

HE SHALL BE GREAT, AND SHALL BE CALLED THE SON OF THE HIGHEST.

There is no doubt that whatever we say to the praise of

the mother we say also to that of the Son: and again, when we honor the Son, we do not detract from the glory of the mother. For, if according to Solomon, "A wise son is the glory of his father," how much more glorious is rendered the mother of Him who is wisdom itself!

But why do I venture upon the praises of one, whom the prophets extol as praiseworthy, whom an angel distinguishes, and with whom the evangelist fills his page? I do not, then praise, because I do not dare to do so: I am content to repeat with reverence what the Holy Spirit has explained by the mouth of the evangelist. He goes on to say: "And the Lord God shall give to Him the throne of His Father David." These are the words of the angel to the virgin concerning the Son promised to her: and who, he assures her, shall possess the kingdom of David, no one doubts. But how, I ask, did God give to Him the throne of David, His ancestor, seeing that He did not reign in Jerusalem, that when the crowd desired to make Him King, He did not yield to their wishes, and that, before Pilate, He protested: "My kingdom is not of this world?" And, after all, what great matter was it to promise to Him who sits throned upon the cherubim, whom the prophet saw seated upon a throne high and lifted up, that He should sit upon the throne of David, His father? But we know that here another Jerusalem is signified, much more noble and rich than that city which is now, and in which David once reigned. That therefore I suppose to be meant here, according to the habitual usage of the sacred writers, who constantly put the sign of the thing signified. Then God truly gave to Him the throne of His Father David, when He set His King upon His holy hill of Sion. But here the prophet seems to have indicated more distinctly of what kingdom he had spoken, in saying not in Sion, but upon

Sion. Therefore perhaps the word upon was used, because David indeed reigned in Sion; but His realm is over Sion, of whom it was said to David: Of the fruit of thy body will I set upon thy seat; and of whom it was said by another prophet: Upon the throne of David and upon his kingdom he shall sit. Now do you see why you find this word upon everywhere? Upon Sion, upon the throne, upon the seat, upon the kingdom. The Lord God will then give to Him the throne of David his Father, not a typical, but a real one; but eternal and heavenly, not temporal and earthly. And that is called, as it is here, the throne of David, because that upon which David sat in this world was a type of that eternal and heavenly one.

"And He shall reign over the House of Jacob forever; and His Kingdom shall have no end." Here also, if we take the word of the temporal House of Jacob, how can He reign forever in it, since it does not endure forever? We must then look for another house of Jacob, which shall endure forever, in which He shall reign with a never-ending dominion. And did not that (former) house of Jacob in its fury deny Him, and in its foolishness repudiate Him, before Pilate, when that Governor said to them: "Shall I crucify your King?" and did not they reply with one voice, "We have no king but Caesar." Inquire then of the apostle, and he will enable you to distinguish between him who is a Jew in secret, from him who is one openly; the circumcision in the spirit from that which is only in the flesh; those who are sons of the faith of Abraham, from those who are his sons only according to the flesh. For they are not all Israel, who are of Israel; neither, because they are the seed of Abraham, are they all children. Apply the same principle then and say: Not all who are of the blood of Jacob, are to be reckoned as of the house of Jacob.

Jacob himself is he who was called Israel. Only those then who shall be found perfect in the faith of Jacob shall be counted as of his house; or, rather, it is only those who are truly of the spiritual and everlasting house of Jacob over whom the Lord Jesus shall reign eternally. Who is there of us who, according to this meaning of the word Jacob, will cast out of his heart the devil, will struggle with his vices and concupiscences, so that sin may not reign in his mortal body, but, that on the contrary, Jesus shall reign in him now through grace, and through eternity in glory? Happy those in whom Jesus shall forever reign, for they shall reign at the same time with Him; and His Kingdom shall have no end. O how glorious is that kingdom in which Kings are gathered to praise and glorify Him who, above all others, is King of kings and Lord of lords; in the glorious beholding of whom the righteous shall shine forth in the kingdom of their Father. Oh! if the blessed Jesus would deign to remember me, a sinner, when He shall come into his Kingdom! O! if He, in that day when He shall deliver up the Kingdom to God and His Father, if He would visit me with His salvation, that I may see the felicity of His chosen ones, and rejoice in the joy of His people, that I, too, may praise Him with His inheritance! But come, Lord Jesus, even now take away the offences out of Thy Kingdom, that is, my soul; so that Thou mayest reign in it, as it is Thy right to do. For avarice has come and claimed a throne in me; boastfulness seeks to rule over me; pride desires to be my lord; luxury says I will reign; ambition, detraction, envy and anger strive within me, whose I shall be. As for me, I resist them as far as I am able and struggle against them to the best of my power. I call upon Jesus, my Lord; I defend myself for Him, because I feel that His is the right over me. I hold to Him as my Lord and my God, and I say: I have no king but Jesus. Come, then, O Lord, scatter them in Thy strength, and do Thou rule over me, for Thou art my Lord and my God, who art the salvation of Jacob.

Then said Mary to the angel, "How shall this be, seeing I know not a man?" First she prudently held her peace while she pondered in doubt of what nature that salutation was, preferring humbly not to reply than to speak rashly of what she knew was not. But having well reflected and being reassured (for while the angel addressed her outwardly God influenced her inwardly), and thus strengthened, faith having put fear to flight and joy diffidence she asked of the angel: "How shall this be?" She did not doubt of the fact, but she inquires respecting the manner and the order in which it would take place, not whether it should do so, but in what way. It is as if she had said: "As my Lord, who is the witness of my conscience, is aware of the vow of His servant not to know a man, by what means and in what order will it please Him that this shall take place? If it shall be needful that I should break by vow in order to become the mother of such a Son, though I rejoice for the Son, yet I grieve for the means proposed, yet His will be done. But if as a virgin I may conceive and bring forth a son, which will not be impossible for Him if He shall so please, then I know in truth that He has had respect unto the lowliness of His servant." 'And the angel answered her: "The Holy Ghost shall come upon thee and the power of the Highest shall overshadow thee." She was just now said to be full of grace, and now in what way is it said the Holy Ghost shall come upon thee? How could she be filled with grace and yet not have the Holy Spirit who is the bestower of graces? If, on the contrary, she already had the Holy Spirit, how could the angel promise that the Holy Spirit should come upon her, as it were, anew? Perhaps it was on this account that it was not said simply, "He shall come," but "He shall come upon," because He was indeed already in her through much grace, but is now announced to superabound (supervene) because of the fullness of more abundant grace, which He was about to pour upon her? But how could she receive more grace, being already filled? If, on the contrary, she was able to receive more, how can she be understood to have been previously filled? Could it be that formerly grace filled her mind, but is now to sanctify her womb for its appointed function, inasmuch as the fullness of the Divinity which was in her previously, as in many of the Saints, dwelt in her spiritually, but is now about to dwell in her corporeally, as it had done in none of the Saints?

He continues then: "And the power of the Highest shall overshadow thee." He who is able to comprehend the meaning of this, let him do so. For who, she alone being excepted who had the immense happiness of knowing by her own experience what is signified, is capable of understanding, or even of forming an idea, how that brightness inaccessible was poured into the chaste womb of the virgin, and how the latter was able to endure the approach of the inacessible when the Spirit vivified instantaneously a minute portion of the same body, of which He overshadowed the whole? And perhaps because of this chiefly it was said shall overshadow thee, because the matter was altogether a mystery, which the Holy Trinity willed to bring about alone and with Mary alone, and which was given to her alone to know, to whom alone it was given to be experienced. Let then the words, "The Holy Ghost shall come upon thee," be thus explained, shall render thee fruitful by His power, and the power of the Highest shall over-

shadow thee as thus: the manner in which thou shalt conceive of the Holy Ghost, Christ, the power of God and the
wisdom of God, shall be so closely veiled and so deeply hidden in the impenetrable shadow of His secret counsels that
the mystery shall be known only to Himself and thee.   It
is as if the angel had replied to the virgin: "Why dost thou
question me upon a matter which thou shalt soon thyself
have experience of? Thou shalt indeed know it, and that
happily, but He who brings about the mystery shall be the
teacher to bring it to thy knowledge.   I have been sent
only to announce to thee thy virginal conception, not to
bring it about.   It can be taught only by Him who effects
it; none but she in whom it shall be brought about can
comprehend it.   Therefore, also, that Holy Thing which
shall be born of thee shall be called the Son of God."   That
is to say, since thou shalt conceive, not of man, but of the
Holy Spirit, but thou shalt conceive the very Power of the
Highest, that is, the Son of God; therefore, that Holy
Thing which shall be born of thee shall be called the Son of
God.   That is to say, not only He who is in the Bosom of
the Father, coming thence into thy womb, shall   overshadow thee, but He shall also, taking of thy substance,
unite it with Himself, and from this He shall be then called
Son of God.   Even as it is He who was begotten by the
Father before all worlds and therefore called Son of God,
so He shall hereafter be called thy Son.   For thus He who
was born of the Father is thy Son, and His son shall be
born of thee, yet not that there are two Sons, but one Son.
And although one be of thee, another of Him, yet shall
there not be to each His own, but one Son, both of the one
and of the other.

Notice, I pray you, how reverently the angel spoke it,
that Holy Thing which shall be born of thee.   Why does he

say simply that Holy Thing without adding more? I believe because there was no name by which he could properly and worthily designate that noble, exalted and reverend being to be formed by the uniting of the soul and the body drawn from the most pure flesh of the virgin, with the only Begotten Son of the Father. If he had said "the holy body," "the holy man" or "the holy child," or any expression of that kind, he would seem to have spoken inadequately. Therefore, no doubt, he used the indefinite expression, that Holy Thing, because whatever were the fruit born of the virgin it was without doubt holy and even uniquely so, both through the sanctification by the Spirit and through its assumption by the Word.

Then the angel added: "Behold, thy cousin Elizabeth, she hath also conceived a son in her old age!" Why was it necessary to announce to the virgin that this barren woman had also conceived a son? Was it perhaps in order to convince, by the news of a miracle so recent, the virgin, whom he saw to be still doubtful and incredulous? By no means. For we read that Zacharias was punished for such incredulity by this very angel, but we do not read that Mary was in any respect blamed. On the contrary, we know that her faith was praised by Elizabeth speaking prophetically: "Blessed is she that believed, for there shall be a performance of those things which were told her from the Lord." But the reason that the angel made known to Mary the conception of her cousin, hitherto barren, was to complete her joy by adding miracle to miracle. Moreover, it was needful that she who was soon about to conceive the Son of the Father's affection with the joy of the Holy Spirit, should, in the first place, be animated by no slight degree of her love and joy, since it was only a heart as full of gladness as of perfect devotedness that was capable of receiving the fullness of happiness and joy. Or it may be that the conception of Elizabeth was announced to Mary because it was fitting that a fact which was soon to be known to all should be declared beforehand to the virgin by an angel, rather than made known to her by the mouth of men and the mother of God appear to be a stranger to the counsels of her Son, if she had remained in ignorance of the events which were taking place so near her upon earth. Or, more probably, the conception of Elizabeth was announced to Mary in order that, being made aware already of the coming of the Saviour and now of that of His forerunner, and knowing the order and the time of each, she would better be able at a later period to declare the truth to the sacred writers and the preachers of the Gospel, as having been fully instructed from on high in all these mysteries from the very beginning. Finally, it is possible that it was made known so that Mary, on learning that a relative already advanced in age was pregnant, she who was still young should hasten as a master of doubtful attentions to visit her, and thus occasion be given to that infant Prophet to pay to his Lord, still younger than he, the first fruit of his duty; and that while the two mothers met, the consciousness felt by the children of each other's presence, should add to one miracle another still more marvelous.

But take care not to suppose that all these events so wonderful, which you hear foretell by the angels, are to be brought to pass by him. If you inquire by whom listen to the angel himself. For with God, he says, nothing shall be impossible. As if he had said "all these things that I promise you so faithfully, rest not upon my power, but upon His by whom I have been sent." And with Him nothing shall be impossible, for what can be impossible to Him who has done all things by his Word? And I am

struck by this in the angel's speech that he markedly says
not "no action" but "no word" is impossible with God.

Does he employ this phrase in order to enable us to
understand that while men are easily able to say all that
they please, but by no means able to do what they please,
God is able as easily and with incomparably greater ease to
carry out in action whatsoever they are able to express in
words? I will explain myself. If it were as easy for men
to do what they wished as to say it, then to them also no
word would be impossible. But now, according to a saying as ancient as well-known, "there is a great difference
between saying and doing," and that is so with men, but
not with God, for with God alone it is the same thing to do
what He shall say, and to express what He wills; most
truly then "no word" shall be impossible with God. For
example, the prophets were able to foresee and foretell that
a sterile virgin should conceive and bring forth, but were
they able to cause her to do so? But God, who gave them
the power to foresee as easily as He was able to predict what
He pleased through them, just so easily was able now when
it pleased Him, to fulfill what He had caused to be predicted. And in fact with God, neither does the word differ
from the intention, because He is truth; nor the act from
the word, because He is power; nor is the manner unsuitable to the act, because He is wisdom. Thus it is that with
God no word shall be impossible.

You have heard, O! virgin, the announcement of that
which is about to take place and the manner in which it
will take place. In each there is matter for wonder and rejoicing. Rejoice, then, daughter of Sion, daughter of Jerusalem. And since you have heard news of gladness and
joy, let us, too, hear from you the glad response for which
we wait, so that the bones which have been humbled by sor-

row may leap for joy. You have heard, I say, the fact and have believed; believe also in the manner in which it shall be accomplished. By the operation of the Holy Spirit, not of a man, shalt thou conceive and bear a Son, and the angel waits only for the reply to return to God who sent him. We, too, O! Lady, we who are weighed down by the sentence of condemnation, wait for the word of pity. The price of our salvation is offered to you. Soon shall we be freed, if you consent (to give yourself to the Divine plan). Alas! we, who all are the creatures of the Eternal Word of God, are perishing; we are to be restored by your brief response and recalled to life. Uphappy Adam, with his miserable progeny, exiled from Paradise, Abraham also and David, entreat this, O! pious virgin, of you. Others join in the entreaty, holy Fathers and ancestors of your own, who also dwell in the valley of the shadow of death. The whole world, prostrate at your knees, waits for your consent, and not without reason, since upon your lips hangs the consolation of the unhappy, the redemption of the captives, the freedom of the condemned, in fine, the safety of the children of Adam, of the whole human race. Reply quickly, O! virgin; give the word which the earth, hell and the heavens themselves wait for us. He, the King and Lord of all things, waits for the word of your consent, by means of which He has proposed to save the world, inasmuch as He has approved of your graces. He whom in silence you have pleased, you will please still more by speech, since He cries to you from heaven: "O! fairest among women, let me hear thy voice." If then thou doest this He will cause thee to see our salvation. Is not this what you desire, what you long for, what you sigh for in daily and nightly prayers? What then? Are you she to whom this was promised, or do we look for another? On the contrary, it is you yourself and not another. You, I say, are that promised, expected and desired one, from whom your Holy ancestor Jacob, already drawing near to death, hoped for everlasting life, saying: "I wait for Thy salvation, O! Lord." In whom, in short, and by means of whom, our God and King Himself, purposed before time began to bring about a salvation in the midst of the earth. Why do you hope for that time from another woman which is offered to you? Why do you expect that to be done by means of another woman which will be speedily made manifest by means of you, provided you reply and yield your assent? Reply, then, quickly to the angel, or rather by the angel to the Lord. Speak a word and receive the Word. Utter but your transitory word and conceive the Word Divine and Eternal. Why do you fear and delay? Believe, consent and conceive. Let humility become bold, let your timidity have confidence. In no wise is it needful even now that virginal simplicity should forget prudence. In this matter alone, O! prudent virgin, you need not fear presumption, for, although reserve is prized by its silence, yet now charity should speak. Open, blessed virgin, your heart to confidence, your lips to consent, your bosom to its Creator. Behold the desire of all nations knocking at its door. If He should pass away while you are delaying and you should begin again with grief to seek Him whom your soul loveth! Arise, then, hasten and open to Him. Rise by faith, hasten by devotion, open by giving consent.

Behold! she said, the handmaid of the Lord, be it unto me according to Thy Word. The virtue of humility is always found closely associated with Divine grace, for God resisteth the proud, but giveth grace unto the humble. She replies then with humility that the dwelling of grace may be prepared. Behold! she says, the handmaid of the Lord.

How sublime is this humility, which is incapable of yielding to the weight of honors, or of being rendered proud by them? The Mother of God is chosen, and she declares herself His handmaid. It is in truth a mark of no ordinary humility, that even when so great an honor is done to her she does not forget to be humble. It is no great thing to be humble when in a low condition, but humility in one that is honored is a great and rare virtue. If, for my sins or for those of others, God should permit that the Church, deceived by my pretensions, should elevate such a miserable and humble man as I to any, even the most ordinary honor, should not I immediately, forgetful of what I am, begin to think myself such an one as men (who do not see the heart) imagine me to be? I should believe in the public opinion, not regarding the testimony of my conscience, not estimating honor by virtues, but virtue by honors. I should believe myself to be the more holy, the higher was the position I occupied. You may frequently see in the church men sprung from the lower ranks who have attained to the higher, and from being poor have become rich, beginning to swell with pride, forgetting their low extraction, being ashamed of their family and disdaining their parents, because they are in humble condition. You may see also wealthy men attaining rapidly to ecclesiastical honors, and then at once regarding themselves as men of great holiness, though they have changed their clothes only and not their minds, and persuading themselves that they are worthy of a dignity to which they have attained by solicitation, and that which they owe (if I dare say so) to their wealth, they ascribe to their merits. I do not speak of those whom ambition blinds, and for whom even honor is a matter of pride.

But I see (much to my regret) some who, after having despised and renounced the pomp of this world in the

school of humility, habituating themselves still more to
pride, and under the wings of a Master who is meek and
humble in heart, become more and more insolent and im-
patient in the cloister than they had been in the world.
And, which is a thing still more perverse, there are very
many who, while in their own homes, they would have had
to bear contempt, cannot endure to do so in the house of
God. They would not have been able to obtain honors in
the world, where all desire to possess them, and yet they
expect to be loaded with honors where all have made profession to despise them. I see others (and it is a thing not
to be seen without grief), after having enrolled themselves
in the army of Christ, entangling themselves anew in the
affairs of the world and plunging again into worldly objects, with earnest zeal they build up walls (muros), but
neglect to build up their own characters (mores), under
pretext of the general good, they sell their words to the
rich and their salutations to matrons. But in spite of the
formal order of their Sovereign, they cast covetous eyes
on the goods of others, and do not shrink from lawsuits to
maintain their own rights, not listening to the proclamation
made by the apostle as a herald bidden by the King. "This
is the very fault among you that ye go to law one with
another. Why do ye not rather endure wrong?" Is it so
that they have crucified themselves to the world and that
the world is crucified to them, that those who before had
scarcely been known in their own town or village, are now
seen traversing provinces, frequenting courts, cultivating
a knowledge of kings and the friendship of the great?
What shall I say of their religious habit itself? In it they
require not so much warmth as color, and they have more
care of the cleanness of their vestment than the culture of
their virtues. I am ashamed to say it, but mere women are

surpassed in their study of dress by monks when costliness
in clothing is studied more than utility. At length every
appearance of the religious state is laid aside, and the soldiers of Christ strive to be adorned, not to be armed. Even
when they are preparing for the struggle and ought to oppose to the powers of the air the ensign of poverty (which
those adversaries greatly fear) they rather prefer to present themselves in carefully studied dress, the sign of peace,
and thus willingly to give themselves unarmed and without
the striking of a blow, to their enemies. All these evils
only come when renouncing those sentiments of humility
which have caused us to quit the world, and finding ourselves thus drawn back to the unprofitable tastes and desires for worldly things, like dogs returning to their vomit.

Whoever we are who find inclinations in ourselves let us
mark well what was the reply of her who was chosen to be
the mother of God, but who did not forget humility. Behold! she said, the handmaid of the Lord; let it be to me
according to Thy Word. Let it be to me is the expression
of a desire, not the indication of a doubt. Even those
words, "according to Thy Word," are to be understood
more as the feeling of one wishing for and desiring, than as
the expression of the doubt of one uncertain. We may
understand let it be to me as words of prayer. And certainly no one prays for anything unless he believes that it
exists and hopes to obtain it. But God wills that what He
has promised should be asked of Him in prayer. And perhaps, therefore, He in the first place promises many things
which He has resolved to give us, that our devotion may
be excited by the promise, and that thus our earnest prayer
may merit what He had been disposed to bestow upon us
freely. This it was that the prudent virgin understood

when she joined the merit of her prayer with the prevenient gift of the promise freely bestowed upon her, saying, let it be to me according to Thy Word. Let it be to me according to Thy Word concerning the Word. Let the Word which was in the beginning with God become flesh from my flesh acording to Thy Word.

Let the Word, I pray, be to me not as a word spoken only to pass away, but conceived and clothed in flesh, not in air, that He may remain with us. Let Him be, not only to be heard with the ears, but to be seen with the eyes, touched with the hands and borne on the shoulders. Let the Word be to me not as a word written and silent, but incarnate and living; that is, not traced with dead signs upon dead parchments, but livingly impressed in human form upon my chaste womb; nor by the tracing of a pen of lifeless reed, but by the operation of the Holy Spirit. Finally, let it thus be to me, as was never done to anyone before me, nor after me shall be done. God hath indeed formerly spoken in divers manners to the fathers by the prophets, and the Word of God is recorded to have been produced in the ear of some, in the mouth of others, and in others again by the hand; but I pray that the Word of God may be formed in my womb according to Thy Word. I desire that He may be formed, not as the Word in preaching, not as a sign in figures, or as a vision in dreams, but silently inspired, personally incarnated, found in the body of my body. Let the Word therefore deign to do in me and for me what He needed not to do and could not do for Himself, according to Thy Word. Let it be done, indeed, generally for the sake of the whole world, but specially let it be done unto me, according to Thy Word.

SERMON No. 12.

Text: "On the words of the Martyrology 'Jesus Christ the Son of God, was born in Bethlehem of Judea.'"

A voice of joy has sounded upon our earth, of salvation and of gladness in the dwellings of sinners. Good tidings have been heard, a word of consolation, a message of great joy, worthy of all acceptation. Sing praise, all ye mountains, and all ye trees of the woods applaud before the Lord, for He comes. Hear, O heaven, and give ear, O earth, wonder and praise, O all creation, but thou especially, O man: "Jesus Christ, the Son of God, is born in Bethlehem of Judea." What man is there of heart so stony-hard that he is not softened at these words? What sweeter news could be anounced to us, or what could be welcomed more? What such news did the world ever hear or receive? Jesus Christ, the Son of God, is born in Bethlehem of Judea. A brief phrase, indeed, to express the Word in His humility, but how full it is of heavenly sweetness. The grateful soul labors and strives to express more completely that sweetfulness of delight, and finds no words to do so; and such is the worth of these few words that if only one iota be changed, the meaning of the whole message is instantly diminished. O Birth of inviolate sanctity, honorable to the whole world, precious to men for the greatness of the benefit which it brings, which even angels desire to look into for the depth of its sacred mystery and the newness of its singular excellence, since before it there was nothing like unto it, nor after it shall be such. O Birth alone with sorrow, or shame, or corruption, which did not open but consecrated the sanctuary of a virginal womb! Nativity that was above nature, but on behalf of

CHRISTMAS MORNING.

nature, surpassing it by the excellence of its miracle, but repairing it by the mysterious virtue which was in it. My brethren, who can narrate such a Birth as this? An angel announces it, the power of the Highest overshadows it, the Holy Spirit intervenes, a virgin believes, conceives by faith, brings forth, yet remains virgin. Who does not wonder? The Son of the Highest, God of God, begotten before the worlds, is born in time; the Word born as an infant, who can wonder sufficiently?

Nor is that nativity unnecessary, nor that condescension of the Divine Majesty unfruitful. Jesus Christ, the Son of God, is born in Bethlehem of Judea. Ye who are in the dust, rise up and render praise to God. Behold, the Lord comes with salvation! With anointing He comes and with glory. For Jesus comes not without salvation, the Christ not without anointing, nor the Son of God without glory, and indeed He Himself is salvation, anointing and glory, as it is written, "A wise son is the glory of his father." Happy the soul, which, having tasted the fruit of His salvation, is drawn by and runs willingly after the perfume of His sweetness, that it may behold His glory, the glory as of the Only Begotten of the Father. Breathe more freely, ye lost ones, for Jesus cometh to seek and to save that which was lost. Return to health, ye who were stricken with death. Christ comes to heal with the balm of His mercy those who are of contrite heart. Rejoice and exult, ye, whosoever ye are, who long for high destinies, the Son of God comes down to you to make you co-heirs of His Kingdom. So heal me, I beseech Thee, O Lord, and I shall be healed; save me and I shall be saved; glorify me and I shall become glorious. "Bless the Lord, O my soul, and all that is within me, bless His holy name, who forgiveth all mine iniquities, who healeth all my diseases, who crowneth me with loving kindness and tender mercies!"

These three reflections, dearly beloved, occur to me, as suggested by the news that Jesus Christ, the Son of God, is born upon the earth. Wherefore do we call His name Jesus, unless that He shall save His people from their sins, or why has He willed to be named Christ, the Anointed One, except because He shall cause the yoke to be destroyed because of the anointing? Wherefore has the Son of God been made man but that He may make men the sons of God? But, then, who shall resist his will? It is Jesus who justifies us, who can condemn us. It is Christ who makes us whole, who could possibly wound us, the Son of God who exalts us and who can humiliate us.

It is the birthday of Jesus. Let each one rejoice whom his conscience condemns as a sinner and deserving eternal damnation, for the love of Jesus overpasses the sins of every offender, whatever be their number or their weight. It is the birthday of Christ; let each who is struggling with his former vices rejoice and be glad, for no disease of the soul, however inveterate it be, can continue in presence of the unction which Christ imparts. It is the birthday of the Son of God; let all those who aspire to high destinies rejoice because the great Rewarder has come. My brethren, here is the Heir of the Father; come let us welcome Him loyally, and His inheritance shall be ours, for He who has given His own Son for us how shall He not with Him freely give us all things? Let no one doubt, let no one hesitate; we have a sure testimony. The Word of God was made Flesh, and dwelt among us. The Only Begotten Son of God has willed to have brethren, that He might be the Firstborn among many brethren. He did not scruple at the fragility and weakness of humanity, before he became the

Brother of Men, He became the Son of Man, He became Man. If man regards this as impossible let him see and he will believe.

Jesus Christ was born in Bethlehem of Judea. Notice the condescension of this. Not in Jerusalem the royal city, but in Bethlehem, which is the least among the thousands of Juda. O Bethlehem, who are small, but rendered great by the Lord! He, who though so great, has deigned to be made small in thee, has rendered thee great. Rejoice then, Bethlehem, and let the festive Alleluia be sung along all thy ways. What city in the world, on learning this great news, will not envy thee that stable, and the glory of that manger? In the whole world thy name is already famous, and all generations call thee blessed. Everywhere glorious things are spoken of thee, O city of God; everywhere the words are chanted: "A Man was born in her, and the Most High has established her." Everywhere, I say, it is proclaimed and preached that Jesus Christ, the Son of God, is born in Bethlehem of Judea. Nor is it useless to add the word "Judea," since it reminds us of the promise made unto the fathers. The sceptre shall not depart from Judah, nor a lawgiver from between his feet, until He who is to be sent forth and who is the Desire of the nations, shall come. For salvation is of the Jews, but a salvation for the whole earth. Judah, says the Patriarch, thy brethren shall praise thee and thy hands shall be upon the necks of thy enemies, and the rest, which we never see accomplished in that Judah, but which is fulfilled in Christ. For He is the Lion of the tribe of Judah, of whom it is added: "Judah is a Lion's whelp; unto the prey, my son, thou hast gone up." That great spoiler, who before he knew how to call by name his father and his mother, takes away the spoil of Samaria, is no other than Christ. Christ is that spoiler, who, ascending up on high, led captivity captive, but as for Himself He has taken from none, but rather has given gifts unto men. These words then in "Bethlehem of Judah" recall to my mind these and similar prophecies which are fulfilled in Christ, of whom indeed they were spoken long before, nor do they leave it doubtful that some good thing should come out of Bethlehem.

But now as to what immediately concerns us we learn from this, in what manner He, who willed to be born at Bethlehem, desires to be received by us. The King of glory might no doubt have thought that it became Him to seek out lofty places, where He might be received with glory, but it was not for such an end that He had descended from His royal throne. In His left hand are riches and glory, and in His right length of days. He possessed all things in abundance in the heavens, but poverty was not found there. Moreover, this abounded and superabounded on the earth, and man knew not its value. This therefore the Son of God loved, and came down that He might choose it for Himself and make it precious in our eyes also by the esteem in which He held it. Deck thy bridal couch, O Sion, but with humility, with poverty. In these marks of poverty He takes delight, and according to the testimony of Mary, these are the silken robes in which it pleases Him to be wrapped. Therefore sacrifice to your God the abominations of the Egyptians.

Consider finally that He is born in Bethlehem of Judea, and strive to become yourself, in a sense, another Bethlehem, that He may condescend to be received also in thee. Bethlehem signifies the house of Bread; Judah signifies confession.

If, then, you fill your soul with the bread of the Divine Word and receive with all the faith of which you are capable, however unworthily that Bread, which came down from heaven and giveth life into the world, the Body, that is, of the Lord Jesus, that new body of the Resurrection shall sustain and renew your former natural body and enable it to contain the new wine (of everlasting life), and if you live by faith you need not lament because you have forgotten to eat your bread; you have become a Bethlehem, truly worthy to receive the Lord, if only you have not failed in confession. Let Judea then be your sanctification. Put upon you an honorable confession, which is the vestment in which the ministers of Christ are most acceptable to Him. Lastly, the apostle briefly commends to you both the one and the other in these words: "With the heart man believeth unto righteousness, and with the mouth confession is made into salvation." Righteousness in the heart is as bread in the dwelling. For righteousness is bread; as it is said, blessed are they that hunger and thirst after righteousness, for they shall be filled. Let then righteousness be in your heart, the righteousness which is of faith, for this alone has glory before God, and by your mouth let confession be made unto salvation. Then you may safely receive Him who is born in Bethlehem of Judea, Jesus Christ, the Son of God.

SERMON No. 13.

Text: "O Judah and Jerusalem fear not; tomorrow ye shall go forth, and the Lord will be with you."

I am addressing those who are truly Jews, not in the letter, but in the spirit: the seed of Abraham, which is multiplied according to the promise that we read was made to him. For not the children of the flesh, but the children of the promise are counted for the seed. Similarly I do not speak here of that Jerusalem which killed the prophets. How, in fact, could I be able to console her, over whom the Lord wept, and which has been given over to destruction? But I speak of that new Jerusalem, which descends from heaven. Fear not, O Judah and Jerusalem! No; fear not at all, ye who are true confessors, who confess the Lord, not only with your mouth, but with your whole being; who are clad with that confession as with a robe; yes, your whole inward natures confess the Lord, whose very bones say: "Lord, who is like unto Thee," not like those who profess that they know God, but in works they deny Him. You confess Him truly, my brethren, if all your works are His works and confess Him. Let them confess Him in two ways, let them be clad, as it were, in a double robe of confession, that is, of your own sins, and of the praise of God. For then you shall be true Jews, confessors of Jehovah, if your whole lives confess that you are sinners, and deserving of the greatest punishments: and that God is supremely good, who foregoes the eternal penalties which you have deserved for these slight and transitory pains. For whosoever does not ardently desire penitence, seems to say by his actions that he has no need of it, and thus does not confess his fault; or that penitence is of no service to him, and thus does not confess the Divine goodness. Do you, then, be true Jews and a true Jerusalem, that you may fear nothing. For Jerusalem is the vision of peace; the vision of it, not the possession; on whose borders the Lord hath established peace: but not at the setting out, nor at the midway thither. If, then, you have not perfect peace, which indeed you are not able to have in this world, at least behold it, look forward to it, meditate upon it and desire it. Fix upon it the eyes of your mind, let your intention direct itself towards peace, do all your actions with a view to attain that peace

which passeth all understanding, and in all you do propose
to yourself no other end than to be reconciled with God and
have peace with Him.

It is to those who do this that I say: Fear not. Those I
console; and not those who have not known the way of
peace. For if to them it is said, "Tomorrow ye shall go
forth," that is not to console, but to threaten. In truth, only
those who behold peace, and know that if the earthly house
of their habitation were dissolved, they shall have another
of God's building—it is only such that desire to be dissolved and depart: not such as are turned towards folly and
delight in their chains. Of such as die in this disposition,
it cannot be said that they go forth into light and liberty,
but rather that they enter into darkness, into prison, into hell.
But to you it is said: "Fear not, tomorrow ye shall go
forth"; and there shall be no fear any longer in your borders. You have, it is true, numerous enemies; the flesh,
than which no enemy can be no nearer to you: the present
evil world which surrounds you on all sides; and, lastly, the
princes of darkness, who are ambushed in the air to beset
your road. Nevertheless, fear not, tomorrow ye shall go
forth; that is, in a short time: for tomorrow means in a
short time. Thus, also, the holy Jacob said: "In time to
come my righteousness shall answer for me." For there
are three epochs, and of these we read: "After two days
He will revive us, and the third day He will raise us up."
One is under Adam, another in Christ, the third with Christ.
Wherefore it is there added: "We shall know, and shall follow to come to the knowledge of the Lord, and as it is said
here, Tomorrow ye shall go forth and the Lord will be with
you." For these words are addressed to those, who have
divided their days, for whom the days in which they were
born have perished: that is, the day of Adam, the day of sin,

on which Jeremiah called down a malediction, saying:
"Cursed be the day on which I was born." All of us were,
in fact, born in that day; would that in all of us, too, it
might perish; that day of darkness and gloominess, of
storm and tempest, which Adam has brought about for us,
which is due to that enemy which said: "Your eyes shall be
opened."

But behold the day of a new redemption for us has
dawned, of the ancient plan of renewal, of an eternal felicity.
This is the day which the Lord hath made. Let us rejoice
and be glad in it, for tomorrow we shall go forth. And
from whence? From our sojourn in this state of existence,
from the prison house of this body, from the fetters of necessity, of restless inquiringness, of vanity, of pleasures which
entangle, in spite of ourselves, the feet of our desire. What
is there really in common between our spirit and earthly
things? Why does it not desire, and seek, and appreciate
spiritual things? O my soul, since thou art from above, what
hast thou to do with these lower subjects? Seek those things
which are above, where Christ sitteth at the right hand of
God. Set your affection on things above, not on things
upon the earth. But the corruptible body presseth down
the soul and the earthly tabernacle weigheth down the
mind, that museth upon many things. Many unhappy
necessities of the body hold us back. The wings of the soul
are clogged with carnal desire and delight, so that they cannot soar; and if even the mind is raised above the earth, it
speedily falls back again. Yet fear not, to-morrow, ye shall
come forth from this abyss of misery, of foul slime; for the
Lord, in order that He might draw you forth thence, has
Himself plunged into it; and ye shall come forth from a
state of mortality and from every corruption of sin. Spend
the day then in Chrst, that ye may walk as He walked;

for he that says that he abideth in Him ought himself also
so to walk, even as He walked. Fear not, then, for to-
morrow ye shall go forth, and so ye shall be ever with the
Lord. Perhaps those striking words and the Lord shall be
with you, are to be understood thus: that while we are in
the body we are able to be with the Lord, that is, in unity
of will with Him; but not He with us, in the sense that He
should be at one with our will. For we would wish to
be freed; we earnestly desire to be released and go forth,
but hitherto, for a certain cause, He delays to grant our
wish. But tomorrow we shall go forth, and the Lord shall
be with us, so that whatever we wish He will wish with us,
and His will and ours will be in complete accord.

Therefore, Judah and Jerusalem, fear not, if you are not
yet able to obtain the perfection which you desire; but let
the humility of confession of your imperfection supply what
is wanting in your daily life, since that imperfection is not
hidden from the eyes of God. If He has commanded that
His precepts should be diligently kept it is in order that,
seeing our constant imperfection and our inability to fulfill
the duty which we ought to do, we may fly to His mercy
and say: "Thy mercy is better than life, and that not being
able to appear clad in innocence or righteousness, we may
be at least covered with the robe of confession. For confession and beauty are in the sight of the Lord if only (as
we have said) it proceeds not from our lips only, but from
our whole nature. If all our bones say: "Lord, who is like
unto Thee, and that in the pure prospect of and desire of
reconciliation with God." For to such as feel thus is the
saying: "Fear not, O Juda and Jerusalem, tomorrow ye
shall go forth; that is to say, speedily your soul shall go
forth from your body; all its affections, all its desires, which
now, like so many bonds, hold it still fast to the things of

the world, shall be dissolved; it shall go forth from this clogging hindrance, and the Lord shall be with thee." Perhaps the time may seem to you very long, if you have regard only to yourself and not to those things which are in relation with you. For is not the whole world in such relation? The creation was made subject to vanity, and on the fall of man, whom the Lord had set over His house as its ruler, and the prince of His whole possession, the whole heritage was infected with Him. Thence are extremities of heat and cold in the atmosphere, the soil being cursed in the labors of Adam, and the subjection of all things to vanity.

Nor, indeed, will the heritage he re-established until the heirs of it return to their first state. Wherefore, according to the testimony of the apostle, it groaneth and travaileth in pain together until now. It is not to the eyes of this world alone, but to those of angels and of men (departed) that we are made a specticle. The righteous, saith in Psalmist, wait for me until Thou shalt restore me. And thus the martyrs, when they earnestly besought the day of judgment, not as being desirous of vengeance, but because they longed for the perfection of blessedness which they shall then obtain, received from God this response: "Endure yet for a little while until the number of your brethren be made up." Each of them, indeed, received a white robe, but they will not be vested in a second until we, too, shall be vested with them. We hold as pledges and hostages their very bodies, without which their glory cannot be consummated, nor will they receive those until the time when we shall receive ours with them. Wherefore the apostle says of the patriarchs and prophets: "God reserving some better thing for us, that without us they might not be perfected." O if we could comprehend with what earnest and eager desire they expect and await our coming! How anxiously they enquire about, and how willingly listen to, any good actions that we do.

Yet why do I speak of these, who have learned compassion by the sufferings they have themselves endured, when our coming is desired by the holy angels themselves? Is it not from such poor worms of the earth and from such dust that the walls of the heavenly Jerusalem are to be raised again? Have you any idea of the ardor with which the citizens of that heavenly country desire the rebuilding of the ruins of their city? With what solicitude do they await the coming of the living stones, who are to be built in together with them? How they pass to and fro between us and God, bearing to Him most faithfully our groans and complaints, and bringing back to us His grace with admirable zeal? Unquestionably they will not disdain to have us for companions, whose helpers they have already become. For are they not all ministering spirits sent forth to minister unto those who shall be heirs of salvation? Let us hasten, then, beloved, I entreat you, let us hasten, since the whole multitude of the heavenly host awaits us. We cause the angels to rejoice when we have turned to penitence. Let us come forward now and hasten to fill them with joy on our behalf. Woe to you, whoever you are, who art meditating a return to the mire and the vomit. Do you suppose that you will thus render favorable to you at the day of judgment those whom you wish to deprive of a joy so great and so much hoped for? They have been glad when we came to penitence, as over those whom they saw turning back from the very gates of hell. What will now be their affliction, if they see returning from the gates of ·Paradise and taking the backward road those who had already one foot within its threshold? For if our bodies are still below yet our hearts are already in heaven.

Hasten, then, my brethren, hasten; for not the angels alone, but the Creator of the angels awaits you. The marriage feast is prepared, but the house is not yet full of guests. Those who shall fill the places at the feast are still being waited for. The Father awaits you and desires your coming; not only because of the great love wherewith He loved you (wherefore also the only Begotten Son, who is in the Bosom of the Father, Himself declared The Father loveth you, but because of His Ownself, as He speaks by the prophet. Because of my Ownself I will do this, not because of you).

Who can doubt that the promise shall be fulfilled which He made to the Son, saying, "Ask of Me and I will give Thee the nations for Thy inheritance." And in another place: "Sit Thou on My Right Hand until I shall make Thine enemies Thy footstool." Now, all His enemies would not be subdued, as long as they shall continue to attack us who are His members. Nor will this promise be fulfilled until the last enemy shall be destroyed, which is death. For who knoweth not how greatly the Son longed for the fruit of His incarnation, and of the whole Life which He lived in the flesh; in short, the fruit of His Cross and Passion, the price of His Precious Blood? Will he not hereafter give over to God, the Father, the Kingdom which He has acquired? Will He not bring back to communion with Him His creatures for whose sake the Father sent Him into the world? The Holy Spirit also awaits us. For He is that charity and loving kindness in which we have been predestinated from all eternity; nor is it doubtful that He wills His predestination to be fulfilled.

Since then the wedding feast is prepared, and all the hosts of the heavenly court are waiting for and desiring our coming. Let us, my brethren, run our Christian course not as uncertainty; let us run with earnest desire and striving after virtue. To set out is to make progress. Let each of us say: "Look upon me and have mercy upon me, as Thou usest to do unto those who love Thy Name. Have mercy upon me, not as I have deserved, but as they have decreed." Let us say also: "Let Thy will be, as it is done in heaven"; or simply Thy will be done. For we know that it is written: "If God be for us who can be against us?" And again: "Who shall lay anything to the charge of God's elect?" It is not lawful for Me, He says, to do what I will with Mine own? Let these words be our consolation, my dear brethren, until we go forth from this world, and may the Lord be with us to the end. May He, in His great mercy, bring us to that blessed departure and that glorious tomorrow; may He, in that tomorrow which is near each of us, deign to visit us and to be near to help us, so that those who find themselves perhaps entangled and held back by some temptation, by His mercy who comes to preach deliverance to the captives, may be able in that tomorrow to go forth free; let us, in the joy of salvation, accept the crown of our new-born King, by His help, who, with the Father and the Holy Ghost, liveth and reigneth, God for ever and ever. Amen.

SERMON No. 14.

CONCERNING THE ERRORS OF HERETICS WITH RESPECT TO MARRIAGE, TO THE BAPTISM OF INFANTS, TO PURGATORY, TO PRAYERS FOR THE DEAD, AND TO THE INVOCATION OF THE SAINTS.

Text: "Take us the foxes, the little foxes, that spoil the vines."—Cant. II. 15.

With these foxes I am still busied. They are those who wander out of the path and lay waste the vineyard. They are not content with quitting the road of right, but turn the vineyard into a desert by their wicked falsehoods. It is not enough for them to be heretics; they must, as if to fill up the measure of their wrongdoings, be hypocrites also. These are they who come in sheep's clothing to strip the sheep and despoil the rams. Does it not seem to you that this is what they have done when, on the one hand, they rob the people of their faith, and, on the other, deprive the priests of their people? Who are these robbers? They are sheep in appearance, but foxes in cunning, and in their actions have the crulety of wolves. They are men who desire to seem good, but are not; who desire not to seem evil, but are so. Evil they are, yet they wish to be thought good, lest they should be left alone in their evil; and they fear to appear evil, lest they should not thus have sufficient power for evil. For open malice has always been less dangerous; nor is a person who is good ever deceived except by a pretense of goodness. They study, then, to appear good in order to do injury to the good, and shrink from appearing evil that they may thus give their evil designs fuller scope. For they do not care to cultivate virtues, but only to color their vices with a delusive tinge of virtues. Under the veil of religion they conceal an impious superstition; they regard the mere refraining from doing wrong openly as innocence, and thus take for themselves an outward appearance of goodness only. For a cloak to their infamy they make a vow of continence. They think that infamy consists only in having wives, whereas it is marriage alone that is pure. Coarse they are and stupid and altogether contemptible; but I assure you, not on that account to be disregarded, for they succeed in doing much evil, and their word eateth as doth a cancer.

Nor has the Holy Spirit overlooked such as these, since He has plainly prophesied of them long since by the mouth of the apostle. Now the Spirit speaketh expressly that in the latter times some shall depart from the faith, giving heed to seducing spirits and doctrines of devils, speaking lies in hypocrisy, having their conscience seared with a hot iron, forbidding to marry, and commanding to abstain from meats, which God hath created to be received with thanksgiving.

It was evidently of those people that He spake. They forbid marriage, they abstain from the food which God created, of which latter subject I will presently speak. But now see if all these things are not rather an illusion of demons than a mere mistake of men, according to that which had been foretold by the Holy Spirit. Ask of them who is the author of their sect; they will name no one. Yet what heresy has not had from such men its own leader? The Manicheans had Manes for chief and for master; the Sabellians, Sabellius; the Arians, Arius; the Eunomians, Eumomius; the Nestorians, Nestorius. So it is with all the other plagues of this kind. Each of them had some man for its master, from whom it has drawn at once its name and its origin. But what name or what title will you consider should be bestowed upon these people? Truly none at all, for their heresy is not of man, nor have they received it of man, nor have they received it by man. God forbid that we should say that they had it by the revelation of Jesus Christ, but rather and without doubt, as the Holy Spirit foretold, by the suggestions and artifices of seducing spirits, speaking lies in hypocrisy and forbidding marriage.

They talk also of hypocrisy, and with a vulpine cunning

pretend that they speak from mere love of chastity, whereas they have no other purpose than to foment and multiply impurity. It is so evident that this is their intention that I wonder how any Christian man could ever be persuaded that it was otherwise, unless, indeed, he were so wanting in insight as not to perceive that he who condemns marriage loosens the reins to every kind of uncleanness, or so full of wickedness and absorbed in diabolical malignity as to shut his eyes to what he cannot but perceive, and rejoice at the destruction of men. It you take away from the church marriage, which is honorable and undefiled, will you not fill the church with persons guilty of every kind of uncleanness? Choose, then, which alternative you prefer; either that all these monsters of wickedness are saved, or that the number of the saved is reduced to the few who have kept continence unbroken. In the one case you include too few, in the other too many. Neither of these alternatives is suited to the Saviour. What shall infamy be crowned? Nothing is less suitable to the source of purity. Or on the other hand, shall men be universally condemned, with the sole exception of the very few who have preserved their continence? That is not to be a Saviour. Continence is rare upon the earth, and if it were not for a very few persons that fulness of grace would have expired altogether. And how have we all received of that fulness, if a share of it is vouchsafed to those who are continent? There is no reply that can be made to that argument, nor yet, I think, to the other alternative. If there is for purity only a place in heaven, if there is no companionship between purity and impurity, just as there is no fellowship of light with darkness, then it is certain that no one who is unclean has any place in the land of salvation. If anyone thinks otherwise, an apostolic voice shall convict him of error, asserting expressly, "They which do such things shall not inherit the Kingdom of God." From what cavern shall this artful fox creep forth? I think that he is taken in his burrow, in which he has made two holes, one to enter by, the other to give him egress. This is his custom to do. See now by what means each of these is closed to him. If he maintains that only the continent have a place in heaven he denies salvation to the vast majority of people; if, on the contrary, he holds that those guilty of every kind of defilement have a place there equally with the continent, he causes purity to perish. But it is more accurate to say that he perishes himself, being unable to escape in either direction, and thus, shut up forever, remains a prisoner in the pit which he has digged.

Certain persons, among them different from the rest, declare that marriage is permitted, but only to those who are virgins. But I do not perceive on what ground of reason they make this distinction, except it be that they contend with each other to tear and rend asunder each at his own pleasure, as it were with the teeth of serpents, the sacraments of the church, which are, so to speak, the bowels of their mother. For as to what they allege, that our first parents were virgins when their marriage took place, what is there I ask in that fact to prejudice the liberty of marriage so that it may not be entered into between those who are not virgins? But I know not what declaration, they whisper, they have found in the Scriptures, which they wrongly imagine favors their absurd folly. I believe that it is the Word which our Lord spake after He had recalled that testimony in the Book of Genesis. "God created man in His own image, in the image of God created He him; male and female created He them." He then added: "What therefore God hath joined together let not man put asunder."

These, they say, were both virgins whom God joined together, and it was then not lawful to separate them; but no union of those who are otherwise than virgin shall be presumed to be from God. But who has told you that God joined these two together, because they were virgins? This the Scripture does not assert. But were they not virgins? replies the objector. They were, but it was not the same thing to unite those who were virgins and to unite them because they were virgins. Again, although they were virgins, you will not find the fact even expressly stated, much less given as a reason for their union. The diversity of sex is expressly stated, not their virginity, since it is declared: "Male and female created He them." And rightly so, for the marriage relation requires, not necessarily virginity of body, but difference of sex in the two persons who enter into it. With entire fitness then, did the Holy Spirit, in the record of the institution of marriage, make mention of sex, but preserve silence as to virginity, so as not to give occasion to those guileful foxes to misapply the text, which unquestionably they would have done with great willingness, but in vain. For what if the Holy Spirit had said that, God created them virgins? Would you not forthwith inferred that it was permitted to virgins alone to be joined in marriage? How you would have assumed airs of triumph upon the strength of this single statement. How scornfully you would have rejected second and third marriages. How you would have insulted the Church Catholic, inasmuch as she willingly joins together even persons who have fallen, and become infamous, because she regards this as assuredly the means of enabling them to pass from a state of shame to a state of honor. Perhaps you would even blame God for having commanded one of His prophets to take to wife a woman of that class; but now the entire ground is wanting for your doing all this, and it pleases you to be a heretic of your own accord. For the statement that you have unjustly adduced to support your error is found, on the contrary, to destroy it; it does nothing in your favor, but much against you.

But now listen to another Scripture which ought to confound you entirely, or correct you, and which at all events, crushes and pulverizes your heresy. The wife is bound by the law as long as her husband liveth; but if her husband be dead, she is at liberty to be married to whom she will: only in the Lord. It is St. Paul who allows to a widow to marry whom she will, and you, on the contrary, prescribe that none but a virgin shall marry; nor may she marry whom she will, but only a man who is likewise virgin. Why do you restrain the hand of God? Why do you restrict the abundant benediction bestowed on marriage, and narrow to the virgin alone that which is vouchsafed to all her sex? St. Paul would not permit this if it were unlawful. But it is too little to say that he permits it: he also desires it to be done. I will therefore, he says, that the younger women marry. and there is no doubt that he speaks of widows. What can be plainer than this? That therefore which he permits, because it is lawful, he also desires, because it is expedient. That then, which is permitted, and is expedient, shall a heretic presume to forbid? He will convince men of nothing by this prohibition, except that he is a heretic.

It remains that we should correct these people a little on the other points included in the Apostolic prophecy. For. they abstain as it is predicted, from various kinds of food which God has created to be received with thanksgiving, and thus prove themselves to be heretics, not simply because they abstain, but because they abstain in an heretical spirit. For, I too, sometimes abstain from food; but my abstinence is a satisfaction for sins, and not due to superstition and impiety. Shall we blame St. Paul when he kept under his body, and brought it into subjection? I will abstain from wine, because in it is excess; or if I am weak, will use a little, according to the counsel of St. Paul. I will abstain from eating flesh, lest it should too much pamper my flesh, and with it the lusts of the flesh. I will study to take even bread by measure that I may not, through fulness of stomach stand wearily and pray reluctantly to God, and that I may not be open to the reproach of the prophet that I have eaten my bread in fulness. I will not accustom myself to drink immoderately even of pure water, lest it may excite in me feelings corrupt. It is quite otherwise with the heretic. He turns from milk, and all that is made of it; in fact from everything which is the result of that function. That would be acting rightly and Christianly, if it were done, not because it was the result of that function, but from a motive of prudence.

But how does it come about that everything thus resulting is to be avoided in this matter? The minute scrutiny of kinds of food, so signficantly expressed, is to me a cause of suspicion? If you bring forward this as a medical rule I do not blame this care for the physical health, provided it be not excessive; for no one ever hated his own flesh. If as a part of the discipline of abstinence, that is, of the school of spiritual medicine, I even approve of it as a virtue, by which you bring the flesh under due rule, and restrain its desires. But if, by the madness of the Manichean, you set bounds to the beneficence of God, so that the food which He has created and given to men to be partaken of with thanksgiving you, as a rash and ungrateful critic, pronounce unclean, and abstain from it as from an evil thing, then far from praising your abstinence, I hold in execration your blasphemy, I hold you to be yourself impure, in considering that anything is impure in itself. "To the pure all things are pure," says an excellent judge of things; and nothing is impure, except to him who regards it as such; but unto them that are defiled and unbelieving, he adds, nothing is pure; but even their mind and conscience is defiled. Woe to you who reject food which God created, judging it impure and unworthy to pass into your bodies; wherefore the Body of Christ, which is the Church, has rejected you yourself as defiled and impure.

I am not unmindful that they boast that they, and they alone, are the body of Christ; but that is not astonishing, since they persuade themselves also that they have the power to consecrate daily at their tables the Body and Blood of Christ, to nourish them to become His members and His body. For they boast that they are successors of the Apostles, and call themselves Aposticals, though they are not able to show any sign of their apostolate. How long shall the lantern remain under a bushel? Ye are the light of the world, was said to the Apostles, and therefore are they set upon a candlestick, that they may enlighten the whole world. Let these successors of the Apostles be ashamed to be the light, not of the world, but of a bushel, and to the world to be but darkness. Let us say to them, Ye are the darkness of the world, and pass on to other things. They say that they are the Church, but they contradict Him who said, a city that is set on a hill cannot be hid. Do you believe that the stone, which was cut out without hands, and then became a great mountain, and filled the whole earth is shut up in your caverns? Nor ought we to stop even here. Their opinion is content with whispering in private, and avoids being known openly. Christ has, and will always have, His entire inheritance, and the ends of the earth are His possession. Those who attempt to withdraw from Him this great inheritance rather cease to form a part of it themselves.

See now those detractors, those dogs. They make it a cause of ridicule against us that we baptize children, that we pray for the dead, that we entreat the suffrages of the saints. They hasten to proscribe Christ in people at every age and of either sex; in children and in adults, in the living and in the dead; forbidding the new birth in Him in baptism, to infants because of the weakness of their age, and to adults also because of the difficulty of continence. They deprive the dead of the succor of the living, and the living of the suffrages of the saints who have died. But God forbid that it should be so. The Lord will not give up His people, who are as the sand of the sea; nor will He who redeemed all be contented with a small number, and those heretics. For His redemption is not small, but great and abounding. What is the pettiness of their number to the greatness of the price He paid? Those who attempt to empty it, of its efficacy, deprive themselves of it. Of what importance is it that an infant is not able to speak for himself, while the voice of the Blood of his Brother, and of a Brother so great and prevailing, cries to God from the ground for him? The Church, which is his mother, arises and lifts up her voice on his behalf also. And what of the child himself? Does it not seem to you that in his inarticulate infantine cries he opens his mouth, gasping, if I may so speak, for the Saviour's fountains of grace, and crying out to God in his plaints, "Lord I am distressed; undertake for me." It cries because it is innocent and unhappy, because it is ignorant and small, because it is weak and doomed to suffer. All these things thus cry out together: the Blood of a Brother, the faithfulness of a Mother, the abandoned condition of the unhappy child, and the misery of it abandoned; and these cries rise up to the Father; and He, because He is the Father, is not able to deny Himself.

Let no one abject to me that a child has not faith, for its Mother, that is the Church, communicates it to her own, wraps it in this faith, so to speak, as in a clotk in the Sacrament of Baptism, which she bestows upon it; so that it becomes worthy to receive and to develop that faith in its purity, if not by its own active powers, yet with its passive assent. Is it not a short and narrow cloak which cannot cover two? The faith of the Church is great. Surely it is not less than the faith of the Canaanitish woman, which we know was sufficient both for her daughter and herself. Therefore she had the happiness to hear: "O woman, great is thy faith; be it unto thee even as thou wilt." Nor is it less than the faith of those who let down the paralytic through the roof before Jesus, and obtained for him, both the saving of his soul and his body. For we read: "Jesus, seeing their faith, said unto the sick of the palsy, Son, be of good cheer, thy sins be forgiven thee"; and a little after: "Arise, take up thy bed, and go into thy house." He who believes these things will be easily persuaded that the Church may presume with good reason, not only of the salvation of those little children who are baptized in her faith, but also of the crown of martyrdom for those infants who were slain for Christ. And as this is the case, those who are regenerate will not suffer prejudice from that which is said in another Scripture, without faith it is impossible to please God; since they who have received the grace of baptism for a testimony, are not without faith. Neither will they be hurt by that other declaration: "He that believeth not shall be damned." For what is it to believe but to have faith? Therefore also a woman, shall be saved in child-bearing, if they continue in faith and charity and holiness, with sobriety; and children shall be succored by the Regeneration of Baptism. Adult persons also, who are not able to contain, redeem themselves by the thirtyfold fruit of marriage. The dead also, who shall have need of the prayers and sacrifices of the living, and shall be worthy of them, shall receive them, by the good offices of the angels; and from those who have already attained, comforts and consolations shall in no wise be wanting to the living, because of the affection which they have in God, Who is everywhere, and the charitable care they feel for those who are absent; for to this end Christ both died and rose and revived, that He might be Lord both of the dead and living. To this end also, He was born as an Infant, and passed all degrees of age, till He became a perfect Man, that He might be wanting to no age.

They do not believe that there remains a purgatorial fire after death; but that the soul, when released from the body, passes at once either to rest or to damnation. Let them, then ask of Him, who declared of a certain sin that it should not be forgiven, "neither in this world, nor in the world to come," why He said this, if there were no forgiveness at all in the world to come. But it is not wonderful that those who do not acknowledge the Church should make light of the Orders of the Church; that they should not receive her institutions; that they should despise her Sacraments, and refuse to obey her commands. The successors of the apostles, they say, are all sinners, archbishops, bishops and presbyters, and therefore are not fit to administer Sacraments or receive them. Are then, these two things, to be a sinner and to be a sinner, so incompatible as that they can never be found in the same person? That is not the case. Caiaphas was a Bishop; and how great a sinner was he, who pronounced sentence of death upon the

Lord? If you deny that he was a Bishop, the testimony of St. John, who declares that he was high priest for that year, and prophesied, shall convict you of error. Judas was an Apostle, and even chosen by the Lord; yet he was covetous and a man accursed. Do you hestitate to allow that he had the apostolate whom the Lord Himself chose? He Himself said: Have I not chosen you twelve, and one of you is a devil? You hear that he was the same man, was chosen Apostle, and showed himself a devil; and do you deny that a man who is a sinner can possibly be a bishop? The Scribes and Pharisees sat in Moses' seat; and those who did not obey them, as obedience is in like manner due to bishops, were guilty, in fact of disobedience to the Lord Himself, who gives these commands, and says: "Whatsoever they bid you observe, that observe and do." It is clear, then, that, although they were Scribes, although they were Pharisees, although they were even the greatest of sinners, yet for the sake of the chair of authority of Moses which they occupy, that saying nevertheless, applies to them: "He that heareth you heareth Me; and he that despiseth you, despiseth Me."

There are many other erroneous and evil opinions which are urged upon this foolish and undiscerning people by those spirits of evil, who speak lies in hypocrisy; but it is not needful to make reply to all. For who is acquainted with all these errors? Besides the labor of doing so would be unending; nor is it in the least necessary. For as for those people, neither are they convinced by reasons, because they do not understand them, nor corrected by the weight of authorities, for they do not receive them; nor are they influenced by persuasions because they are entirely perverted. It has been shown by experience that they prefer to die rather than be converted. Of these men the end is destruction; at last the fire awaits them. Long ago the

type of them was shown forth in the foxes to whose tails
Samson applied the fire. Often the faithful have laid hands
on some of them, and brought them into public notice.
When they have been questioned upon these points of their
belief on which they were suspected, they according to
their custom, refused entirely to give any answer; and when
examined by the judgment of water, they have been found
liars. But when they have been discovered, and were not
able to make denial, nor received the water at all; then taking, as the saying is, the bit in their teeth, they were so unhappy as to profess openly their impiety, to maintain it as
the true faith, and to declare that they were prepared to
suffer death on its behalf. Nor were those who were present less prepared to inflict it. Therefore the people rush-
ing in upon them, made of them new martyrs to their un-
belief. Their zeal we approve, but we do not advise the
imitation of their action, because faith is to be produced
by persuasion, not imposed by force. Although it would,
without doubt, be better that they should be coerced by the
sword of him "who beareth not the sword in vain," than
that they should be allowed to draw away many other persons into their error.

Some persons are astonished that they go to their death,
not only patiently, but as it seems, even with joy; but such
persons do not consider how great is the power of the devil,
not only over the bodies, but also over the hearts of those
whom, when once permitted, he has taken possession of.
Is it not more astonishing still that a man should lay violent
hands upon himself than that he should endure violence
willingly from another person? But we know by experience that the devil has frequently exerted that power,
namely, over many whom he has caused to drown or hang
themselves. Thus Judas hanged himself doubtless by the

instigation of the devil. Yet I find it strange, and a greater cause for wonder, that he should have been able to put it in the heart of Judas to betray his Lord than he should have caused him to hang himself. There is nothing resembling the constancy of the martyrs in the obstinacy of these men, because in the former it is piety, in the latter hardness of heart, that causes a contempt of death. Also the Psalmist has said, perhaps with the voice of a martyr: Their heart is curdled like milk; but I have meditated on Thy law, to show that, although the suffering seemed the same, yet the intention was very different; for whilst the one was hardening his heart against the Lord, the other was meditating on His holy law.

This being the case, there is no need, as I have said, to say much against men who are foolish and obstinate in the extreme; it suffices to take note of them that they may be avoided. Wherefore, that they may be discovered, they must be obliged either to send away the women, by retaining whom in their houses they give scandal to the Church, or to leave the Church. It is much to be lamented that not only secular princes, but also, as it is said, certain of the clergy, and even of the order of Bishops, whose special duty it is to seek them out, support them for the sake of gain, and for the presents which they receive from them. How, they say, shall we condemn men who do not confess error, nor are convicted of it? By this means alone, if there were no other, you will easily discover them; if as I have said, you separate the one from the other, obliging the women to live with those of their own sex who have taken the same vow as themselves, and the men to do likewise. In this way you will have consulted both the interest of their vow, and their reputation, in giving them both witnesses and guardians of their good behavior. If they do not submit to this, they will most justly be expelled from the Church to which they give scandal. Let this sacrifice, then, for the discovery of the wiles of those foxes that they may be known and guarded against by the Church, which is the beloved and glorious bride of our Lord Jesus Christ, who is above all, God blessed forever.   Amen.

SERMON No. 15.

OF THE SUPREME AND INFINITE SPIRIT, WHO IS GOD; AND OF THE SENSE IN WHICH MERCY AND JUDGMENT ARE CALLED THE FEET OF GOD.

In order that this sermon may be continuous with that which went before it, let me remind you of what was last said, that the Supreme and Infinite Spirit, and He alone, has no need of the help of any body or of the agency of any bodily organ to do whatever He wills to do.   We have then, no difficulty in saying that as God alone is truly immortal, so He alone is incorporeal, because He alone of all spirits, is so raised above the entire nature of a body, and transcends it to such a degree, that He has no need of its ministry in any of His works, but when it so pleases Him, acts by the sole Fiat of His will, and thus performs whatever is His good pleasure.   It is that Divine Majesty alone, therefore, which has no need of any bodily organization, neither on its own account, nor for the sake of others, because to its omnipotent bidding, obedience is swiftly rendered; every high thing bends before it, every obstacle yields, every created thing submits, and this without the intervention or help of any creature, corporeal or spiritual. He teaches or He warns without a tongue; He gives or

CHRIST TAKING LEAVE OF HIS MOTHER—BY HOFMANN.

withholds without the use of hands; without feet He runs, and comes to the succor of those who perish.

Thus He was wont to do with our fathers in former ages. Men felt a continual stream of benefits, but they did not know who was their Benefactor. By His strength He did indeed order all things from the height even unto the depth; but as He at this same time disposed them sweetly and gently, His action though perpetual, was unfelt by men. In the good gifts of the Lord they rejoiced, but the Lord of Sabaoth was unknown to them, because all His judgments were calm and tranquil. From Him were men, but they were not with Him; by Him they lived, but not for Him; it was from Him that they had wisdom, but they did not use it to gain knowledge of Him; they were insensate, ungrateful, and altogether alienated from Him. Thus at length it came about that they no longer attributed their being, their life, their reason to their Creator, but to nature, or even, which was still more utterly unreasonable, to chance; while there were many who attributed not a few of the good things which came to them to their own labor and skill. How great praise these seducing spirits thus arrogated to themselves! How much was given to the sun and the moon! How much attributed to earth and to water! Even things which the hand of man had made, plants, shrubs, and the commonest of seeds, were honored as divinities.

Alas! It is thus that men have degraded the object of their worship, and changed their glory into the similitude of a calf that eateth hay. And God had pity upon their errors; He deigned to come forth from the clouds and darkness of His holy mountain, and to set His tabernacle in the light of the sun. To those who knew only the flesh, He offered His flesh, in order to teach them by it to know also the Spirit. For whilst He was in the Flesh, He made use of the Flesh indeed, but to do by it, not the works of the flesh, but the works of God; commanding nature, fixing and rendering certain the uncertainty of chance, rendering the wisdom of men foolishness, and breaking down the tyranny of the demons, and thus plainly manifested that it was He by whom the same wonders were worked in former ages also. He did, I repeat, in the flesh and by means of the flesh, actions of power, plainly miraculous; He spake words of salvation, He endured cruel indignities; and yet He showed evidently that it was He who had created the world by His power, sovereign, though invisible; who ruled it by His wisdom, and protected it in His love and mercy. Lastly, when He preached the Gospel to those ungrateful ones, when He prayed even for those who crucified Him, did He not clearly declare Himself to be that High and Lofty One, who, with His Father, makes His sun to shine daily upon the just and the unjust? As He Himself said: "If I do not the works of My Father, believe Me not."

Behold Him! He who in a deep adorable silence imparts eternal wisdom to the angels in heaven, He in the flesh opens His mouth and teaches His disciples upon the mouth. See how the leper is healed at the mere touch of His hands, how blindness is dispersed, hearing restored, the silent tongue set free, the disciple about to be whelmed in the deep caught by the hand and saved: and can you fail to recognize that great Being to whom David had said long before: "Thou openest Thine hand and satisfiest the desire of every living thing;" and again, "Thou openest Thine hand and they all are filled with good." See how the woman that was a sinner, now penitent and upon her knees at His feet, hears Him say: "Thy sins are forgiven," and recognize Him of whom she may have read what had been written many ages before: "The devil shall go forth from before His feet." For where sin is remitted, there, without doubt, the devil is driven forth from the heart of the sinner. Therefore it is that He speaks in general terms of all true penitents: "Now is the judgment of this world; now shall the prince of this world be cast out," because God forgives sins to him who humbly confesses them; and thus the devil loses the dominion which he had usurped in the sinner's heart.

Lastly, He walks with the Feet of His flesh upon the waves; He of whom the Psalmist had sung before as yet He was incarnate: "Thy way is in the sea, and Thy path in the great waters." That is to say, Thou shalt tread under foot the swelling hearts of the proud, and repress the disordered desires of carnal men; shalt render the ungodly righteous, and lower the pride of the arrogant. Yet because He does this invisibly, the carnal man does not recognize whose hand it is that brings it to pass. Wherefore also it is that the Psalmist adds: "And Thy footsteps are not known." Hence also the Almighty Father saith to the Son: "Sit Thou at My right hand until I make Thine enemies Thy footstool," that is, until I shall render all those who despise Thee subject to Thy will, whether unwillingly and to their destruction, or gladly and to their happiness. Now since the flesh was not capable of comprehending this, which is a work of the Spirit (for the natural man receiveth not the things of the Spirit of God), it was needful that the sinner should prostrate herself in the body, kneeling upon mortal knees, and with mortal lips imprinting a kiss upon the feet of the Redeemer and thus receive the pardon of her sins. Thus is this change which the Right Hand of the Most High hath wrought, by which He marvelously, yet invisibly, justifies the unrighteous, made apparent even to carnal men.

But I must not omit to refer to those spiritual Feet of God which it behooved the penitent, first of all, in a spiritual and mystical sense to kiss. I know the inquiring temper of your minds, which will not, with its own good will, pass over the least detail without thorough examination. Nor is it a matter to be neglected as of small importance to know what is meant by the Feet of God, so frequently referred to in the Scripture. At one time He is represented as standing, as in this: "We will worship in the place where His Feet have stood;" at another as walking, as in the verse, "I will dwell in them and walk in them;" at another even as running, as here: "He rejoiceth as a strong man to run a race." If it seemed right to the apostle to speak of the Head of Christ as the deity, then I think that we may not unfitly speak of His Feet as the humanity, and call the one mercy, the other judgment. These two words are well known to you, and if you reflect, many passages of Scripture will occur to you, in which they are each so employed. That God has taken the Foot of Mercy, in assuming the Flesh which he united with Himself, is taught in the epistle to the Hebrews, whence we learn that Christ was tempted 'in all points like as we are, though without sin, that He might be compassionate and merciful. And as for that other which has been named the Foot of Judgment, does not He who is God and Man plainly signify that it belongs to Himself as Incarnate, where He declares that the Father hath given Him authority to execute judgment also, because He is the Son of Man?

With these two feet then, fitly conjoined under one Divine Head, it was that the invisible Emmanuel was born of a woman, made under the law, was seen upon earth, and had converse among men. It is, again, on these feet, that He passes to and fro even now, but spiritually and invisibly, benefiting and healing all those vowed to His service, enlightening and penetrating constantly the hearts and reins of the faithful. These are it may be, the legs of the Bridegroom which are so strikingly commended by the Bride in a latter part of the Book, where she likens them, if I do not mistake, to pillars of marble, set upon blocks of fine gold. And this is very beautifully phrased, for it is in the Incarnate Wisdom of God, which is represented as gold, that mercy and truth have met together, and elsewhere it is said that all the paths of the Lord are mercy and truth.

Happy is the soul in which the Lord Jesus has once set His Feet! There are two signs by which you may recognize the soul in which this is the case, and such a soul bears of necessity the prints of those Divine footsteps. These are fear and hope: the one bearing the print of judgment, the other of mercy. With reason it is that God taketh pleasure in them that fear Him, in them that hope in His mercy; since the fear of the Lord is the beginning of wisdom; hope, the progress in it, and charity its consummation and perfectness. And since that is the case, the benefit is of no small value which is derived from that first kiss which is imprinted upon the Feet of Jesus, provided only that neither one nor the other of them be neglected. For if you are deeply touched with grief for your sins and with fear of God's judgment, then you have pressed your lips upon the footprints of truth and of judgment. If you temper that fear and that grief by a consideration of the Divine goodness, and by the hope of obtaining pardon, then you may know that you are embracing the Foot of Mercy. But to embrace the one without the other is not expedient, for the remembrance of judgment alone precipitates the soul into the abyss of despair, and a deceptive assurance of mercy wherewith a mind flatters itself, generates a most pernicious security.

It has been given to me, a miserable sinner, sometimes to sit at the feet of the Lord Jesus, and to embrace now the one, now the other, with a devotion as full and complete as His benignity deigned to enable me to feel. But if it ever happened that pressed by the reproaches of conscience, I was forgetful of mercy, and attached myself too long to judgment, I was soon cast down by incredible fear and pitiable shame, and surrounded by the darkness of horror, so that, trembling in the shadow, I could only cry: "Who knoweth the power of Thy anger: even according to Thy fear, so is Thy wrath." But if, on the other hand, leaving that, I had embraced the other, the Foot of Mercy, more than was meet, I was dissolved into negligence and indifference so great that I speedily became less earnest in prayer, less prompt in action, more inconsiderate in speech, more given to idle laughter—in short, less steady and stable in every part of my nature, whether of the inward or outward man. Therefore having learned from that best of teachers, experience, I no longer dwell upon judgment alone, any more than upon mercy alone; but unto Thee, O Lord, will I sing of mercy and judgment. Those two sources of righteousness forever I will not forget; they shall both equally be my songs in the house of my pilgrimage until mercy having been exalted high above judgment, my unhappy condition shall cease and come to a full end, and the glory which shall be granted to me shall alone inspire my hymns of praise to Thee, without the least mingling of pain or grief, forever.

SERMON NO. 16.

Text: "Tomorrow the Lord shall come; and in the morning ye shall behold His glory."—Exod. XVI. 6, 7.

Dwellers on the earth, children of men, hearken; ye who sleep in the dust, awake and sing the praises of God: for One who shall come, who is to the sick a Healer, to those who are sold into slavery a Redeemer, to the wandering a Guide, and Life to the dead. Yes, He comes who shall cast all our sins into the depth of the sea, who shall heal all our infirmities, who shall bear us upon His own shoulders to our own original greatness. Great is His power, but His mercy is more wonderful still; that He who was able to help should have been willing thus to come. To-morrow, says our text, the Lord shall come. These words have indeed their own first fulfillment in place and time recorded in the Scripture; but our Mother Church has not unfitly adapted them to the Vigil of our Lord's coming in the flesh. The Church I say, who has with her the guidance and the spirit of Him who is God and her Spouse, who is the well-beloved, and rests upon her bosom, which He alone possesses and makes His throne. It may be said that she, opening her heart, has plunged the eye of her contemplation into the deep abyss of the secret purposes of God, so as to prepare for Him a perpetual habitation in her heart, and for herself in His. When then she either transfers or varies the words of Holy Scripture, that transference is even of as much more weight than the original sense as the truth is more than the figure, the full light than the shadow, the mistress than the servant.

You shall see then even to-day that the Lord will come. In my opinion these words give me clearly the idea of two kinds of days; the first has begun with the fall of the first man, and continues even until the end of the world; a day on which the saints have often poured their maledictions. For on that day Adam was driven out from that brightness of light in which he was created; and being thrust upon the things of this world, he entered upon a day of darkness, and was deprived almost wholly of the light of the truth. We are all born into this day when we come into the world, if indeed it ought not rather to be called night, not day, except that the sovereign mercy of God has left to us the light of reason, as it were a certain glimmering of day. But the second day shall be that of the glory of the saints, and shall endure throughout endless eternities, when that peaceful morrow shall dawn, which is the obtaining of the promised mercy, when death shall be swallowed up in victory: when clouds and shadows shall be dispersed, and all things both within and without, above and below, shall be equally filled with the splendor of the true light. Thus a saint says: "Cause me to hear Thy loving kindness in the morning, and in the morning we were filled with Thy mercy." But let us return to our day, which for its shortness is called a watch of the night, a shadow and a nothing, by the inspiration of the Holy Spirit: "My days are as a shadow that declineth; they are consumed like smoke." "Few and evil have the days of the years of my life been," says that holy patriarch, who saw the Lord face to face, and talked with Him as with a friend. And indeed in this day God has endowed man with reason, He has left to him intelligence; but it is needful for man that when he goes forth from this world he should be enlightened by God with the light of the knowledge of Him, lest if he should leave this prison-house, quelled, as it were, by the completeness of its gloom, he should be forever unable to receive any light. Therefore it was that the only begotten Son of God, the brightness of righteousness, has enlightened and warmed the prison-house

of this world, as it were, with a torch of brilliant and un-
measured light; so that all who desire to be enlightened may
be fired by His glory, may be united to Him so closely that
nothing may intervene between. For it is our sins that
come between us and God. Let them be taken away, and
we are at once enlightened by the true light, are united, and
as it were absorbed into Him. Thus if an extinguished
light be brought near to one still burning and shining, so
that nothing intervenes between, it is at once relighted. So
by an example taken from visible things, we may learn the
working of the invisible.

Let us follow then the counsel of the prophet; let us light
up for ourselves the light of knowledge at this star so great
and so effulgent, before we go forth from the shadows of
this world, that we may not pass away into the darkness
which is eternal. But what is that knowledge? Plainly it
consists in knowing that the Lord will come, though when
He will come, we cannot know. This is all that is asked of
us. But you reply, that knowledge belongs to all. For
who is there, being a Christian even in name only, who
knows not that the Lord will come; that He will come to
judge the quick and the dead, and to render to every man
according to his works? No, my brethren, that knowledge
does not belong to all: it belongs even to few, because in
truth there are few that are saved. Do you think, for example, that those who are happy when they have done
wrong, who take pleasure in the worst of actions, that they
either consider or know that the Lord will come? If they
should say that they do so, do you not believe them: for
he that says I know God, and keepth not His commandments, is a liar. They confess, says the Apostle, that they
know God, but in works they deny Him, for faith without
works is dead. They would not thus pollute themselves

with every kind of impurity, if they knew or feared that the Lord would come; on the contrary, they would watch, and not suffer their consciences to be wounded thus grievously.

For this knowledge works, in the first place, in the soul penitence and sorrow. It changes laughter into weeping, songs into groans, joy into sorrow. It causes those things to displease you in which you had before taken extreme pleasure; and to have a special horror of those which you were wont specially to desire. For thus it is written, He who increaseth knowledge increaseth sorrow, so that the consequence which follows true and holy knowledge is sorrow. In the second stage it brings about correction; so that you no longer employ your members as instruments of iniquity unto sin; you restrain gluttony, you strangle luxury, you lower pride, and make your body, which before had been the slave of iniquity, the servant of holiness. For penitence profits not without correction, as says the wise man: "If one builds and another destroys, of what profit is their labor? If one prays and another curses, whose voice shall the Lord hear? If one who is washed after having touched a dead body again touches it, his washing profits him nothing." It is, on the contrary, to be feared, according to the word of the Saviour Himself, that a worse thing will happen to a man who does this. But as these two conditions cannot be long maintained, unless the mind watches and strives in all things with unwearied circumspection; knowledge in the third stage produces solicitude, so that a man begins to walk with continual care·in his God, and to examine himself in every part, lest he should offend in the smallest matter the sight of His awful majesty. Thus repentance lights up the soul, correction makes it earnest, solicitude gives it brightness and light; and thus the whole man is renewed both within and without.

But here he begins to breathe a little from the depression and griefs which his sins have caused him, and to temper the extremity of his fear with spiritual joy, that he may not be swallowed up with overmuch sorrow on account of the greatness of his crimes. Hence, although he fears his judge, he has good hope in his Saviour; and since joy and fear exist together in his soul, they conflict and war with each other; often fear prevails over joy; but still more frequently joy triumphs over fear, by its secret strength. Happy is the conscience in which such a conflict goes on without ceasing, until mortality is swallowed up in life; until fear, which is only in part, shall be done away, and joy which is complete and perfect shall take its place; for its fear is but for a time, but its joy eternal. But the soul, though thus burning and shining with the fire of love, must nevertheless not as yet believe itself to be in the House where the lighted torch of Love may be ever borne, without any fear of hostile winds; it must remember that it is still under the open sky, and carefully shield with either hand the light which it carries, and distrust the winds, even though the air seems peaceful. For suddenly, and at an hour when he expects it not, a change will come: and if he shall have removed his sheltering hand ever so little, the light will be extinguished. Even if the heat of its flames should have burned (as sometimes happens) the hands of him who bears it, prefers rather to endure this, than to withdraw his hands; because he knows that in a moment, in a twinkling of an eye, the flame may be blown out. If we were in that house not made with hands, which is eternal in the heavens, where no enemy enters, and no friend goes forth, there would be nothing to fear. But now we are exposed to three winds most malign and strong; the world, the flesh and the devil; which strive to extinguish the light in the conscience, blow-ing upon our hearts with evil desires, unlawful impulses, and so disordering us with sudden trouble, that we scarcely know any longer whence we came or whither we go. Two of these fierce winds are often at rest; but from the blast of the third none is ever free. This is why we ought to protect our soul, with the hands as it were, both of the heart and of the body, lest the light of the soul, once lit up, should be extinguished; we must neither yield to the tempest, nor recoil before it, even though the extreme violence of temptation has broken upon either element of our human nature; but we must say with the Psalmist: "My soul is always in my hands." Let us rather endure the pain than yield to the temptation. And as we cannot easily forget that which we hold in our hands: so let us never forget the care of our souls, but apply ourselves earnestly and with all powers to carry it out perfectly.

With our loins girded, therefore, and with lamps burning, let us, during the watches of this night, keep under strict control the multitude of our thoughts and actions; so that the Lord when He shall come, whether it be in the first, or the second, or the third watch, may find us ready. The first watch is rightness of action; and it consists in endeavoring to fashion your whole life according to the Rule which you have sworn to observe; in not transgressing the limits which your fathers have laid down in all the details of duty and of this your calling, not declining to the right hand nor to the left.. The second is purity of intention, so that your eye being without guile may render your whole body full of light, in so far that whatsoever you may do you shall do it as unto God, and so the graces which you have received will return again to their source and come back to you anew. The third consists in the preservation of unity amongst yourselves, so that being placed in a community you should study to prefer the wishes of others to your own wishes; thus you will live with your brethren not only without quarrel, but also with good understanding and kindly feeling, each one praying for all the rest, so that it may be said of each of us: He is a lover of the brethren and of the people of Israel, he has much at heart the good of his people and of the holy city Jerusalem. Thus, then, on this day the coming of the Only Begotten Son lights up in us the flame of a true knowledge; of that knowledge, I say, which teaches us that the Lord will come, and is a constant and firm foundation of goodness in us.

And in the morning ye shall behold His glory. O what a morning! O day which art in the courts of the Lord, and better than a thousand passed elsewhere! When shall we see month succeed to month and Sabbath to Sabbath, when shall the splendor of light and the glow of charity enlighten the dwellers upon the earth, even to the discerning of the loftiest wonders of God? Who shall presume to think of Thy wonders, much less to speak of them? Yet in the meanwhile, brethren, let us build our faith, that if we cannot behold those wonders which God has reserved for us, we may at least contemplate some small part of the marvels which are done on our account upon the earth. The Almighty Majesty of God has done three things, accomplished three blendings in taking our flesh; so uniquely wonderful and so wonderfully unique that nothing similar was ever done or is to be done again upon the earth. That is to say, there were joined closely together: God and man, (the characters of) mother and virgin, faith and a human heart. Marvelous indeed are those blendings, but that which is more marvelous than any miracle is the manner in which things so diverse in character and so mutually distinct from each other are yet able to be mutually conjoined.

And in the first place consider the creation, the position, and the arrangement of things. What great power, that is to say, is manifested in their creation, what great wisdom in their position, what great goodness in their arrangement. In creation see how many things were created, and with how great power; in position, with what wisdom all things were placed; in arrangement, with what goodness, with what wonderful and engaging love, things which were highest were united to those which were lowest.

For to the dust of the earth He has united a vital force which, in the trees, for example, causes beauty to arise in the leaves, brilliance in the flowers, taste and healthful qualities in the fruits. And not being content with this He has added to our dust another power still, that of feeling, as in the lower animals, which have not only life, but also rejoice in a five-fold power of sense. Again, He did something more; and honored our dust by giving to it the power of reason that we see in men who not only have life, and have feeling, but who also are able to discern between what is fitting and what is unfitting, between good and evil, between what is true and what is false. He willed after that to raise up our weakness to a more lofty glory still, and His Majesty emptied itself so as to unite to our dust that which was loftiest in Him, that is to say, Himself, and to unite in one and the same person God and the dust of the earth, majesty and weakness, loftiness so exalted and lowness so extreme. For nothing is higher than God, nothing lower than the dust of the earth: and yet with condescension so great God descended to the dust, and with such great elevation the dust arose to God; so that whatever God did in our dust it might be believed by our faith that it was done even by our dust; and whatever our dust suffered and went through God might be said to have gone through in it, by a mystery as unspeakable as it is incapable of being grasped. And remark again, that as in the one and only God there is a Trinity of Persons, but a Unity of Substance; so in this unique blending there is a Trinity of Substance; but a Unity of Person; and as in that the three Persons do not destroy the Unity nor the Unity diminish the Trinity: so also this, the Unity of Person does not cause a confusion of Natures; nor the Natures take away the Unity of Person. The Supreme and blessed Trinity has thus put before us a trinity; a work wonderful and surpassing all things, and which among all things stands absolutely alone. For the Word of God, a soul, and a body, unite to form one Person; and these Three are One, and this One is Three, not by confusion of Substance, but by Unity of Person. This is the first and supremely excellent blending; and it is first among three. Consider, O man, that thou art dust, and be not proud: consider also that thou art united to God, and be not ungrateful.

The second blending is that of (the characters of) virgin and mother: a wonderful event indeed, and obviously unexampled. From the beginning of the world has it not been heard, that there was a Virgin who was a Mother, or a Mother who remained Virgin. Never in the ordinary course of things is virginity found, where fecundity exists; nor fecundity where virginity remains intact. There is only this instance, in which virginity and fecundity have met each other. In this one case was that done which had never been done before, nor ever shall be done again; it had no precedent, nor shall have any repetition. The third blending is of faith and a human heart: it is no doubt inferior to the first and second, but perhaps not less as a proof of power. For that a human heart has entertained faith is wonderful, as well as that God could be believed to be Man, and that one who has just become a mother should have remained a virgin. Just as iron and clay are not capable of being united; so these two cannot be blended, unless by the uniting power of the Spirit of God. Is it then to be believed that He is God great and boundless, who is laid in a manger, who weeps in a cradle, who endures the pains of infantile necessities, who is scourged, spit upon, crucified, laid in the sepulchre and enclosed between two stones? Shall she be a virgin, who suckles her child, whose husband shares her table and couch, and leads her into Egypt, brings her back thence, making alone with her a journey so long and so solitary? How could the human race, and the whole world, be persuaded of this? And yet it was persuaded; so easily and so powerfully, that the multitude of believers in it makes it credible to me. Young men and maidens, old men and children, have chosen rather to die a thousand deaths, than to fall from the faith even for a moment.

This first blending is indeed excellent, the second more so, but the third surpasses these. The ear has heard the first, but the eye has not seen it: because that great mystery of piety is heard and believed even to the ends of the earth; but yet the eye of man has not seen. O God, none has seen but Thou, in what manner Thou has united to Thyself a body similar to ours, in the narrow space of a Virgin's womb. The second blending, the eye of man has seen, because that Queen highly favored saw herself fruitful and yet a virgin, as she kept in memory all these words, and pondered them in her heart: Joseph too, who was the witness as well as the guardian of so wonderful a virginity, had knowledge of it. Finally, the third has found place in the heart of man, because he has believed that which was done, as having been done; since we give greater credence to the voice that speaks to us from above than to our own sight, when we hold and most firmly believe, nothing doubting, what was done and handed down to us. See then in the first mystery what God has given to you; in the second, by what means He has given it; in the third, for what motive He has given it. He has given to you Christ by means of Mary, in order to restore you to spiritual health. In the first blending is a remedy: a remedy, God-and-man to heal all your spiritual ills.

The two were crushed and mingled in the womb of the Virgin, as in a mortar; and the Holy Spirit, as it were a pestle, gently mingled them. But as to you were unworthy on whom He should be bestowed, He was given to Mary, so that you might receive of her whatsoever you might have: and Mary, inasmuch as she is a mother, has brought forth for you Him who was God: and inasmuch as she is a virgin, she has, for her reverence, been heard in your cause and in that of the whole human race. If she were only a mother, it would suffice for her that she should be saved through the generation of her children; if she were only a virgin, it would suffice for her: but the fruit of her womb would not be blessed, nor the price of the world's (redemption). Since then in the first mystery there is a remedy, in the second the remedy is applied; since according to the will of God, all that we have received comes to us by means of Mary. But in the third, merit found, since when we firmly believe these things, then we have a degree of merit: and in faith there is salvation; for he who believes the same shall be saved.

SERMON No. 17.

Text: "Rejoice in the Lord always; again I say, Rejoice."-- Phil. IV. 4.

The custom of our Order does not require a sermon today: but as the Celebration of Masses will occupy us longer than usual to-morrow, and the short time remaining will not admit of a sermon, I think it not amiss to prepare your hearts to-day for a solemnity so great; especially as in considering the profundity and the immeasurable height of this great mystery, it seems nothing less than a source of living water, of which we may drink the more abundantly, that it can never be exhausted. And as I know how greatly your tribulation for Christ's sake abounds, I would that your consolation through Him should abound also: since I am neither able, nor desirous, to offer you the consolation of the world. That is of no value, and of no utility: and (which is a thing more to be feared) it is an obstacle to true and salutary consolations. Therefore it is that He who is the delight and the glory of the Angels has made Himself the salvation and the consolation of the unhappy. He who, being great and highly exalted in His heavenly city, made the citizens of it perfectly happy, has come as a poor and humble Child into the exile of this world, and brings great joy unto us exiles: and He who in the highest heaven is the glory of the Father, upon earth is made Peace to men of good will. He is given, a lowly Child, to us who are lowly, so that we may become great and receive Him in His real greatness: and that those whom as a Child He justifies. He may at a later time, make great and glorious when He shall have resumed his glory. Hence without doubt that vessel of election, who had received of the fulness of that little Child (for although He were a child He was filled, filled with grace and truth, and in Him dwelt all the fulness of the Godhead bodily); hence, I say, no doubt St. Paul spoke those words of blessed meaning which during these days have been frequently sounding in our ears. Rejoice in the Lord alway: and again I say, Rejoice! Rejoice, he says, for the blessing that is before your eyes, and rejoice for that which is promised in the future; since the fact accomplished, and the future promised, are alike full of joy. Rejoice, because from the Left Hand of God you have already received gifts; and from His Right Hand also you hope for them. "His left hand," it is said, "shall be under my head, and His right hand shall embrace me." The left hand sustains us, the right hand lifts us up: the left hand heals and justifies: the right blesses in embracing. In the left are contained merits (to redeem): in the right promises (to sanctify): in the right, delights: in the left, remedies.

But notice how good and how wise is our Physician. Consider diligently how new the remedies which He brings; and not only new, but costly and beautiful; not only priceless for the restoration of health, but sweet to the taste and pleasant to the eye. Think of the first remedy which he brings in His left hand: you will find it to be His Miraculous Conception. Reflect what a wonderful and novel a fact that is, as well as how admirable and lovable. What more admirable than a holy generation? What more glorious than a conception holy and pure, unstained by shame or corruption? But as we should be perhaps less struck by admiration of this new thing, however welcome, if our mind were not delighted by the thought of the usefulness and salvation which comes with it: that conception manifests itself to us as not only glorious in outward appearance, but also precious in inward virtue: since in it is found, according to that which is written, in the left hand of the Lord riches and honor; the riches of salvation, the honor of newness. For who can make pure that which is conceived of an impure stock, but He who alone was conceived without evil concupiscence? In my very root and origin I was infected and defiled: in sin was I conceived: but He by whom it is taken away, upon Him did it fall.

I have seen the riches of salvation, the most pure conception of Christ, by which I am redeemed from the stain of my own conception. Add to these, O Lord Jesus, abiding signs, unchanged marvels: for the first have lost their wonder by our very familiarity with them. For although the sun's rising and setting, the fruitfulness of the earth, the alternation of the seasons, are evidently miracles and great ones: yet they are so often renewed before our eyes, that no one now notices them. But behold, He says, "I make all things new." Who says this? It is the Lamb that sat upon the throne. The Lamb who is altogether sweetness and delight, who is in short, the Anointed One; for this is the interpretation of the name Christ. To whom can He appear harsh or stern, when not even to His mother at His birth did He bring injury or suffering? These were marvels truly new; without sin was He conceived, and without pain born. In our Virgin the malediction of Eve was changed; for without sorrow she brought forth. A malediction was changed, I say, into a benediction, as it was foretold by the Angel Gabriel: "Blessed art thou among women." O woman happy in being blessed not cursed, alone free from the general malediction, and exempted from the pains of childbirth. Nor is it strange, brethren, that He should bring no sorrow to His mother, who bore the sorrows of the whole world: who, according to the saying of Isaiah, Himself carried our sorrows. There are two things which human weakness fears, shame and suffering. Each of these Christ came to take away, wherefore He bore both the one and the other, when (not to speak of other endurances) He was condemned by wicked men to a shameful death. Therefore, that He might give us confidence that He would preserve us from these evils, He first preserved His mother in safety from each: and thus she conceived without sin and brought forth without suffering.

Riches still increase, glory is augmented, new signs appear, miracles change their nature. Not only is the Son of Man conceived without stain, but brought forth without suffering, and His Mother is without corruption. O novelty truly unheard of! A Virgin has brought forth, and after childbirth has remained a virgin, has obtained fruitfulness in posterity while retaining integrity of the flesh, and has both the joy of maternity and the honor of virginity. Now I await with confidence the promised glory of incorruption in my flesh, since by Him incorruption has been preserved in His Mother. It will be easy for Him, who did not suffer His Mother to see corruption in bringing forth a Son, to make me the corruptible, to put on incorruption, when He raises me from the dead.

Yet you have riches greater and glory more abounding ever than this. A woman becomes Mother without loss of virginity; a Son is born without any stain of sin. Upon that Mother the malediction pronounced upon Eve does not fall; the Child born of her is also free from the common lot of which the prophet speaks: "None is free from the stain of uncleanness, not even the infant, whose life upon the earth is but of one day." Behold an Infant without spot, alone true among men, who is even more—the very Truth itself. Behold the Lamb without spot, the Lamb of God, who taketh away the sins of the world. For who can better take away sins than He upon whom sin has not descended? He is without doubt able to cleanse me from sin, who is evidently free from any. Let His hand, screened in clay, yet which is alone without earthly stain, purge my eyes from their darkness. Let Him who has no beam in His eye, pluck forth the mote out of mine; yea, rather, let Him pluck forth the beam from mine, who has not in His own the smallest grain of dust.

We have seen in truth the riches of life and salvation: we have seen His glory, glory as of the Only-Begotten of the Father. If I am asked, of what Father? I reply in the words of the prophet: "And He shall be called the Son of the Highest." It is plain what is meant by "the Highest." But that there may be no place for hesitation about this, the Angel Gabriel himself says to Mary: "That Holy One who shall be born of thee shall be called the Son of God." O truly Holy One! Thou, O Lord, shall not suffer Thy Holy One to see corruption, who has kept corruption even from His Mother. Miracles grow greater and greater, the treasure house of grace is opened, and its riches are poured forth in profusion. She who bears, is mother and yet Virgin: He who is born is God-and-man. But are holy things to be given to dogs, or pearls thrown unto swine? Let our treasure then be that hidden in a field, our money kept safely in the purse. Let the miraculous conception be sheltered by the betrothal of the Mother; the painless Birth by the wails and suffering of the Child. Let the purity too of the newly made mother be hidden by undergoing the purification of the Law, and the innocency of the Child by the accustomed circumcision. Hide, I say, O Mary, hide the splendor of that Sun newly rising: lay thy Infant in the manger, fold around Him the swathing bands, for they are our riches. The bands which bound the Saviour are more precious than any purple, and this manger more filled with glory than the gilded thrones of Kings; in fine, the poverty of Christ is more costly than all riches and treasures. For what is found richer or more precious than the humility by which grace is acquired and even the Kingdom of Heaven attained? as it is written, "Blessed are the poor in spirit, for theirs is the Kingdom of heaven;" and by the Apostle: "God resisteth the proud, and giveth grace unto the humble." In the Nativity you have humility commended by God Himself. For in it He emptied Himself, taking upon Him the form of a servant, and was found in the likeness of a man.

Do you seek riches more precious still, and a glory still more excellent? You have it in the love shown in His Passion: "Greater love hath no man than this, that one should lay down his life for his friends." This riches and glory of salvation, is the Precious Blood wherewith we have been redeemed; and the Cross of Jesus, in which we glory with the Apostle. "God forbid," he says, "that I should glory, save in the Cross of our Lord Jesus Christ;" and again: "I determined to know nothing among you, but Jesus Christ, and Him crucified." The Left Hand of God (in the text) is then Christ Jesus, but Him crucified; and the Right Hand is still Christ Jesus, but Him glorified. We ourselves, perhaps, are the cross, upon which we are told that He was nailed; for man has himself the form of a cross; and more manifestly when he extends his hands. For Christ says in the Psalm: "I am sunk in the deep mire where there is no standing." It is plain that the mire is nothing but ourselves, for we are made of the dust of the earth: though then we were of the dust of Paradise, but now the dust of the abyss. "I am sunk in it," he says: not, I have passed through it, or I have come out of it. "I am with you even to the end of the world." For He is Emmanuel, God with us. He is with us indeed, but as it were, by the left hand. Thus we see that once when Tamar was in labor, and Zara first put forth his hand, it was bound with a thread of scarlet, which is a symbol of the Lord's Passion.

We hold fast then now by the Left Hand of God: but yet it is needful for us to cry: "Stretch out, O Lord, Thy Right

Hand to the work of Thy Hands, for at Thy Right Hand there are pleasures for evermore. Lord, stretch out to us Thy Right Hand, and it suffereth us.

Glory, He says, and riches are in His house, that is to say, of him who fears the Lord; but in Thy House, Lord, there is the voice of praise and the giving of thanks.

"Blessed are they who dwell in Thy House," etc. For eye hath not seen nor ear heard, neither have entered into the heart of man, the things which God hath prepared for them that love Him. For there is light inaccesible, peace which passeth all understanding; a spring which never waxes nor wanes. The eye hath not seen the inaccesible light; the ear hath not heard the peace which cannot be comprehended. Beautiful indeed are the feet of those who bring good tidings of peace, but their sound hath gone forth into the whole world; while the peace which passeth all understanding is far from being comprehended in its fulness by men, nor has it entered into their ears. For Paul himself says: "Brethren, I count not myself to have apprehended. Faith cometh by hearing indeed, and hearing by the word of God: but faith not sight; the promise of peace, not the manifestation of it." And indeed there is peace even now to men of good will, even upon the earth: but what is that peace to the plenitude and fulness of that farther gift? Wherefore the Lord Himself also says: "My peace I give unto you, peace I leave with you. That peace of mind indeed which passeth all understanding, and is a peace above peace, you are not capable of experiencing; wherefore I give unto you the land of peace, and leave to you in the meantime the way of peace."

But why these words, into the heart of man it hath not ascended? Doubtless because it is a spring and does not flow upwards. For we know that the nature of springs is to follow the streams of the valleys and to fall upon the steeps of the mountains, as it is written: "Who sendeth the springs into the valleys which run among the hills." For this is why I study frequently to admonish your charity that God resisteth the proud, but giveth grace to the humble, for a spring does not rise higher than the spot where it takes its beginning. It might at first sight appear that according to this rule, the paths of grace are not hindered by pride: especially because he who was the first to be proud, whom Scripture calls the King over all the sons of pride, is not said in the Scripture to have declared, "I will be higher than I am," but "I will be like unto the Most High." And yet the Apostle was not wrong in saying that he exalteth himself above all that is called God or that is worshipped. Man cannot hear the statement without a shudder of horror; but would that he shuddered equally at evil thoughts and sentiments. For I say unto you, that not the evil one alone, but every one that is proud exalteth himself against God. For the will of God is that which He commands should be done: and the proud desires to do his own will. These two things may seem to be equally legitimate: but notice how different are the conditions of the two. God does indeed will that His commands should be obeyed, but in those particulars only which reason approves (as reason always does approve the holy commands of God): he who is proud on the contrary, desires that His will should be done, whether it be conformable to reason or not. Do you not see how high he holds himself, and that the streams of grace are not able to reach him? Unless ye be converted, it is said, and become as little children (He says this who is the Source of Life, in whom dwelleth and from whom floweth forth the fulness of all graces) ye shall not enter into the kingdom of heaven. Prepare then the channels, level the barriers of

proud and earthly thoughts, become like, not to the first man
Adam, but to the Son of Man: because the source of grace
does not ascend into the heart of man while it remains carnal and earthly.   Purify thine eye also, that it may be able
to behold the purest light; and incline thine ear to obedience,
that thou mayest sometime attain to perpetual peace, which
is above all peace.   That is light which is the cause of serenity, peace which possesses tranquility, and a fount, that
which is a source of eternal and full satisfaction.   By the
source understand the Father, from whom is born the Son,
and from whom proceeds the Holy Spirit: by the light the
Son, who is, as it were, the splendor of Eternal Life, and
the true Light, which lighteth every man who cometh into
the world: by the peace the Holy Spirit, who rests upon
the heart that is humble and peaceful.   But I do not say
this as if these qualities were the propria of the several
Persons: for the Father is Light also, as the Son is Light of
Light; and the Son is Peace, He is our peace, who has made
both one: and the Holy Spirit is a Source of living water,
which springeth up unto eternal life.

    But when shall we reach this?   When wilt Thou satisfy
me, O Lord, with the joy of Thy countenance?   We indeed
rejoice in Thee, because Thou hast visited us, as the Son
rising from the height of heaven: and again we rejoice in
the blessed hope of my Second Advent.   But when shall
come the fulness of joy, not from Thy remembrance, but in
Thy presence; not from expectation, but in the fulfillment
of our hope?   Let your moderation, says the Apostle, be
known unto all men; the Lord is at hand.   For it is proper
that your moderation should be known to all, as was that
of the Lord.   For what is more incongruous that man, who
cannot but be conscious of his own weakness, should act
pretentiously when the Lord of Glory has shown Himself

unpretending among men? Learn of me, He says, for I am
meek and lowly in heart, that so your moderation may be
known among men.   By the words which follow, the Lord
is at hand, are to be understood His Right Hand: as when
He says, "Lo, I am with you always, even to the end of
the world," the words are to be understood of His Left.
The Lord is at hand, brethren, therefore be anxious for
nothing: He is very near, and shall speedily come to our
sight.   Fail not, be not wearied: seek Him while he may be
found, call upon Him while He is near.   The Lord is nigh
unto them that are of a broken heart: He is near to them
that wait for Him, that wait for Him with true hearts.
Finally, would you know how near He is?   Listen to the
song of the Bride when she speaks of her Bridegroom:
"Lo, He standeth behind our very wall."   By that wall, understand thy body, which is the hindrance interposed, so
that though He is near, yet thou art not able to behold Him.
Because of this Paul desired to be dissolved and to be with
Christ; and elsewhere he exclaims in sorrow: "O wretched
man that I am, who shall deliver me from the body of this
death?"   So also the Psalmist: "Bring my soul out of
prison that I may praise Thy name."

OUR LADY OF PERPETUAL HELP.

OUR LADY OF PERPETUAL HELP.

HISTORICAL SKETCH OF THE MIRACULOUS PICTURE.

Towards the latter half of the XV century there lived in the Island of Crete, a pious merchant, whose name, however, has not come down to us. He was particularly devout to Our Lady, and the most precious treasure he possessed was a picture of Our Lady of Perpetual Help, which he held in the highest veneration and before which he performed his daily devotions.

At that period, the Turks were at the height of their power and were making inroads into Southern Europe. In order to escape these barbarous and cruel invaders, a number of inhabitants of the Island of Crete resolved to leave their homes and seek refuge in Italy. Amongst them was our pious merchant, who took with him the holy picture, to prevent its desecration by the enemies of the Faith.

Yet scarce had they set sail, when dark clouds gathered overhead and a terrible storm arose. All that human strength and ingenuity could do to save the ship, was done, yet in vain. The tempest raged on with unabated fury so that all gave themselves up for lost. The merchant alone remained calm and unmoved. When all were on deck expecting each moment to be their last, he went and brought forth from his cabin the holy picture and holding it up, that all on board might see it, he exhorted them to place themselves under the protection of Mary, the mother of Perpetual Help, and invoke her aid.

At his bidding, they all knelt down before the picture and with sighs and tears offered their petitions to Mary, the Star of the Sea. They had hardly gone on their knees, when the fury of the storm began to abate. Peace and calm were soon restored, and in a short time they safely reached an Italian port whence the merchant with his miraculous picture proceeded to Rome.

The conception of the Picture is grand. The Holy Child has been asleep on His mother's arm, when he is roused from His slumbers by a terrifying vision, two angels bearing the signs of His future Passion and Death, the Cross, the nails, the spear to pierce His side, the sponge fastened to a reed giving Him gall and vinegar to drink. In His tender human frame, He shrinks from that fearful sight: hence His painful look: hence His clinging to Mary for help. Yet, as in Gethsemane, so here, He accepts His sufferings in obedience to the will of His heavenly Father. "Not my will, but thy will be done." Mary is fully aware of all that is in store for her divine Son. The sword of anguish has already commenced to pierce her heart. Hence her look of sorrow. Yet she, too, is patient and resigned. Her look is turned to us and not to Her Divine Son. For she is appealing to us to place our sorrows at her feet, since she is the Mother of Sorrows and to confide in her, since she holds in her arms Him who is the Saviour of the world. In the East, where numerous copies of the Picture are to be found, it is known under the title of "The Terrible Vision;" with us it is always known under the title of Our Lady of Perpetual Help.

It was on the 26th of April, 1866, when the miraculous Picture was brought in solemn procession from the Convent of the Redemptorists and carried through the streets previous to its solemn installment in its new Sanctuary. The houses were decorated with banners and the streets strewn with flowers. It is impossible to describe the enthusiasm of the people. The streets were too narrow to contain the vast crowds that had flocked together. Yet their whole bearing was marked with piety and devotion. Nothing was heard save the solemn chants of hymns and canticles which filled the air and the low murmuring of the fervent prayers that arose from the lips of the multitudes.

The procession was followed by a solemn Triduum in honor of Our Lady of Perpetual Help. Each day there was in the morning a Pontifical High Mass and a special sermon, followed by coronation of the Madonna of Perpetual Help. The right to grant this favor was from time immemorial possessed by the Chapter of St. Peter's. The Chapter unanimously granted the petition and charged the Dean of the Chapter, Monsignore Antici Mattei, Patriarch of Constantinople, to perform the solemn ceremony. In consequence of this, the Cardinal Vicar of Rome issued in the name of His Holiness, Pius IX, the following address to the Roman people, dated June 2d, 1867: "Last year we invited you to venerate the ancient miraculous Picture of Our Lady of Perpetual Help. Upon that occasion, you vied with one another in your public display of love and veneration to the Mother of God. Since then, numbers of you have invoked her again and again and received extraordinary favors from her merciful hands. In a few days hence, the miraculous Madonna is to be solemnly crowned. We invite you, therefore, once more to hasten forth and manifest your love and veneration to the powerful Queen of Heaven. Show to the faithful who have come to Rome from every part of the globe (by reason of the Jubilee celebrations of the Holy Apostles SS. Peter and Paul) how much you are devoted to Our Lady of Perpetual Help. Let them be edified by your noble example, that they may join you in prayer to implore Mary's protection upon Rome and the Universal Church.

The picture is in Byzantine style, painted on wood and evidently belongs to the XIII or XIV century. It measures about 15 by 12 inches. Upon a background of gold is seen the Blessed Virgin Mary, carrying the Infant Jesus on her left arm. Her outer covering is of dark blue color, her garment is red edged with gold. The halo around her head is artistically ornamented with beautiful designs. Above the halo is a brilliant star, and above that again are four Greek characters, two on either side, M. R. and Th. U., standing for Meter Theou, which means Mother of God. The Holy Child has His eyes turned to the left where His gaze is met with an object which causes His lovely features to be overspread with an expression of pain; with His two little hands He has seized hold of the right hand of His mother, as if for protection. He is clothed with a garment of green, held together with a girdle of red, and partially covered by a mantle of dark yellow. His head is likewise surrounded with a halo and above His left shoulder are four Greek characters J. S. Ch. S., standing for Jesous Christos, meaning Jesus Christ.

The bearing of the Holy Child and the painful expression on His countenance is explained by the two angels seen above Him, one to the left, the other to the right of Our Lady. The one to the left holds in his hands a Cross along with four nails which he seems to present to the Holy Child. This Angel is St. Gabriel and is expressed by the Greek initials seen above him, O. A. G., meaning the Archangel Gabriel. The Angel to the right holds in his hands a vessel, out of which stand forth a spear and a reed with a sponge. This is St. Michael, expressed by the Greek initials O. A. M.

The characteristic feature of the Picture consists in this that Mary's look, which likewise expresses a deep yet patient sorrow, coupled with tender compassion, is turned to the beholders as though she would say to them: "I, too, have suffered and know how to pity the sorrows of others. Confide in me: for I am the Mother of Perpetual Help."

The Holy See has encouraged this devotion to Our Lady under the title of "Perpetual Succor" in many ways. Pius IX granted the Redemptorists the privilege to commemorate the anniversary of the coronation of the Madonna by the celebration of a solemn feast with a proper Office and Mass. In 1871 a sodality was erected under the invocation of Our Lady of Perpetual Succor, which since 1876, has been raised to the rank of an Archconfraternity.

CONFESSIO VIATORIS.

Unum scio, quia cæcus cum essem, modo video.

By

C. KEGAN PAUL.

In my early childhood I knew of no church other than that in which my father ministered, and was vaguely conscious that from it there were some dissidents. These were spoken of in the county as Ranters, in the town as Wesleyans and Quakers, the only sects with which I was, however slightly, brought in contact.

The village in which we lived was in the Somersetshire coal-field; the fabric of the church was disgraceful, but no one had dreamed of restoration, the communion-table was a plain four-legged piece of carpentry without a cover, such as might have stood in our kitchen, the whole Service, when there was no Communion, was read in the desk, the Sacrament was administered about four or five times in the year; the surplice was a full white gown unrelieved by any stole or scarf. My father's reading of the prayers was grave and dignified, his doctrine old-fashioned orthodox, his sermons moral essays far over the heads of his congregation, his parochial ministrations above the average of those days.

We were wont to move into the neighboring city of Bath for the winter, where we attended the Octagon Chapel, later Margaret's Chapel, and, on very rare occasions, the Abbey. I believe my elders found something in the Services which aided their piety, but I remember nothing which helped my own. I loathed church-going, but was not an irreligious child. My mother always prayed with her children, and till long after I was grown up always came to me after I was in bed and read me a chapter in the Bible. This nightly reading is among the happiest memories of my youth.

In Bath there were still persons who retained some of the traditions of the High Churchism of Queen Anne's time, and we learnt from them that it was an old and pious use to attend Services on Wednesday and Friday. There was even one chapel attached to an hospital for old men which retained daily prayer. There also lingered the tradition that it was well to practice some self-denial in Lent. An old physician who was very kind to us as children then gave up snuff, and it was the only season in which we could approach him without sneezing.

The first time I was conscious of a dignified Church beyond the Anglican, and no mere body of Dissenters, was when my mother went one Holy Thursday to the Tenebrae Service at Prior Park, and gave me an account of it. She had made acquaintance, how I do not know, with a certain Father Logan, who preached the Three Hours' devotions on that occasion. I think my mother went to Prior Park at times for some years, and all that she told me impressed me deeply.

This was first when I was about ten years old, and then also, or soon afterwards, I found in my father's library a work called Downside Discussions, and read it with profound interest, though as may be well imagined, with little understanding. Some Protestant controversialist had challenged the Downside Fathers to a public argument on the points of difference between Rome and the Protestant Churches, and, strange to say, the challenge was accepted. A public disputation took place, and the matter ended as such encounters usually end, without apparent result. I do not remember any details, but it was clear to me that the Protestant champion had not answered all that was said on the other side.

When I was twelve or thereabouts, two books fell in my way which would have done much to make me a Catholic had there been any one to guide me; but the impression left on me by them was quite indelible. One was the well-known tale, Father Clement. In his recently published life of Mr. Philip Gosse, the naturalist, his son, Mr. Edmund Gosse, tells us that the reading of this work gave his father the strong abhorrence of Rome which remained with him all through his life; and no doubt such was the effect intended by the author.

On me the influence was quite the other way. The Protestant clergyman in the book, a Presbyterian, but put forward as a type of a Protestant minister, is asked where was his Church before the Reformation. His answer is at once so evasive and so fatuous that it was, to me, impossible to accept it for a moment, while the practices of piety inculcated on the young Papists, and held up for scorn, such as veneration for the saints, fasting, the sign of the Cross, etc., seemed to me meritorious, or at least perfectly innocent. And in so far as the hero, Father Clement, had Protestant leanings, he appeared to be leaving the more for the less worthy course.

The second book was The Nun, published anonymously, but known to be written by Mrs. Sherwood, the author of The Fairchild Family, Little Henry and His Bearer, and other books of a vehemently Protestant character. It is of high literary merit, and is far more true to fact than Father Clement. Subtracting certain absurdities of nuns kept in dungeons for heretical opinions, and secret meetings in underground chapels, when the Bishop urges putting a recalcitrant nun to death; "when a limb is affected with gangrene, my daughter, no ideas of false compassion should prevent our cutting it off"; convent life is not ill-described, as seen through distorted spectacles.

This book had been given to my mother by her dearest friend, and for that friend's sake it always lay on a table in her room. I read it for its literary charm, till I knew it almost by heart, and here again my sympathies were wholly with the orthodox Nun Annunciatia, the Abbess, and the Bishop, who were not I was sure, guilty of the deeds attributed to them, rather than with Pauline and Angelique, who escape in the Revolution troubles to become wives and mothers. But there was no one to deepen these vague impressions; and Roman priests and nuns, however interesting, were much like the characters in my fairy tales, denizens of a world into which I never expected to enter.

From the age of eight, when I went to a private school, till my entrance into Eton at thirteen, my school life had little influence on my religious life. Such as it had was harmful. Crossman's Catechism, which we learnt, is to me now a mere name. The head master and his wife, who gave us religious instructions, were cruel in temper and disposition, so that many of us were set against all that came from them, though I have no doubt they meant to teach us aright.

At Eton much was changed. There, for the first time, I heard a chanted "Cathedral Service," and weekday prayers in church without the weariness of a sermon; there, in 1841, such of us boys who were inclined to think, and who read the newspapers, became conscious of the great stir in Church matters which was going on at Oxford; a few of our masters were falling under the influence of the new theology, and this could not be without its effect on the boys.

It had its bearing on our minds, but to an extremely limited extent on our lives. There are lads who, by the grace of God, have in them a natural and ingrained purity of soul, and a revolt from every wrong word and deed, an instinct against evil, which preserves them in ignorant innocence through the perils of boyhood; but as a rule an average English lad is neither ignorant nor innocent. When he ceases to say his nightly prayer at his mother's knee, there is no one who enforces on him the connection between religion and morals; no one, except from the distant pulpit, ever speaks to him of his soul; no one deals with him individually, or attempts to help him in his special trials. A father is, as a rule, shy of his son, tutors are apt to treat all moral transgressions as school offences, and are unwilling to see what is not forced on them, so that the boy's soul shifts for itself, and for the most part fares badly. I can truly say that for the five years I was at Eton, between the ages of thirteen and eighteen, no one ever said one word to me about my own religious life, save always my mother, but she could know nothing of a boy's dangers, and was as one that fought the air.

But as a mere matter of intellectual opinion, Church questions were extremely interesting. The Christian Year became known to me almost by heart; it, and still more the Lyra Apostolica, Miss Sewell's books, and among them especially Margaret Perceval, put before me the Anglican Church theory, which I accepted with eagerness; nor was my pleasure and acquiescence in it disturbed even by the caricature of it which I found in Hawkstone, a foolish and impudent book, though written by a very able man, Miss Sewell's brother, the Rev. William Sewell, soon to become my tutor at Exeter College, Oxford.

I went to Oxford prepared to be a very High Churchman, and matriculated at Exeter, then a High Church College, the Rev. Joseph Richards being Rector, and Sewell senior tutor. A first cousin, who had obtained a scholarship at Trinity the year before, was already among the very highest of high undergraduates, and I became intimate also with a set of Christ Church students greatly under the influence of Dr. Pusey; so that on the religious side of Oxford life there was much to affect me.

My most intimate friend among the more thoughtful men in college, had brought up to Oxford far more definite Church tradition and practices than I. Had Sewell not been my tutor, I should have been, no doubt, wholly and completely a member of the High Church party; but no man ever made a serious cause more ridiculous than he. To a minute and scrupulous insistence on ritual, as then understood, and a burthensome and penitential life urged on all without reference to previous training or individual fitness, he joined a distrust and horror of Rome that were comic in their exaggerations. It was said that, like the old lady in Cranford, who rolled a ball under her bed each night, and only when it came out on the other side, was sure no burglar was concealed there, Sewell looked in the same hiding place to find a Jesuit; and it is certain that even Eugene Sue's belief in the machinations of the Society was not more intense than his.

The set with which I mainly lived was not a religious one, but rather the cricketing, boating and riding set, men of good morals for the most part, who were in no degree devout. In more serious hours, however, my sympathies were all with the High Church party. I was careful to attend any church at which Dr. Pusey was announced to preach, read Newman's sermons to my mother and sister in the vacations, and, unknown to my Oxford friends, endeavored to do some little district visiting among the poor, in a fitful way, under the direction of Rev. William Knott, Fellow of Brasenose, afterwards Vicar of St. Saviour's, Leeds.

In my third year I knew well a lady living in Oxford, who was herself in the habit of going to confession to Dr. Pusey, and was by her introduced to him. He invited me to see him, and I came to know him fairly well, but was never attracted by him, and should not have dreamt of making him my confessor or my familiar friend. The lady in question, much to her husband's annoyance, fitted up an oratory in her house, in which she had strange Services, more Roman than Anglican, but I never attended them, nor could I enter into her feeling when on meeting her one day in the street, she said, "Oh, my dear friend, the Father (Pusey) tells me we may not go to Rome." I assured her that I had no intention of going, but that, if I had, the Father's saying I was not to go would have no weight with me. I am afraid she never foregave me, though I remained an intimate friend of her excellent husband rather than of herself during the remainder of my Oxford career.

In my vacations, more than in Oxford, I saw the High Church party at its best. Much of my time was spent with the family of a member of my College. They indeed "lived the life," holding much Catholic doctrine, adopting many Catholic practices with a simplicity, earnest piety, and thoroughness very beautiful to witness. The eldest daughter was then an intimate friend of Miss Sellon, taking much interest in the attempt at the revival of Sisterhoods in the Church of England, and is now a Catholic nun of the Order of St. Dominic. The remainder of the family are still satisfied with their half-way house. I should probably have been more closely identified with them and their opinions but for the influence on my life of one of the most remarkable personalities I ever met, who drew me off for some years in quite another direction.

This man was Charles Kingsley. When I first knew him he was about eight or nine and twenty, in the full vigor of his manhood, and had just become celebrated among us young Oxford men by the publication of The Saint's Tragedy. I first met him at a breakfast given by his old schoolfellow, Cowley Powles, one of our Exeter tutors. Kingsley and I, Powles being engaged with his lectures, walked to Iffley on that morning, and the geniality and versatility of his nature impressed me as I have never been impressed by any other man, save one who in a degree resembled him in his enthusiasm and high-bred courtesy, James Brooke, Rajah of Sarawak.

Kingsley had come to Oxford to see some young men who were intending to take Orders, one of whom might serve him as a curate at Eversley. He selected one of my old school fellows, whom I visited in the following summer. The curate's lodgings were limited in accommodation, and I had to sleep at the village inn. We dined with the Kingsleys on the first evening of my stay, and early next day I received a note characteristically dated, "Bed, this morning," asking me to transfer myself and baggage to the Rectory. I did so, stayed weeks instead of days, and for some years thereafter Eversley Rectory became to me a second home.

A large part of Kingsley's character, and a charming description of his life, is given in the Memoir by his widow. The defect of the book is explained by the fact that it was written when the sense of her bereavement was very recent, so that the work is pervaded by a certain solemnity and gloom which were quite alien to the nature of the man as his friends knew him. No doubt like most persons of exhuberant temperament, Kingsley had his moment of deep depression, and he was towards the end of his life a disappointed man, but at the time of which I speak he was characterized by a sunny joyousness, an abounding vitality, and a contagious energy which were most attractive. He was in no sense a learned man, nor a sound scholar, nor a deep theologian, nor a well-read historian; he knew more of science than of all these put together, yet was not really scientific. But on almost all subjects conceivable he had read enough to talk brilliantly without any inconvenient doubt of his entirely sufficient equipment.

To young men, still in course of formation, this coruscating person, ten years older than ourselves, but young in mind, and a born leader of men, came as a kind of revelation. We had never met any one like him, nor indeed have I ever since encountered any one so impressive to the young. What was most attractive to me, and, of course, not to me alone, was that this man, so varied in knowledge and so brilliant in talk, athletic in habits and frame, a first-rate horseman, keen sportsman, good quoit player, was also a man of prayer and piety, filled with a personal, even passionate, love of Christ, whom he realized as his Friend and Brother in a fashion almost peculiar to the saints.

His reading of the Bible, whether at family prayer, or in church, sounded like a true message from God; his sermons, thoroughly unconventional, written in admirable English, were vigorous, reverent, and inspiring. He knew every man. woman and child in his scattered parish, and, with less effort than I have ever seen, with less sense of incongruity, could pass from light badinage in any casual meeting to deep·religious talk on the state of his interlocutor's soul. He was, theology apart, the ideal pastor of his people, living

among them and for them, rarely in those days going beyond the bounds of his parish, wholly devoted to what he
believed his divinely given work.

In his opinions Kingsley belonged to what was called
the Broad Church School, though he disliked the term, and
never would allow it to be used. The Athanasian Creed was
not recited in Eversley Church in those days, though
Kingsley joined a society for its defense towards the end of
his life, and the absence of anything which now would be
called ritual was remarkable.

I remember that when the curate preached, and Kingsley's
part of the Service was over, he was wont to put off his surplice, and take his place in his usual dress in the pew under
the pulpit by his wife's side. When the sermon was ended,
he would stand up thre in the pew and give the blessing in
his cut-away coat, without vestige of ecclesiastical garment.

But the Services, if unconventional, were reverent, and
whatever deductions might be drawn from his omissions,
Kingsley's teaching was sound on the great doctrines of the
Christian faith, as expounded in the Anglican formularies.
He was kind and tolerant to Nonconformists and their doc-
trines, and the whole vials of his wrath were reserved for
Rome and the priests of Rome. On the Catholic laity he
looked with compassion as foolish souls beguiled by liars.
In his first novel, Yeast, he introduces a priest named Padre
Bugiardo.

A man of this vehement and vigorous nature could not but
have great influence on young men. My own desire for
many years had been to take Orders in the Church of England. But my career at Oxford had brought doubts
about religion, still more about my own fitness for
the work; the High Anglican theory had broken down, and
with it had gone much of my childhood's faith, no authori-

tative interpretation of Scripture had ever been presented to me, and I was attracted by the plausible ingenuities of German criticism. I began to wonder whether there were indeed a Divine message for men, and if there were, whether I had the skill or the worthiness to hear it and deliver it again. The formularies of the Church had come to seem fetters on free research, which, as I now see, means only that each man may think what he pleases.

Kingsley, who mixed with his religion eager democratic politics, a care for the poor which verged on socialism, and a strong hatred of shams, endeavored, and with success, to persuade such as I that work brought the solution of all doubts; that not in cut and dried forms of theology, but in a zeal for God, lay the motive power of a parson's work; that if the Church of England needed widening it was to be done from within. I was moved with his enthusiasm, and felt with his feelings; to be a parson after his pattern was my aim, and a desire to help my fellow-men seemed as a call from God. My mother had always wished to see me a clergyman, and her death, with the deeper feelings it brought, gave me a push forward in the same direction. I accepted the curacy of Tew, in the diocese of Oxford, and was ordained deacon in the Lent of 1851.

Though Tew was a small parish, the work was considerable. Like most young clergymen of that date I had absolutely no theological training, and the mere duty of preparing sermons sent me to a course of reading which kept me well employed. When I consulted Kingsley on what to read, before my ordination, he advised me to read the Bible, without note or comment, and to let it tell me its own story, and Maurice's Kingdom of Christ. That seemed to him sufficient theology for the task, and the Bishop's requirements were hardly more. It is difficult to recall with precision what books were my study in my year and a half at Tew, but it was in a degree systematic and thorough, and gained me some grasp of scientific theology.

The clergy around were High Churchmen, some of them extremely so, and it soon became plain to me, that whatever the doctrinal teaching, the whole work of a parish, to be effective at all, except in the hands of a Kingsley, must be conducted on Catholic lines. And so, putting any deep thought aside under the stress of work, I became a more decided High Churchman in practice, and in some points of doctrine, while in others I remained latitudinarian. The standard of parochial work was high, and the clergy were kept up to the mark in this by the Bishop. Samuel Wilberforce was never to me an attractive person, indeed I disliked and distrusted him, but there has rarely been his equal for impressing a uniform stamp on the men who came under his sway, and for exacting to the full the tale of mechanical work. As all readers of his Life now know, he was always intensely Protestant, and his gross unfairness to Rome made me more tender to her supposed errors. But in Oxfordshire, as in Somerset in my youth, I knew no Catholics, and the murmurs and airs that reached me from the Church soon died away.

After eighteen months at Tew the work grew lighter; the schools had been organized, the church at Little Tew was built, mainly through me, I knew every soul in the two villages, and wished for a larger parish. The Bishop came to Tew for a confirmation, and asked me to take charge of Bloxham, a large and neglected village a few miles off, close to Banbury, a charge which I accepted with pleasure.

The circumstances of the parish were remarkable, as showing what was then the state of the Church in some byeplaces of England, even in so stirring a diocese as Oxford.

The incumbent was ninety years old, but hale and strong. He had been appointed to the living more than fifty years before, in exchange with a man who had died soon thereafter, so that Eton College, with whom rested the patronage, had in fact been kept from its exercise for half a century. His neglect of the parish had been scandalous; the Communion was administered but thrice a year, on Christmas Day, Good Friday, and Easter Day.

Not long before I became curate, the wine for this rite, which was always set on the table in a black bottle, was unopened. The Vicar turned to the communicants and asked "if any lady or gentleman had a corkscrew"; one in a pocket-knife was produced, and the Service proceeded. The curate was over seventy, but in much feebler health, and not more active than the Vicar. The scandals connected with the Services, and the neglect of parochial visiting became so flagrant, that the Bishop suspended the curate from the exercise of his functions, and made the Vicar place the whole administration of the parish in the Bishop's hands, in consideration of which the Bishop promised not to proceed against him. It was a somewhat high-handed and arbitrary measure, but no doubt substantial justice was done.

On the day my ministry at Bloxham began, the Vicar died suddenly, but as the Provost of Eton at once announced his intention of offering the living to a gentleman who was a chaplain in India, it was clear that six months of work lay before me, and I turned to this with a will. Never did a neglected parish respond so cordially to what was done for it. The Bishop made a great point of my endeavoring to know all the parishioners, to revive the schools, which had dwindled almost to non-existence; he insisted on frequent services, celebrations of Holy Communion monthly, and announced a confirmation, for which I had to prepare the candidates. The people welcomed zeal, often I fear without knowledge, and the duties were so incessant that there was no time for thought, or for reading.

At the end if six months the living was filled, and, somewhat overwrought by a spell of exciting and laborious work, I accepted a tutorship to teach two little boys in a family who were going to reside in Germany for at least a year. We went abroad in the late autumn of 1852. I had now settled down into that phase of thought which seemed to satisfy me. I was a latitudinarian in teaching and a High Churchman in external observances; the controversy between the Churches had ceased to interest me, and there was no reason to suppose I should adopt other opinions than those into which I had drifted. The friends with whom I was traveling were themselves average English Church people, with a strong desire that they, and especially the children, should not lose touch of English ways. We had, therefore, our own Services each Sunday. I rarely strayed into the Catholic churches, either at Carlsruhe, or afterwards at Constance.

I made the acquaintance of no or but few, Catholics, and the tuition of the boys, and my own German studies, left scanty leisure for much else. It was a dreary, stagnant time, in which I found no intellectual companions, and at Constance, in the following spring, a long and serious illness left me weak and prostrate. Pauci infirmitate meliorantur, says Thomas a Kempis, and his words were found most true. I began to pine for some real·work in my clerical capacity once more.

This came in most pleasant shape. My old tutor became Head Master of Eton, and, always one of my kindest friends, wrote to tell me that a conductship or chaplaincy at Eton was vacant, which might be mine for the asking.

This involved Services in the College chapel, and also the curacy of the parish. I accepted the work gladly, and entered on it in the autumn of 1853. My tutor had wished this chaplaincy to be a stepping-stone to another post, which he was soon able to offer me in conjunction with it; that of Master in College, in which I was to have the supervision of the seventy scholars on the foundation, my rooms adjoining and communicating with the boys' buildings:

In dealing with this task, very arduous, but at the same time one of exceeding interest, the necessity of one of the main practices of the Church soon became manifest to me, though I was far from grasping all that it meant. To direct a boy's conscience, to aid him to resist sin, to gain his confidence, without any fear that his transgressions would be considered as school offenses, and with a certainty that all he said was absolutely inviolable, it was necessary that something very like confession should enter into the relation between many of those entrusted to my charge and myself.

It was certainly a help such as they had never had before, one for which I had sighed in vain in my own school days, but even when I saw the blessing I recognized only the human side of it. It was a relief to tell another person all the actions and all the thoughts which interfered with a holy life, and the fact that the recipient of the tale did not turn away, but rather gave sympathy, advice and consolation, became a sign and pledge that God, more loving than man, would not reject the pentient, and induced those who might have despaired or become hardened, to cast themselves on the mercies of God. But there was in all this no belief and no teachings of true sacramental confession, itself the access to God, followed by valid absolution ratified at the time in heaven, thus, and thus only, communicated to the sinner.

There were those among the authorities, both Fellows and Tutors, who objected strongly to the influence I gained over some of the boys, and to my supposed High Church teaching and practices, but the Head Master gave me his full sympathy, and his entire sanction for coming as near to the administration of the Sacrament of Penance as in my position, and in my ignorance, it was possible to come.

But I was far from being a High Churchman in creed. Neologian criticism, which I read more and more, took increasing hold on me, and I had got completely on the wrong path. The traditional teaching of the Church once set aside, or rather never understood, the student necessarily dwells on the human, to the exclusion of the Divine, element in Holy Scripture, and wanders in the Bible like the Ethiopian servant with no man to guide him. My reading taught me to minimize dogmatic teachings, to hold the least possible doctrine compatible with a love for a somewhat stately ritual, chanted Services, and frequent celebrations of Communion, in which pious remembrance of Christ's Death, for it was to me no more than this, there seemed for myself and others great help towards a spiritual life.

The work among the boys was thoroughly happy. Some of those who had been at the head of the school when I was first appointed Master in College returned to work as Assistant Masters, and with these I lived in pleasant, elder-brotherly intimacy.

But the Head Master became Provost, and I was not on the same terms with his successor; the rooms appointed for the Master in College were no longer suited to the needs of my family; it was necessary to think of a change.

A College living in Dorset was offered to, and accepted by me, and I left Eton once again, with regret for the past and hope for the future. I remembered Kingsley's happy work at Eversley, and hoped to carry it out in my own sphere. He, however, had believed with all his might the faith he professed, I was soon to find doubts and perplexities at every turn.

The chaotic state of parties, dogma and discipline in the Church of England was forced at once on my attention. For many years, up to about four before the time of which I am now speaking, the Vicar had been non-resident, and the curate in charge was a pronounced, even extreme, Low Churchman. On the death of the Vicar, the living fell into the hands of a very prominent member of the ultra-Tractarian party, who at once established daily Services, and ornate ritual, restoring the church well, and contradicting in his every word and deed the teaching and example of his predecessor, who moved only to the next parish, and did all that in him lay to neutralize the work of the new Vicar.

When this gentleman was preferred to a benefice in another county, the Bishop frankly told me he wished for no Broad Churchman, and would, if it were possible, have refused to accept a man of my opinions, which had become known by various essays contributed from time to time to current literature. But as he could not help himself, he trusted I would at least continue the outward character of the Services now fixed in the parish, which indeed was quite in accordance with my own intention.

It struck me, however, as most grotesque, that the chief pastor of a diocese should have no voice whatever in the selection of the men appointed to serve under him, no power to inhibit what he considered false doctrine, and should have to appeal to the forbearance and good sense of his clergy to hinder a complete reversal of an established ritual approved by himself. The failure of his attempt to declare Dr. Rowland Williams an heretic, one of the writers in the then notorious volume, Essays and Reviews, brought into still greater prominence the weakness of the Anglican Episcopate.

All through the ministrations of three clerygmen, Low, High, Broad, the villagers, the farmers, and in great measure the few resident and educated gentry were scarce aware that there were any other than outward differences in the mode of conducting worship; these, and not the doctrines, were points to which objection was occasionally raised, and provided the parson went on the principle of quieta non movere, he might preach what he pleased, orthodoxy or heterodoxy, the doctrines of Rome, or Wittenberg or Geneva.

Yet again, for some years, my doubts were silent. The work of a parish was once more profoundly interesting, and the social problems which faced the worker in Dorset were so pressing as to throw for a time intellectual problems into the background. The condition of the agricultural laborer, then adscriptus gleboe almost as truly as any serf of old; his wages, sometimes, as low as eight shillings a week, with a dole of mouldy corn, and, if he were a shepherd, the chance of a joint of "braxy" mutton from a sheep which had died; his cottage, in which decency was impossible, cried aloud for reform, and made a parson who did his work into an agitator rather than a theologian.

Then came the great wave of the Temperance movement in Dorset, and the splendid crusade against drunkenness in my immediate neighborhood by one of the bravest and best women it has been my lot to know. The Laborers' Union and the Dorset County Temperance Association, added to my parish work, and to the preparation for College of pupils under my roof, made acquiescence possible in formulas, which if they did not appeal to me as absolute truth, seemed at least a plausible statement of all that in this life we could attain to know.

But the Laborers' Union accomplished its intention, raising wages by a dead lift at least two shillings a week, while public light, turned on the cottages, brought about there also a reform. We had done much for the Temperance organization, the parson's social and political work had been carried as far as possible; but meantime faith had not grown firmer, rather it had insensibly slipped away.

It is always difficult to say at what moment an intellectual position, long held with loosening grasp, becomes untenable; it is so easy to acquiesce for a while, so hard to deny what after all the heart continues to desire when the intellect rejects it; but at last I had to face the fact that I could no longer use in any honest sense the Prayer Book of the Church of England, nor minister at her altars, nor preach a definite message when all my mind was clouded with a doubt. I resigned my living, and came to London to take up a literary life.

Now for the first time during many years, I was able to consider my position calmly and fairly. While doing my duties as best I could, it had not been easy to realize how completely I had fallen away from the faith. Now, as a layman, with no external obligation to use words in which it was necessary to find some meaning consistent with my opinions, the whole Services of the Church of England seemed distasteful and untrue. The outward scaffolding on which I had striven to climb to God, every sacramental sign under which I had sought to find Him, had crumbled into nothingness. I was in no conscious relation to Him, God had practically no part in my life; though I did not deny Him, nor cease to believe that a First Cause existed; simple atheism is a rare, and perhaps an impossible position. I was content not to know, and to wait.

But in the meantime certain things were abundantly clear. Human relationships exist, the family, society, our country, the race; towards all these we have duties which must be organized; some conception of history, philosophy, and science must be framed, if not depending on God, at least in relation to man. The system formulated by Auguste Comte had long attracted me on its historical and social sides; a friend who, in and since Oxford days, had swayed my life more than he knew, had found it sufficient for himself, and he placed before me the religious side also of this grave and austere philosophy.

It is not a paradox, but sober truth, to say that Positivism is Catholicism without God. And it does, after a fashion, give order and regularity to life, inculcates simplicity of manners, aims at a certain amount of discipline, and caricatures, unconsciously, and with some effect, the sacraments, the cultus of Saints, the place of our Lady in worship, making of Humanity the ideal woman, the great Mother and Mistress of all.

It should in fairness be said that in this faith, if so it may be called, men and women live high, restrained, ascetic lives, and find in Humanity an object, not self, for their devotion. Like the men of Athens, they would seem ignorantly, and under false names, to worship God. And for myself I may say that I doubt if I should have known the faith, but for Positivism, which gave me a rule and discipline of which I had been unaware. The historical side of Comte's teaching still remains in large measure true to my mind, based as it is on the teaching of the Church. Comte had the inestimable advantage of having been Catholic in his youth, and could not even, when he tried, put aside the lessons he had learnt from her.

But Auguste Comte did more for me than this. It may seem strange, but, till I did so under his direction, I had never read the Imitation of Christ. Comte bids all his followers meditate on this holy book, telling them to substitute Humanity for God. The daily study of the Imitation for several years did more than aught else to bring me back to faith, and faith back to me.

So long as my Positivism lasted, I brought into it a fervor and enthusiasm to which I had been a stranger, and I was therefore long in discovering that these were unreal and forced. On many Sundays, when the Service was over, I was wont to walk home with a younger friend, whose experiences had been largely my own, save that his loss of faith had arisen from revolt against the extreme Calvinism which had been presented to him in his youth. He also had wandered out into Agnosticism, and discovered that he needed an external rule against the temptations of life, which for awhile he thought to find in the Religion of Humanity. In long walks across the park homewards in summer and winter noons we both found that the fervor of the Services evaporated, and left nothing behind them; there was none of that sense of a power abiding within us, which the Catholic worshipper brings away from before the Tabernacle, even if he cannot always maintain the intensity of devotion which has been granted him during the action of Holy Mass, or in the Benediction Service.

Once more I saw that my soul was stripped and bare, when it had seemed fully clothed. Such also was my friend's experience; and God has given him grace to find, as I have found, the truth after which we both were seeking.

Positivism is a fair-weather creed, when men are strong, happy, untempted, or ignorant that they are tempted, and so long as a future life and its dread possibilities do not enter their thoughts; but it has no message for the sorry and the sinful, no restoration for the erring, no succor in the hour of death.

In the training of my intellect and literary faculty, such as it is, one man had always held predominant sway. Those young men who entered on their Oxford careers towards the end of the decade 1840-1850, found that one prophet at least had gained honor in his own country, even if he had experienced also scorn and rejection. John Henry Newman was a moving intellectual force along with Tennyson, Browning, Ruskin and Carlyle. I came to know the two poets as I know my Bible, if it be not irreverent to say so, in such a way that after a time I needed no longer to read them, because the exact words surged up in memory when thought was directed to them, and there was no need of the printed page. Ruskin and Carlyle delivered their message, and passed on, but Newman abode, and his intellectual influence developed into one that was moral and spiritual, preparing my soul for the great grace and revelation which God had yet in store.

Like Thomas a Kempis, so Newman studied day by day, sank into my soul and changed it. Since Pascal none has put so plainly as he the dread alternative, all or nothing, faith or unfaith, God or the denial of God. I had not denied Him, but had left Him on one side, and now, as it were, God took His revenge. This is no place to explain in detail how in sorrow and desolation of Spirit God left His servant alone for awhile, to clutch in vain for some help in temptation, for some solution of doubt, and find none, if it were not God and the old creeds. It were to lay the secrets of the soul too bare to declare minutely, how each hesitation to submit to what was becoming intellectually clear, was followed by some moral or spiritual fall, as though the Father would allow His child to slip in miry ways, if nothing else would teach the need of guidance.

But apart from the direct leadings of God's grace, and the general effect of the Imitation and Newman, it may be well to specify more closely some of the arguments which weighed with me to accept the faith I had so long set at naught.

First, and above all, was the overwhelming evidence for modern miracles, and the conclusions from their occurrence. A study of Pascal's Life, when I was engaged in translating the Pensees, directed my special attention to the cure of Pascal's niece of a lachrymal fistula, by the touch of the Holy Thorn preserved at Port Royal. It is impossible to find anything of the kind better attested, and readers may judge for themselves in the narrative written of the facts by Racine, and the searching investigations by unprejudiced, and certainly not too credulous critics, Sainte-Beuve and the late Charles Beard.

Next in importance were the miracles of Lourdes, one of which as wrought on a friend of my own, came under my notice. I do not mean, especially in the former case, that these facts proved any doctrines; that the miracle of the Thorn made for Jansenist teaching, or those at Lourdes for the Immaculate Conception; but rather, that the Thorn must from its effects, have been one that had touched the Sacred Head, that the spring at Lourdes could only have had its healing powers by the gift of God, through Our Lady. It was .not that miracles having been declared in the Bible made these later occurrences possible, but that these, properly attested in our own days, and times so near our own, made the Bible miracles more credible than they were before, adding their testimony to that which the Church bears to Holy Scripture. And it was on the testimony of a living Church that I would accept the Scripture, if I accepted it at all, for surely of all absurd figments, that of a closed revelation, to be its own interpreter, is the most absurd.

The books which mainly aided me at this period, when I had accepted in a more definite way than ever before, the being of a God, who actively, daily, and visibly interposes in His creation, were the Grammar of Assent, by Cardinal Newman, and Religio Viatoris, by Cardinal Manning. Both works postulate God and the Human Soul, and on that foundation built up the Catholic faith. They are very different in their method, and perhaps, as a rule, helpful to different classes of mind, but both aided me. The re-reading of Grammar of Assent as a theological treatise, and with the wish to believe, was quite a different matter to my earlier study of it on its publication, when I regarded it only as an intellectual effort, interesting as the revelation of a great mind, but not as yet recognizing that it had any special message for me. But in these later days it proved to be the crowning gift of the many I received from that great teacher, who had been my guide through the years of my pilgrimage, little though I knew it.

It is not possible to state precisely the moment at which definite light came upon my soul, in preparation for the fuller day. As Clough says truly of earthly dawn:—

"And not by eastern windows only,
    When daylight comes, comes in the light,
In front, the sun climbs slow, how slowly,
    But westward, look, the land is bright."

About 1888 I had light enough to attend Mass pretty frequently, but even then was not definitely Catholic in my belief and sympathies. There was one of my own family, having a right to speak, who distrusted my evident leanings, not so much from want of sympathy with religion, as from a fear that as my opinions had been so long in a state of change, this also might be a passing phase. I said to myself, whether rightly or wrongly I cannot judge, that a year should elapse before I made up my mind on the question, though I began to see which way it must be answered. This was in the spring of 1889; but so weak is memory that towards the end of the year I was misled by a date, and supposed it had been in the late summer.

In May, 1890, I went for a short tour in France, as I had done for some years past, and a profound sense of dissatisfaction with myself filled my whole soul. In other days the cathedrals and their services, the shrines and their relics, places of pilgrimage, venerated images, had all been connected with a faith in which no one who studied the workings of the human mind could fail to take an interest, but they had no relation to my own soul. Now it seemed to me that I was an alien from the family of God, unable to take a part in that which was my heritage, shut out by my own coldness of heart, my own want of will. And as had long been the case, what attracted me most were just those things in the cult of Rome which most offended my companions.

A distinguished ecclesiastic was talking in Rome with a lady who while in England had shown some disposition towards the Church, but lamented that in the Holy City she had seen much that was to her disedifying, and quite unlike the pious practices she had known at home. He replied, "Ah, madame, il ne faut pas regarder de si pres la cuisine du

Bon Dieu." It was this which interested me and drew me to it. At Tours, the heap of crutches in the house devoted to the cultus of the Holy Face, the pathetic agony of the engraving of the same, seen in so many churches of that diocese, appealed more to me than the celebration of High Mass in the Cathedral; the rude image of our Lady at Chartres more than many a fairer statue.

At Beaulieu, near Loches, the end came. We had walked there from Loches, and while my companions were resting under the trees in the little Place, and taking a photograph of a neighboring mill, I remained in the church in conversation with the Cure, who was superintending some change in the arrangements of the altar. We spoke of Tours and St. Martin, of the revived cult of the Holy Face, of M. Dupont, "the holy man of Tours," whom the Cure had known, and at last he said, after a word about English Protestantism, "Mais, Monsieur est sans doute Catholique?" I was tempted to answer, "A peu pres," but the thought came with overwhelming force that this was a matter in which there was "no lore of nicely calculated less or more"; we were Catholics or not, my interlocutor was within the fold, and I without, and if without, then against knowledge, against warning, for I recognized that my full conviction had at last gone where my heart had gone before, the call of God had sounded in my ears, and I must perforce obey. But when?

The promise which I had made to myself that I would wait a year was binding on me as though made to one for whose sake I had made it, and the date at which the promise would expire seemed far off. But early in August I discovered that I had been in error as to the time, and that I was already free. On the 12th of August, at Fulham, in the Church of the Servites, an Order to which I had long felt an attraction, I made my submission to the Church, with deep thankfulness to God.

It was the day after Cardinal Newman's death, and the one bitter drop in a brimming cup of joy was that he could not know all that he had done for me, that his was the hand which had drawn me in, when I sought the ark floating on the stormy seas of the world. But in a few days afterwards, as I knelt by his coffin at Edgbaston, and heard the Requiem Mass said for him, I felt that indeed he knew, that he was in a land where there was no need to tell him anything, for he sees all things in the heart of God.

Those who are not Catholics are apt to think and say that converts join the Roman communion in a certain exaltation of spirit, but that when it cools they regret what has been done, and would return but for very shame. It has been said of marriage that every one finds, when the ceremony is over, that he or she has married another, and not the bride or groom who seemed to have been won, and Clough takes the story of Jacob as a parable representing this fact. We wed Rachel, as we think, and in the morning behold it is Leah. So the Church bears one aspect when seen from a distance, ab extra, another when we have given ourselves into her keeping.

But the Church is no Leah, rather a fairer Rachel than we dared to dream, her blessings are greater than we had hoped. I may say for myself that the happy tears shed at the tribunal of Penance, on that 12th of August, the fervor of my first Communion, were as nothing to what I feel now. Day by day the Mystery of the Altar seems greater, the unseen world nearer, God more a Father, our Lady more tender, the great company of saints more friendly, if I dare use the word, my guardian angel closer to my side. All human relationships become holier, all human friends dearer,

because they are explained and sanctified by the relationships and the friendships of another life. Sorrows have
come to me in abundance since God gave me grace to enter
His Church, but I can bear them better than of old and
the blessing He has given me outweighs them all. May He
forgive me that I so long resisted Him, and lead those I
love unto the fair land wherein He has brought me to dwell!
It will be said, and said with truth, that I am very confident.
My experience is like that of the blind man in the Gospel
who also was sure. He was still ignorant of much, nor
could he fully explain how Jesus opened his eyes, but this
he could say with unfaltering certainty, "One thing I know,
that whereas I was blind, now I see."

SAINT AUGUSTINE AND THE EUCHARISTIC SACRIFICE.

By

VERY REVEREND ALEXANDER MACDONALD, D. D.,

Of Nova Scotia.

———

In the roll of those who rank as Fathers of the Church there is no name more illustrious than that of St. Augustine. In loftiness of genius, subtlety and grasp of intellect, in range and accuracy of theological knowledge, it is not too much to say that he is without a peer. The greatest witness for the faith in his own day, and its stoutest defender, he still holds a place of preeminence among the men who have enlightened the whole Church by their learning. In every age since his own, he has been looked up to as an authority; so much so that in the religious revolt of four centuries ago, even the men who turned so completely away from the whole teaching and spirit of this great Catholic Doctor, would still fain claim him for their own, and shelter themselves beneath the aegis of his mighty name.

St. Augustine is thus singularly competent to tell us what the belief of the early Church was respecting the Eucharistic Sacrifice. Did the early Christians believe the Mass to be identically the same sacrifice with that of the Cross? Or, to put the question in a form better suited to the purpose of our inquiry, did they believe the sacrificial idea in the Mass, the formal reason why the Mass is a sacrifice, to be one and the same with the sacrificial idea in the bloody oblation of Calvary? I propose to seek an answer to this question in the pages of St. Augustine.

There are, in the voluminous works of the Bishop of Hippo, references almost without number to the Eucharistic Sacrifice. Nowhere, however, does the Saint set himself to determine the formal reason why the Mass is a sacrifice. Nor does he, so far at least as I have been able to see, define anywhere in precise words what a sacrifice is. In his De Civit Dei, he describes sacrifice as being "any work performed with a view of uniting us to God in holy fellowship;" but it is obvious that he does not in these words define sacrifice in the strict sense. That he looks upon immolation as an essential element of sacrifice in the strict sense, at least when there is question of sacrificing to God that which has life in it, is plain from a passage in his homily on the feast of SS. Peter and Paul. "To be immolated," he there observes, "is to die for God. The word is borrowed from the ritual of sacrifice. Whatsoever is sacrificed is slain unto God." Elsewhere he speaks of the sacrifice of the New Law as an "immolation," and in his epistle to Boniface writes: "Christ was immolated but once in Himself, and yet in the sacrament (or mystic rite) He is immolated, not only on every Paschal solemnity, but every day, for the people; nor would it be in any sense untrue, if one were asked whether He is immolated, to reply that He is." Here, then, we have the twofold immolation of the Victim, the real and the mystic, the bloody and the unbloody. Is it this latter that, in the eyes of St. Augustine, makes the Mass to be the distinctive sacrifice of the New Law, which he so often refers to as "sacrificium Christianorum," or "sacrificium Novi Testamenti?" It needs no deep study of his words to satisfy one's self that it is not; that it is, on the contrary, the real immolation of Crist upon the Cross which is, for St. Augustine, the ratio formalis sacrificii Christianorum. He does not say so expressly, it is true, but he clearly, and, I think necessarily implies it (1) in passages where he uses a language in speaking of the Mass which, at first sight, would seem to imply and has in fact been quoted by Protestant writers as implying, that it is not in itself a sacrifice, but a commemoration of the sacrifice offered up on Calvary; (2) in passages where he speaks of the Mass as being not merely a sacrifice, but the one and only sacrifice of the New Law; (3) in passages where he refers to the Mass as identically the same sacrifice with that of the Cross; (4) in passages where he insists upon the absolute oneness of the sacrifice of the New Testament. I shall examine these four sets of passages in the order named

In the passage, already cited, of his epistle to Boniface, the Saint says that we speak of Christ as being daily immolated on the altar in the same sense that we speak of His Resurrection from the dead year after year, as being, that is, a memorial or commemoration of what once took place. And in Contra Faustum Manichaeum he says that the mystic rites of the Old Law foreshadowed, in many and divers ways, "the one Sacrifice of which we celebrate the commemoration." Later, in the same work, he repeats this, saying that "Christians now celebrate the memory of that same completed sacrifice by the most holy oblation and participation of the Body and Blood of Christ;" and in the next chapter but two: "This sacrifice of the Body and Blood of Christ was promised before His coming in type and figure; in the passion of Christ it was offered in verity; after the Ascension of Christ it is celebrated in the Sacrament of commemoration." Does St. Augustine here mean to say that the Mass is only a commemoration of a sacrifice, and not itself a real sacrifice? Far from it, as we shall presently see. What, then, does he mean? In these and similar passages he is considering only one aspect of the Eucharistic Sacrifice. Viewing it precisely as distinct from the Sacrifice of the Cross, he pronounces it only a memorial or commemoration of that Sacrifice. Now, it is distinct just because in it there is a mystic and unbloody immolation of the Victim. Therefore, according to St. Augustine, the mystic immolation, or any immolation other than the real, does but make the Mass a memorial and representation of a "completed sacrifice;" it is the real immolation, and that alone, which makes it a sacrifice "in verity."

The passages are very numerous in which the Saint speaks of the Mass as being the one and only Sacrifice of the New Law. In his Confessions he says simply that "the Sacrifice of our ransom was offered" for the soul of his mother Monica. In his epistle to the catechumen Honoratus he writes: "Hence we give thanks to the Lord our God, which is a great sacrament mystery or (mystic rite) in the sacrifice of the New Testament. This latter, when you have been baptized, you will learn where and when and how it is offered." "There was formerly, as you know," he says, "the Jewish sacrifice of goats and oxen after the order of Aaron, and this in figure; there was not as yet the sacrifice of the Lord's Body and Blood, which the faithful know, as those also do who read the Gospel, the sacrifice that is now found over all the earth." So, also, in his commentary on the thirty-ninth Psalm. And, De Civ. Dei, "God clearly foretold by the mouths of the Hebrew prophets that there should be an end of the sacrifices which the Jews offered to shadow forth the one that was to be, and that this one sacrifice the Gentiles should offer from the rising of the sun to its setting." In the Tract. adv. Judaeos he declares that "the sacrifice of the Christians is offered in every place," and in the work Contra Adver. Leg. et Prophet., 1. 1, c. 18, that "former sacrifices of whatever kind were figures of that which the faithful know in the Church." So again, Tom. 9, pp. 154, 462; Tom. 10, pp. 211, 481; and in his homily De Sacramento altaris and infantes, where he refers to the Mass as the "sacrifice so pure and so simple (easy), which is not offered in the early city of Jerusalem only, not in the tabernacle built by Moses, or in that temple which Solomon erected, all which were figures of the future; but in which, from the rising of the sun to its going down, is immolated and offered to God a Victim of praise according to the grace of the New Testament. No longer," he adds, "is the victim singled out from the flock, nor is sheep or he-goat led to the altar. The sacrifice of our time is the Body and Blood of the Priest Himself; for of Him it was foretold so long before in the Psalms, 'Thou art a priest forever according to the order of Melchisedech.'" How could St. Augustine see in the Mass the one and only Sacrifice of the New Law, did he not regard it as being formally, that is to say, in ratione formali sacrificii, identical with that bloody sacrifice on Calvary in which Christ became a Victim forevermore? Certainly the bloody sacrifices of the Old Law foreshadowed first and foremost the Sacrifice of the Cross, and the Eucharistic Sacrifice only on the supposition that it is identical as a sacrifice, not materially merely, but formally, with that of Calvary.

But there are passages in which the Saint affirms, at least equivalently and by implication, the formal identity of the Eucharistic Sacrifice with the Sacrifice of the Cross. In his Confessions he tells us that his mother had never absented herself for one day from the altar of God, "whence she knew that Holy Victim to be dispensed, by which 'the hand-writing that was against us is blotted out.'" Again, in his Quaest, in Hept., he says: "What means it that the (Jewish) people were so strictly forbidden to taste the blood of sacrifices offered for sins, if by those sacrifices was prefigured this one sacrifice, in which the remission of sins is really effected, while no one is forbidden to take the blood of this sacrifice as food, but all rather are exhorted to drink, who would have life?" And in his Contra Cresconium Donatistam, "Although our Lord Himself says of His own Body and Blood, the alone sacrifice of our redemption, 'Unless ye eat of the flesh of the Son of Man and drink of His blood, ye shall not have life in you,' does not the Apostle teach us that even this becomes pernicious to those who use it amiss? For he says, 'Whosoever shall eat the bread and drink the chalice of the Lord unworthily, shall be guilty of the Body and Blood of the Lord.'" See also De Civ. Dei. Now, one who assigns as the formal reason why the Mass is a sacrifice aught else than its formal identity with the Sacrifice of the Cross, is logically compelled to agree with Saurez that the Eucharistic Sacrifice is not only distinct from, but, strictly speaking, different (simpliciter diversum) from the sacrifice

RETURN FROM GOLGOTHA—BY DELAROCHE.

offered on Calvary, though the same in a certain sense (idem secundum quid). In view of the passages quoted above, it does seem certain that such an idea was altogether foreign to the mind of St. Augustine.

Finally, there are many passages in which the Saint affirms in the most categorical and emphatic way, the oneness of the Sacrifice of the New Law. Over and over again he repeats this; he rings the changes upon it. Now it is "unum hoc sacrificium," now "unico sacrificio pro salute nostra," again "verum et unicum sacrificium pro peccatis," at another time "verissimo et singulari sarificio," and once more "singulari et solo vero sacrificio." Immediately after the words last cited, he goes on to say: "Accordingly, in the olden time, God ordered that the animals offered to Him in sacrifice should be without blemish, to foreshadow in such types this sacrifice; so that, as those (victims) were spotless and free from bodily defect, ground should be given for the hope that there would be immolated for us One who alone was spotless from sin." And a few sentences further on: "All of which the faithful are made to know in the sacrifice of the Church (Ecclesiae sacrificio), whereof all former species of sacrifice were but adumbrations."

The oneness of a thing is bound up with the being of a thing, for as much as a thing derives its unity from the same principle from which it derives its exsitence. Whence, then, has sacrifice its being? All are familiar with the fourfold division of cause into efficient, material, formal, and final. As for the efficient, final and material causes, there is no question, but these are identically the same in the Sacrifice of the Mass as they were in the Sacrifice of the Cross. In respect of these at least the Mass is absolutely one and the same sacrifice with that offered up on Calvary. The whole question is about the formal cause. Is this, too, one and the same in both? Sacrifice, in its first intention, denotes an action, rather than a thing; the sacrificial action, to speak precisely, is the sacrifice. This, so far at least as regards our sacrifice, is the act of immolation. Now, intrinsic unity of sacrifice depends more upon this than upon any of the other three causes for the reason that the intrinsic essence of sacrifice depends more upon it. The efficient and final causes, though they determine the being and therefore the unity of sacrifice, are yet extrinsic to it; and the material cause, the victim in actu primo, is not an intrinsic cause of sacrifice until it receives its determination from the formal cause, i. e., until the victim is actually immolated. The Paschal lamb, which prefigured Christ our Pasch, was not a sacrifice until it was slain. The lamb as such was no sacrifice! the lamb as victim, the lamb offered and immolated, was the sacrifice.

Does St. Augustine, then, regard the Mass as one and the same sacrifice, in the formal sense of the word, with the Sacrifice of the Cross, or as one and the same in the material sense only? It does not seem to admit of doubt that he is speaking of oneness and sameness in the formal sense. The Sacrifice of the New Law might indeed be called "unum sacrificium," in a loose, material sense, even if the Mass differed in ratione formali sacrificii from the sacrifice offered on Calvary. But such unity as this would hardly warrant the language used by the Saint in speaking of it. The expression, "unicum sacrificium," for instance, would imply more than this, for "unicum" is exclusive, as when we say of our Lord that He is unicus, Filius Mariae Virginis. So, again, the term "singulaire" implies formal oneness, expressing, as it does, the highest degree of oneness, namely, that of the individual. It is this formal oneness of the sacrifice that St. Thomas, too, seems to have in view when he says that "the Victim offered by Christ, who is both God and Man, has an everlasting power of sanctifying;" and the Council of Trent when it declares that the unbloody immolation in the Mass serves but to represent and to commemorate the Sacrifice in which Christ "by His own Blood entered once into the Holies, having obtained eternal redemption."

REV. ABRAM J. RYAN. TAKEN FROM THE LATEST PHOTOGRAPH

THEIR STORY RUNNETH THUS.

By

Rev. Abram J. Ryan.

———

Two little children played among the flowers,
Their mothers were of kin, tho' far apart;
The children's ages were the very same
E'en to an hour—and Ethel was her name,
A fair, sweet girl, with great, brown, wond'ring eyes
That seemed to listen just as if they held
The gift of hearing with the power of sight.
Six summers slept upon her low white brow,
And dreamed amid the roses of her cheeks.
Her voice was sweetly low; and when she spoke
Her words were music; and her laughter rang
So like an altar-bell that, had you heard
Its silvery sound a-ringing, you would think
Of kneeling down and worshiping the pure.

They played among the roses—it was May—
And "hide and seek," and "seek and hide," all eve
They played together till the sun went down.
Earth held no happier hearts than theirs that day:
And tired at last she plucked a crimson rose
And gave to him, her playmate, cousin-kin;
And he went thro' the garden till he found
The whitest rose of all the roses there,
And placed it in her long, brown, waving hair.
"I give you red—and you—you give me white:
What is the meaning?" said she, while a smile,
As radiant as the light of angel's wings,

Swept bright across her face; the while her eyes
Seemed infinite purities half asleep
In sweetest pearls: and he did make reply:
"Sweet Ethel! white dies first; you know, the snow,
(And it is not as white as thy pure face)
Melts soon away; but roses red as mine
Will bloom when all the snow hath passed away."

She sighed a little sigh, then laughed again,
And hand in hand they walked the winding ways
Of that fair garden till they reached her home.
A good-bye and a kiss—and he was gone.

She leaned her head upon her mother's breast,
And ere she fell asleep she, sighing, called:
"Does white die first? my mother! and does red
Live longer?" And her mother wondered much
At such strange speech. She fell asleep
With murmurs on her lips of red and white.

Those children loved as only children can—
With nothing in their love save their whole selves.
When in their cradles they had been betroth'd;
They knew it in a manner vague and dim—
Unconscious yet of what betrothal meant.

The boy—she called him Merlin—a love name—
(And he—he called her always Ullainee,
No matter why); the boy was full of moods.
Upon his soul and face the dark and bright
Were strangely intermingled. Hours would pass
Rippling with his bright prattle; and then, hours
Would come and go, and never hear a word

Fall from his lips, and never see a smile
Upon his face. He was so like a cloud
With ever-changeful hues, as she was like
A golden sunbeam shining on its face.

* * * * * * * *

Ten years passed on. They parted and they met
Not often in each year; yet as they grew
In years, a consciousness unto them came
Of human love.
           But it was sweet and pure.
There was no passion in it. Reverence,
Like Guardian-Angel, watched o'er Innocence.

One night in mid of May their faces met
As pure as all the stars that gazed on them.
They met to part from themselves and the world;
Their hearts just touched to separate and bleed;
Their eyes were linked in look, while saddest tears
Fell down, like rain, upon the cheeks of each:
They were to meet no more.
           Their hands were clasped
To tear the clasp in twain; and all the stars
Looked proudly down on them, while shadows knelt,
Or seemed to kneel, around them with the awe
Evoked from any heart by sacrifice.
And in the heart of that last parting hour
Eternity was beating. And he said:
"We part to go to Calvary and to God—
This is our garden of Gethsemane;
And here we bow our heads and breathe His prayer
Whose heart was bleeding, while the angels heard:
Not my will, Father! but Thine own be done."

Raptures meet agonies in such heart-hours;
Gladness doth often fling her bright, warm arms
Around the cold, white neck of grief—and thus
The while they parted—sorrow swept their hearts
Like a great, dark stormy sea—but sudden
A joy, like sunshine—did it come from God?—

Flung over every wave that swept o'er them
A more than golden glory.
       Merlin said:
"Our loves must soar aloft to spheres divine;
The human satisfies nor you nor me,
(No human love shall ever satisfy—
Or ever did—the hearts that lean on it);
You sigh for something higher as do I,
So let our spirits be espoused in God,
And let our wedlock be as soul to soul;
And prayer shall be the golden marriage ring,
And God will bless us both."
       She sweetly said:
"Your words are echoes of my own soul's thoughts;
Let God's own heart be our own holy home
And let us live as only angels live;
And let us love as our own angels love.
'Tis hard to part—but it is better so—
God's will is ours, and—Merlin let us go."

And then she sobbed as if her heart would break—
Perhaps it did; an awful minute passed,
Long as an age and briefer than a flash
Of lightning in the skies. No word was said—
Only a look which never was forgot.
Between them fell the shadows of the night.
Their faces went away into the dark,

And never met again; and yet their souls
Were twined together in the heart of Christ.

And Ethel went from earthland long ago;
But Merlin stays, still hanging on his cross.
He would not move a nail that nails him there,
He would not pluck a thorn that crowns him there.
He hung himself upon the blessed cross
With Ethel; she has gone to wear the crown
That wreathes the brows of virgins who have kept
Their bodies with their souls from earthly taint.

And years and years, and weary years, passed on
Into the past.　One Autumn afternoon,
When flowers were in their agony of death,
And winds sang "De Profundis" over them,
And skies were sad with shadows, he did walk
Where, in a resting place as calm as sweet,
The dead were lying down; the Autumn sun
Was half way down the west; the hour was three—
The holiest of all the twenty-four,
For Jesus leaned His head on it, and died.
He walked alone amid the virgins' graves
Where virgins slept; a convent stood near by,
And from the solitary cells of nuns
Unto the cells of death the way was short.
Low, simple stones and white watched o'er each grave,
While in the hollows 'tween them sweet flowers grew,
Entwining grave and grave.　He read the names
Engraven on the stones, and "Rest in peace"
Was written 'neath them all, and o'er each name
A cross was graven on the lowly stone.
He passed each grave with reverential awe,
As if he passed an altar, where the Host

Had left a memory of its sacrifice.
And o'er the buried virgins' virgin dust
He walked as prayerfully as tho' he trod
The holy floor of fair Loretta's shrine.
He passed from grave to grave, and read the names
Of those whose own pure lips had changed the names
By which this world had known them into names
Of sacrifice known only to their God;
Veiling their faces they had veiled their names;
The very ones who played with them as girls,
Had they passed there, would know no more than he
Or any stranger where their playmates slept;
And then he wondered all about their lives, their hearts,
Their thoughts, their feelings, and their dreams,
Their joys and sorrows, and their smiles and tears.
He wondered at the stories that were hid
Forever down within those simple graves.
In a lone corner of that resting-place
Uprose a low white slab that marked a grave
Apart from all the others; long, sad grass
Drooped o'er the little mound, and mantled it
With veil of purest green; around the slab
The whitest of white roses 'twined their arms—
Roses cold as the snows and pure as songs
Of angels—and the pale leaflets and thorns
Hid e'en the very name of her who slept
Beneath. He walked on to the grave, but when
He reached its side a spell fell on his' heart
So suddenly—he knew not why—and tears
Went up into his eyes and trickled down
Upon the grass; he was so strangely moved
As if he met a long-gone face he loved.
I believe he prayed. He lifted then the leaves

That hid the name; but as he did, the thorns
Did pierce his hand, and lo! amazed, he read
The very word—the very, very name
He gave the girl in golden days before—
"ULLAINEE."
He sat beside that lonely grave for long,
He took its grasses in his trembling hand,
He toyed with them and wet them with his tears,
He read the name again, and still again,
He thought a thousand thoughts, and then he thought
It all might be a dream—then rubbed his eyes
And read the name again to be more sure:
Then wondered and then wept—then asked himself:
"What means it all? Can this be Ethel's grave?
I dreamed her soul had fled.
Was she the white dove that I saw in dream
Fly o'er the sleeping sea so long ago?"
The convent bell
Rang sweet upon the breeze, and answered him
His question. And he rose and went his way
Unto the convent gate; long shadows marked
One hour before the sunset, and the birds
Were singing Vespers in the convent trees.
As silent as a star-gleam came a nun
In answer to his summons at the gate;
Her face was like the picture of a saint,
Or like an angel's smile; her downcast eyes
Were like a half-closed tabernacle, where
God's presence glowed; her lips were pale and worn
By ceaseless prayer; and when she sweetly spoke,
And bade him enter, 'twas in such a tone
As only voices own which day and night
Sing hymns to God.

She locked the massive gate.
He followed her along a flower-fringed walk
That, gently rising, led up to the home
Of virgin hearts. The very flowers that bloomed
Within the place, in beds of sacred shapes,
(For they had fashioned them with holy care,
Into all holy forms—a chalice, a cross,
And sacred hearts—and many saintly names,
That, when their eyes would fall upon the flowers,
Their souls might feast upon some mystic sign),
Were fairer far within the convent walls,
And purer in their fragrance and their bloom
Than all their sisters in the outer world.

He went into a wide and humble room—
The floor was painted, and upon the walls,
In humble frames, most holy paintings hung;
Jesus and Mary and many an olden saint
Were there. And she, the veil-clad Sister, spoke:
"I'll call the mother," and she bowed and went.

He waited in the wide and humble room,
The only room in that unworldly place
This world could enter; and the pictures looked
Upon his face and down into his soul,
And strangely stirred him. On the mantle stood
A crucifix, the figured Christ of which
Did seem to suffer; and he rose to look
More nearly on to it; but he shrank in awe
When he beheld a something in its face
Like his own face.
But more amazed he grew, when, at the foot
Of that strange crucifix he read the name—
              "ULLAINEE."

A whirl of thought swept o'er his startled soul—
When to the door he heard a footstep come,
And then a voice—the Mother of the nuns
Had entered—and in calmest tone began:
"Forgive, kind sir, my stay; our Matin song
Had not yet ended when you came; our rule
Forbids our leaving choir; this my excuse."
She bent her head—the rustle of her veil
Was like the trembling of an angel's wing,
Her voice's tone as sweet. She turned to him
And seemed to ask him with her still, calm look
What brought him there, and waited his reply.
"I am a stranger, Sister, hither come,"
He said, "upon an errand still more strange;
But thou wilt pardon me and bid me go
If what I crave you cannot rightly grant;
I would not dare intrude, nor claim your time,
Save that a friendship, deep as death, and strong
As life, has brought me to this holy place."

He paused. She looked at him an instant, bent
Her lustrous eyes upon the floor, but gave
Him no reply, save that her very look
Encouraged him to speak, and he went on:

He told her Ethel's story from the first,
He told her of the day amid the flowers,
When they were only six sweet summers old;
He told her of the night when all the flowers,
A list'ning, heard the words of sacrifice—
He told her all; then said: "I saw a stone
In yonder graveyard where your Sisters sleep,
And writ on it, all hid by roses white,
I saw a name I never ought forget."

She wore a startled look, but soon repressed
The wonder that had come into her face.
"Whose name?" she calmly spoke. But when he said

"ULLAINEE."

She forward bent her face and pierced his own
With look intensest; and he thought he heard
The trembling of her veil, as if the brow
It mantled throbbed with many thrilling thoughts,
But quickly rose she, and, in hurried tone,
Spoke thus: " 'Tis hour of sunset, 'tis our rule
To close the gates to all till to-morrow's morn.
Return to-morrow; then, if so God wills,
I'll see you."

         He gave many thanks, passed out
From that unworldly place into the world.
Straight to the lonely graveyard went his steps—
Swift to the "White-Rose-Grave," his heart: he knelt
Upon its grass and prayed that God might will
The mystery's solution; then he took,
Where it was drooping on the slab, a rose,
The whiteness of whose leaves was like the foam
Of summer waves upon a summer sea.

         Then thro' the night he went
And reached his room, where, weary of his thoughts,
Sleep came, and coming found the dew of tears
Undried within his eyes, and flung her veil
Around him. Then he dreamt a strange, weird dream.
A rock, dark waves, white roses and a grave,
And cloistered flowers, and cloistered nuns, and tears
That shone like jewels on a diadem,

And two great angels with such shining wings—
All these and more were in most curious way
Blended in one dream or many dreams.   Then
He woke wearier in his mind.   Then slept
Again and had another dream.
His dream ran thus—
(He told me all of it many years ago,
But I forgot the most.   I remember this):
A dove, whiter than whiteness' very self,
Fluttered thro' his sleep in vision or dream,
Bearing in its flight a spotless rose.   It
Flew away across great, long distances,
Thro' forests where the trees were all in dream,
And over wastes where silences held reign,
And down pure valleys, till it reached a shore
By which blushed a sea in the ev'ning sun;
The dove rested there awhile, rose again
And flew across the sea into the sun;
And then from near or far (he could not say)
Came sound as faint as echo's own echo—
A low sweet hymn it seemed—and now
And then he heard, or else he thought he heard,
As if it were the hymn's refrain, the words:
"White dies first!"   "White dies first!"

The sun had passed his noon and westward sloped;
He hurried to the cloister and was told
The Mother waited him.   He entered in,
Into the wide and pictured room, and there
The Mother sat and gave him welcome twice.
"I prayed last night," she spoke, "to know God's will;
I prayed to Holy Mary and the saints
That they might pray for me, and I might know

My conduct in the matter. Now, kind sir,
What wouldst thou? Tell thy errand." He replied
"It was not idle curiosity
That brought me hither, or that prompts my lips
To ask the story of the 'White-Rose-Grave,'
To seek the story of the sleeper there
Whose name I knew so long and far away.
Who was she, pray? Dost deem it right to tell?"
There was a pause before the answer came,
As if there was a comfort in her heart,
There was a tremor in her voice when she
Unclosed two palest lips, and spoke in tone
Of whisper more than word:

          "She was a child
Of lofty gift and grace who fills that grave,
And who has filled it long—and yet it seems
To me but one short hour ago we laid
Her body there. Her mem'ry clings around
Our hearts, our cloisters, fresh, and fair, and sweet.
We often look for her in places where
Her face was wont to be: among the flowers,
In chapel, underneath those trees. Long years
Have passed and mouldered her pure face, and yet
It seems to hover here and haunt us all.
I cannot tell you all. It is enough
To see one ray of light for us to judge
The glory of the sun; it is enough
To catch one glimpse of heaven's blue
For us to know the beauty of the sky.
It is enough to tell a little part
Of her most holy life, that you may know
The hidden grace and splendor of the whole."

"Nay, nay," he interrupted her; "all! all!
Thou'lt tell me all, kind Mother."

She went on,
Unheeding his abruptness:
"One sweet day—
A feast of Holy Virgin, in the month
Of May, at early morn, ere yet the dew
Had passed from off the flowers and grass—ere yet
Our nuns had come from holy Mass—there came
With summons quick, unto our convent gate
A fair young girl. Her feet were wet with dew—
Another dew was moist within her eyes—
Her large, brown, wond'ring eyes. She asked for me
And as I went she rushed into my arms—
Like weary bird into the leaf-roofed branch
That sheltered it from storm. She sobbed and sobbed
Until I thought her very soul would rush
From her frail body, in a sob, to God.
I let her sob her sorrow all away.
My words were waiting for a calm. Her sobs
Sank into sighs—and they too sank and died
In faintest breath. I bore her to a seat
In this same room—and gently spoke to her,
And held her hand in mine—and soothed her
With words of sympathy, until she seemed
As tranquil as myself.

"And then I asked:
'What brought thee hither, child? and what wilt thou?'
'Mother!' she said, 'wilt let me wear the veil?
Wilt let me serve my God as e'en you serve
Him in this cloistered place? I pray to be—
Unworthy tho' I be—to be His spouse.

Nay, Mother—say not nay—'twill break a heart
Already broken;' and she looked on me
With those brown, wond'ring eyes, which pleaded more,
More strongly and more sadly than her lips
That I might grant her sudden, strange request.
'Hast thou a mother?' questioned I. 'I had,'
She said, 'but heaven has her now; and thou
Wilt be my mother—and the orphan girl
Will make her life her thanks.'
        'Thy father, child?'
'Ere I was cradled he was in his grave.'
'And hast not sister nor brother?' 'No,' she said,
'God gave my mother only me; one year
This very day He parted us.' 'Poor child,'
I murmured. 'Nay, kind Sister,' she replied,
'I have much wealth—they left me ample means—
I have true friends who love me and protect.
I was a minor until yesterday;
But yesterday all guardianship did cease,
And I am mistress of myself and all
My worldly means—and, Sister, they are thine
If thou but take myself—nay—don't refuse.'
'Nay—nay—my child!' I said; 'the only wealth
We wish for is the wealth of soul—of grace.
Not all your gold could unlock yonder gate,
Or buy a single thread of Virgin's veil.
Not all the coins in coffers of a king
Could bribe an entrance here for any one.
God's voice alone can claim a cell—a veil,
For any one He sends.
        Who sent you here,
My child? Thyself? Or did some holy one
Direct thy steps? Or else some sudden grief?

Or, mayhap, disappointment? Or, perhaps,
A sickly weariness of that bright world
Hath cloyed thy spirit? Tell me, which is it.'
'Neither,' she quickly, almost proudly spoke.
'Who sent you, then?'
                        'A youthful Christ,' she said,
'Who, had he lived in those far days of Christ,
Would have been His belov'd Disciple, sure—
Would have been His own gentle John; and would
Have leaned on Thursday night upon His breast,
And stood on Friday eve beneath His cross
To take His Mother from Him when He died.
He sent me here—he said the word last night
In my own garden; this the word he said—
Oh! had you heard him whisper: "Ethel, dear!
Your heart was born with veil of virgin on;
I hear it rustle every time we meet,
In all your words and smiles; and when you weep
I hear it rustle more. Go—wear your veil—
And outwardly be what inwardly thou art,
And hast been from the first. And, Ethel, list:
My heart was born with priestly vestments on,
And at Dream-Altars I have ofttimes stood,
And said such sweet Dream-Masses in my sleep—
And when I lifted up a white Dream-Host,
A silver Dream-Bell rang—and angels knelt,
Or seemed to kneel, in worship. Ethel say—
Thou wouldst not take the vestments from my heart
Nor more than I would tear the veil from thine.
My vested and thy veiled heart part to-night
To climb our Calvary and to meet in God;
And this, fair Ethel, is Gethsemane—
And He is here, who, in that other, bled;

And they are here who came to comfort Him—
His angels and our own; and His great prayer,
Ethel, is ours to-night—let's say it, then:
Father! Thy will be done! Go find your veil
And I my vestments." He did send me here.'

"She paused—a few stray tears had dropped upon
Her closing words and softened them to sighs.
I listened, inward moved, but outward calm and cold
To the girl's strange story. Then, smiling said:
'I see it is a love-tale after all,
With much of folly and some of fact in it;
It is a heart affair, and in such' things
There's little logic, and there's less of sense.
You brought your heart, dear child, but left your head
Outside the gates; nay, go, and find the head
You lost last night—and then, I am quite sure,
You'll not be anxious to confine your heart
Within this cloistered place.'
            She seemed to wince
Beneath my words one moment—then replied:
'If e'en a wounded heart did bring me here,
Dost thou do well, Sister, to wound it more?
If merely warmth of feelings urge me here,
Dost thou do well to chill them into ice?
And were I disappointed in yon world,
Should that bar me from a purer place?
You say it is a love-tale—so it is; .
The vase was human—but the flower divine;
And if I break the vase with my own hands,
Will you forbid that I should humbly ask
The heart of God to be my lily's vase?
I'd trust my lily to no heart on earth

Save his who yesternight did send me here
To dip it in the very blood of Christ,
And plant it here.'
        And then she sobbed outright
A long, deep sob.
        I gently said to her:
'Nay, child, I spoke to test thee—do not weep.
If thou art called of God, thou shalt come
And fiind e'en here a home. But God is slow
In all his works and ways, and slower still
When He would deck a bridge to grace His Court,
Go, now, and in one year—if thou dost come
Thy veil and cell shall be prepared for thee;
Nay—urge me not—it is our holy rule—
A year of trial! I must to choir, and thou
Into the world to watch and wait and pray
Until the Bridegroom comes.'
        She rose and went
Without a word.

        "And twelvemonth after came,
True to the very day and hour, and said:
'Wilt keep thy promise made one year ago?
Where is my cell—and where my virgin's veil?
Wilt try me more? Wilt send me back again?
I came once with my wealth and was refused:
And now I come as poor as Holy Christ
Who had no place to rest his weary head—
My wealth is gone; I offered it to him
Who sent me here; he sent me speedy word
"Give all unto the poor in quiet way—
And hide the giving—ere you give yourself
To God!" Wilt take me now for my own sake?

I bring my soul—'tis little worth I ween,
And yet it cost sweet Christ a priceless price.'

" 'My child,' I said, 'thrice welcome—enter here;
A few short days of silence and of prayer,
And thou shalt be the Holy Bridegroom's bride.'

"Her novice days went on; much sickness fell
Upon her. Oft she lay for weary weeks
In awful agonies, and no one heard
A murmur from her lips. She oft would smile
A sunny, playful smile, that she might hide
Her sufferings from us all. When she was well
She was the first to meet the hour of prayer—
The last to leave it—and they named her well:
The 'Angel of the Cloister.' Once I heard
The Father of our souls say when she passed
'Beneath that veil of sacrificial black
She wears the white robe of her innocence.'
And we—we believed it. There are sisters here
Of three-score years of service who would say:
'Within our memory never moved a veil
That hid so saintly and so pure a heart.'
And we—we felt it, and we loved her so,
We treated her as angel and as child.
I never heard her speak about the past,
I never heard her mention e'en a name
Of any in the world. She little spake;
She seemed to have rapt moments—then she grew
Absent-minded, and would come and ask me
To walk alone and say her Rosary
Beneath the trees. She had a voice divine;
And when she sang for us, in truth it seemed

The very heart of song was breaking on her lips.
The dower of her mind as of her heart,
Was of the richest, and she mastered art
By instinct more than study. Her weak hands
Moved ceaselessly amid the beautiful.
There is a picture hanging in our choir
She painted. I remember well the morn
She came to me and told me she had dreamt
A dream; then asked me if I would let her paint
Her dream. I gave permission. Weeks and weeks
Went by, and ev'ry spare hour of the day
She kept her cell all busy with her work.
At last 'twas finished, and she brought it forth—
A picture my poor words may not portray.
But you must gaze on it with your own eyes,
And drink its magic and its meanings in;
I'll show it thee, kind sir, before you go.

"In every May for two whole days she kept
Her cell. We humored her in that; but when
The days had passed, and she came forth again,
Her face was tender as a lily's leaf,
With God's smile on it; and for days and days
Thereafter, she would scarce ope her lips
Save when in prayer, and then her every look
Was rapt, as if her soul did hold with God
Strange converse. And, who knows? mayhap she did.

"I half forgot—on yonder mantelpiece
You see that wondrous crucifix; one year
She spent on it, and begged to put beneath
That most mysterious word—'Ullainee.'

"At last the cloister's angel disappeared;

Her face was missed at choir, her voice was missed-
Her words were missed where every day we met
In recreation's hour. And those who passed
The angel's cell would lightly tread, and breathe
A prayer that death might pass the angel by
And let her longer stay, for she lay ill—
Her frail, pure life was ebbing fast away.
Ah! many were the orisons that rose
From all our hearts that God might spare her still;
At Benediction and at holy Mass
Our hands were lifted, and strong pleadings went
To heaven for her; we did love her so—
Perhaps too much we loved her, and perhaps
Our love was far too human. Slow and slow
She faded like a flower. And slow and slow
Her pale cheeks whitened more. And slow and slow
Her large, brown, wondering eyes sank deep and dim.
Hope died on all our faces; but on her's
Another and a different hope did shine,
And from her wasted lips sweet prayers arose
That made her watchers weep. Fast came the end.
Never such silence o'er the cloister hung—
We walked more softly, and, whene'er we spoke,
Our voices fell to whispers, lest a sound
Might jar upon her ear. The sisters watched
In turns beside her couch; to each she gave
A gentle word, a smile, a thankful look.
At times her mind did wander; no wild words
Escaped her lips—she seemed to float away
To far-gone days, and live again in scenes
Whose hours were bright and happy. In her sleep
She ofttimes spoke low,, gentle, holy words
About her mother; and sometimes she sang

The fragments of sweet olden songs—and when
She woke again, she timidly would ask
If she had spoken in her sleep, and what
She said, as if, indeed, her heart did fear
That sleep might open there some long-closed gate
She would keep locked. And softly as a cloud,
A golden cloud upon a summer's day,
Floats from the heart of land out o'er the sea,
So her sweet life was passing. One bright eve,
The fourteenth day of August, when the sun
Was wrapping, like a king, a purple cloud
Around him on descending day's bright throne,
She sent for me and bade me come in haste.
I went into her cell. There was a light
Upon her face, unearthly; and it shone
Like gleam of star upon a dying rose.
I sat beside her on the couch, and took her hand
In mine—a fair, frail hand that scarcely seem'd
Of flesh—so wasted, white and wan it was.
Her great, brown, wond'ring eyes had sunk away
Deep in their sockets—and their light shone dim
As tapers dying on an altar. Soft
As a dream of beauty on me fell low,
Last words.
          'Mother, the tide is ebbing fast;
But ere it leaves this shore to cross the deep
And seek another, calmer, I would say
A few last words—and, Mother, I would ask
One favor more, which thou wilt not refuse.
Thou wert a mother to the orphan girl,
Thou gav'st her heart a home, her love a vase,
Her weariness a rest, her sacrifice a shrine—
And thou didst love me, Mother, as she loved

Whom I shall meet to-morrow, far away—
But no, it is not far—that other heaven
Touches this, Mother; I have felt its touch,
And now I feel its clasp upon my soul.
I'm going from this heaven into that,
To-morrow, Mother. Yes, I dreamt it all.
It was the sunset of Our Lady's feast.
My soul passed upwards thro' the golden clouds
To sing the second vespers of the day
With all the angels. Mother, ere I go,
Thou'lt listen, Mother sweet, to my last words,
Which, like all last words, tell whate'er was first
In life or tenderest in heart. I came
Unto my convent cell and virgin veil,
Sent by a spirit that had touched my own
As wings of angels touch—to fly apart
Upon their missions—till they meet again
In heaven, heart to heart, wing to wing.
The "Angel of the Cloister" you called me—
Unworthy sure of such a beauteous name—
My mission's over—and your angel goes
To-morrow home. This earthly part which stays
You'll lay away within a simple grave—
But, Mother, on its slab thou'lt grave this name,
"Ullainee!" (she spelt the letters out),
Nor ask me why—tho' if thou wilt I'll tell;
It is my soul name, given long ago
By one who found it in some Eastern book,
Or dreamt it in a dream, and gave it me—
Nor ever told the meaning of the name;
And, Mother, should he ever come and read
That name upon my grave, and come to thee
And ask the tidings of "Ullainee,"

Thou'lt tell him all—and watch him if he weeps,
Show him the crucifix my poor hands carved—
Show him the picture in the chapel choir—
And watch him if he weeps; and then
There are three humble scrolls in yonder drawer';
(She pointed to the table in her room);
'Some words of mine and words of his are there.
And keep these simple scrolls until he comes,
And put them in his hands; and, Mother, watch—
Watch him if he weeps; and tell him this:
I tasted all the sweets of sacrifice,
I kissed my cross a thousand times a day,
I hung and bled upon it in my dreams,
I lived on it—I loved it to the last.'   And then
A low, soft sigh crept thro' the virgin's cell;
I looked upon her face, and death was there."
There was a pause—and in the pause one wave
Of shining tears swept thro' the Mother's eyes.
"And thus," she said, "our angel passed away.
We buried her, and at her last request
We wrote upon the slab, 'Ullainee.'
And I—(for she asked me one day thus,
The day she hung her picture in the choir)—
I planted o'er her grave a white rose tree.
The roses crept around the slab and hid
The graven name—and still we sometimes cull
Her sweet, white roses, and we place them on
Our Chapel-Altar."
                    Then the Mother rose,
Without another word, and led him thro'
A long, vast hall, then up a flight of stairs
Unto an oaken door, which turned upon its hinge
Noiselessly—then into a Chapel dim,

On gospel side of which there was a gate
From ceiling down to floor, and back of that
A long and narrow choir, with many stalls,
Brown-oaken; all along the walls were hung
Saint-pictures, whose sweet faces looked upon
The faces of the Sisters in their prayers.
Beside a "Mater Dolorosa" hung
The picture of the "Angel of the Choir."
He sees it now thro' vista of the years,
Which stretch between him and that long-gone day,
It hangs within his memory as fresh
In tint and touch and look as long ago.
There was a power in it, as if the soul
Of her who painted it had shrined in it
Its very self; there was a spell in it
That fell upon his spirit thro' his eyes,
And made him dream of God's own holy heart.
The shadow of the picture, in weak words,
Was this, or something very like to this:
————A wild, wierd wold,
Just like the desolation of a heart,
Stretched far away into infinity;
Above it low, gray skies drooped sadly down,
As if they fain would weep, and all was bare
As bleakness' own bleak self; a mountain stood
All mantled with the glory of a light
That flashed out from the heavens, and a cross
With such a pale Christ hanging in its arms
Did crown the mount; and either side the cross
There were two crosses lying on the rocks—
One of the whitest roses—ULLAINEE
Was woven into it with buds of Red;
And one of reddest roses—Merlin's name

Was woven into it with buds of white.
Below the cross and crosses and the mount
The earth-place lay so dark and bleak and drear;
Above, a golden glory seemed to hang
Like God's own benediction o'er the names.
I saw the picture once; it moved me so
I ne'er forgot its beauty or its truth;
But words as weak as mine can never paint
The Crucifixion's picture.
                    Merlin said to me:
"Some day—some far-off day—when I am dead,
You have the simple rhymings of two hearts,
And if you think it best, the world may know
A love-tale crowned by purest SACRIFICE."

SONG OF THE MYSTIC

I WALK down the Valley of Silence—
　　Down the dim, voiceless valley—alone!
And I hear not the fall of a footstep
　　Around me, save God's and my own;
And the hush of my heart is as holy
　　As hovers where angels have flown!

Long ago was I weary of voices
　　Whose music my heart could not win;
Long ago was I weary of noises
　　That fretted my sould with their din;
Long ago was I weary of places
　　Where I met but the human—and sin.

I walked in the world with the worldly;
　　I craved what the world never gave;
And I said: "In the world each Ideal,
　　That shines like a star on life's wave,
Is wrecked on the shores of the Real,
　　And sleeps like a dream in a grave."

And still did I pine for the Perfect,
　　And still found the False with the True;
I sought 'mid the Human for Heaven,
　　But caught a mere glimpse of its Blue:
And I wept when the clouds of the Mortal
　　Veiled even that glimpse from my view.

And I toiled on, heart-tired, of the Human,
   And I moaned, 'mid the mazes of men,
Till I knelt, long ago, at an altar,
   And I heard a voice call me. Since then
I walk down the Valley of Silence
   That lies far beyond mortal ken.

Do you ask what I found in the Valley?
   'Tis my Trysting Place with the Divine.
And I fell at the feet of the Holy,
   And above me a voice said: "Be mine."
And there arose from the depths of my spirit
   An echo—"My heart shall be Thine."

Do you ask how I live in the Valley?
   I weep—and I dream—and I pray.
But my tears are as sweet as the dewdrops
   That fall on the roses in May;
And my prayer, like a perfume from censers,
   Ascendeth to God night and day.

In the hush of the Valley of Silence
   I dream all the songs that I sing;
And the music floats down the dim Valley
   Till each finds a word for a wing,
That to hearts, like the Dove of the Deluge,
   A message of Peace they may bring.

But far on the deep there are billows
   That never shall break on the beach;
And I have heard songs in the Silence
   That never shall float into speech;
And I have had dreams in the Valley
   Too lofty for language to reach.

And I have seen Thoughts in the Valley—
    Ah! me, how my spirit was stirred!
And they wear holy veils on their faces,
    Their footsteps can scarcely be heard;
They pass through the Valley like virgins,
    Too pure for the touch of a word!

Do you ask me the place of the Valley,
    Ye hearts that are harrowed by Care?
It lieth afar between mountains,
    And God and His angels are there:
And one is the dark mount of Sorrow,
    And one the bright mountain of Prayer.

ERIN'S FLAG

UNROLL Erin's flag! fling its folds to the breeze!
Let it float o'er the land, let it flash o'er the seas!
Lift it out of the dust—let it wave as of yore,
When its chiefs with their clans stood around it and swore
That never! no, never! while God gave them life,
And they had an arm and a sword for the strife,
That never! no, never! that banner should yield
As long as the heart of a Celt was its shield:
While the hand of a Celt had a weapon to wield
And his last drop of blood was unshed on the field.

Lift it up! wave it high! 'tis as bright as of old!
Not a stain on its green, not a blot on its gold,
Tho' the woes and the wrongs of three hundred long years
Have drenched Erin's sunburst with blood and with tears!
Though the clouds of oppression enshroud it in gloom,
And around it the thunders of Tyranny boom.
Look aloft! look aloft! the clouds drifting by,
There's a gleam through the gloom, there's a light in the sky,
'Tis the sunburst resplendent—far, flashing on high!
Erin's dark night is waning, her day-dawn is nigh!

Lift it up! lift it up! the old Banner of Green!
The blood of its sons has but brightened it sheen;
What though the tyrant has trampled it down,
Are not its folds emblazoned with deeds of renown?
What though for ages it droops in the dust,
Shall it droop thus forever? No, no! God is just!
Take it up! take it up! from the tyrant's foul tread,
Let him tear the Green Flag—we will snatch its last shred,
And beneath it we'll bleed as our forefathers bled,
And we'll swear by the blood which the Briton has shed,
And we'll vow by the wrecks which through Erin he spread,
And we'll swear by the thousands who, famished, unfed,
Died down in the ditches, wild-howling for bread;
And we'll vow by our heroes, whose spirits have fled,
And we'll swear by the bones in each coffinless bed,
That we'll battle the Briton through danger and dread;
That we'll cling to the cause which we glory to wed,
'Til the gleam of our steel and the shock of our lead
Shall prove to our foe that we meant what we said—
That we'll lift up the green, and we'll tear down the red!

Lift up the Green Flag! oh! it wants to go home,
Full long has its lot been to wander and roam,
It has followed the fate of its sons o'er the world,
But its folds, like their hopes, are not faded nor furled;
Like a weary-winged bird, to the East and the West,
It has flitted and fled—but it never shall rest
'Til, pluming its pinions, it sweeps o'er the main,
And speeds to the shores of its old home again,
Where its fetterless folds o'er each mountain and plain
Shall wave with a glory that never shall wane.

Take it up! take it up! bear it back from afar!
That banner must blaze 'mid the lightnings of war;
Lay your hands on its folds, lift your gaze to the sky,
And swear that you'll bear it triumphant or die,
And shout to the clans scattered far o'er the earth
To join in the march to the land of their birth;
And wherever the Exiles, 'neath heaven's broad dome,
Have been fated to suffer, to sorrow and roam,
They'll bound on the sea, and away o'er the foam,
They'll sail to the music of "Home, Sweet Home!"

A CHILD'S WISH.

I wish I were the little key
  That locks Love's Captive in,
And lets Him out to go and free
  A sinful heart from sin.

I wish I were the little bell
  That tinkles for the Host,
When God comes down each day to dwell
  With hearts He loves the most.

I wish I were the chalice fair,
  That holds the Blood of Love,
When every flash lights holy prayer
  Upon its way above.

I wish I were the little flower
  So near the Host's sweet face,
Or like the light that half an hour
  Burns on the shrine of grace.

I wish I were the altar where,
  As on His mother's breast,
Christ nestles, like a child, fore'er
  In Eucharistic rest.

But, oh! my God, I wish the most
  That my poor heart may be
A home all holy for each Host
  That comes in love to me.

MY BEADS.

Sweet, blessed beads! I would not part
    With one of you for richest gem
    That gleams in kingly diadem;
Ye know the history of my heart.

For I have told you every grief
    In all the days of twenty years,
    And I have moistened you with tears,
And in your decades found relief.

Ah! time has fled, and friends have failed
    And joys have died; but in my needs
    Ye were my friends, my blessed beads!
And ye consoled me when I wailed.

For many and many a time, in grief,
    My weary fingers wandered round
    Thy circled chain, and always found
In some Hail Mary sweet relief.

How many a story you might tell
    Of inner life, to all unknown;
    I trusted you and you alone,
But ah! ye keep my secrets well.

Ye are the only chain I wear—
    A sign that I am but the slave,
    In life, in death, beyond the grave,
Of Jesus and His Mother fair.

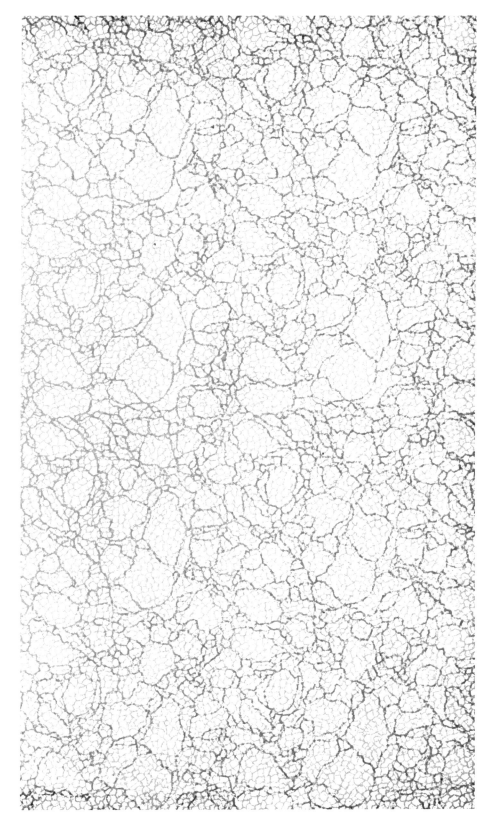

ImThe Story.com

Personalized Classic Books in many genre's

Unique gift for kids, partners, friends, colleagues

Customize:

- Character Names
- Upload your own front/back cover images (optional)
- Inscribe a personal message/dedication on the
  inside page (optional)

Customize many titles Including
- Alice in Wonderland
- Romeo and Juliet
- The Wizard of Oz
- A Christmas Carol
- Dracula
- Dr. Jekyll & Mr. Hyde
- And more...

Lightning Source UK Ltd.
Milton Keynes UK
UKHW022038070619
344049UK00014B/1365/P

9 781314 517323